MW01274079

VOYAGE

OF

DISCOVERY AND RESEARCH

IN THE

SOUTHERN AND ANTARCTIC REGIONS,

DURING THE YEARS 1839—43.

BY

CAPTAIN SIR JAMES CLARK ROSS, R.N.

KNT., D.C.L. OXON., F.R.S., ETC.

WITH PLATES, MAPS, AND WOODCUTS.

IN TWO VOLUMES.

VOL. I.

LONDON:

JOHN MURRAY, ALBEMARLE STREET.

1847.

LONDON :
SPOTTISWOODE and SHAW,
New-street-Square.

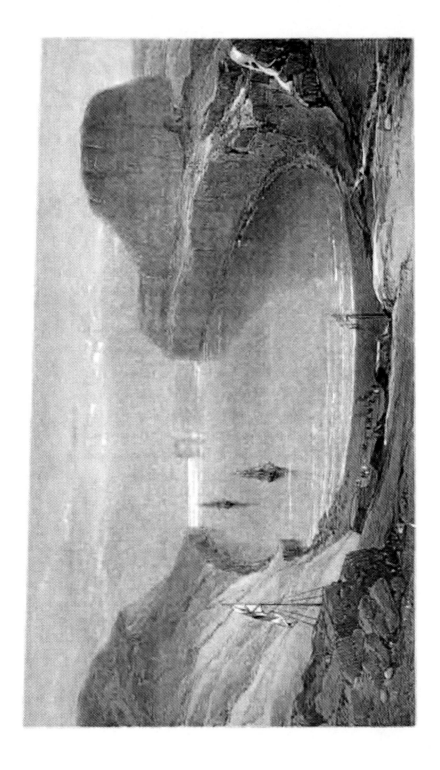

TO

THE RIGHT HONOURABLE

THE EARL OF MINTO, G.C.B.

LORD PRIVY SEAL,

LATE FIRST LORD COMMISSIONER OF THE ADMIRALTY,

UNDER WHOSE AUSPICES

THE EXPEDITION OF SCIENTIFIC RESEARCH TO THE ANTARCTIC REGIONS

WAS SENT FORTH,

THIS NARRATIVE OF ITS PROCEEDINGS

IS,

WITH GRATITUDE AND RESPECT,

BY PERMISSION,

Dedicated,

BY HIS LORDSHIP'S OBEDIENT AND FAITHFUL SERVANT,

JAMES CLARK ROSS.

Aston House, Aylesbury,
1st *June,* 1847.

INTRODUCTION.

AT the eighth meeting of the British Association for the Advancement of Science, held at Newcastle, in August, 1838, the attention of the physical section of that body was directed to the number and importance of desiderata in that great practical branch of science called Terrestrial Magnetism, by Lieutenant-Colonel Sabine of the Royal Artillery; and a Committee was appointed, consisting of Sir John Herschel, Mr. Whewell (now Master of Trinity College, Cambridge), Mr. Peacock (now Dean of Ely), and Professor Lloyd, of Trinity College, Dublin, to represent to Her Majesty's Government a series of resolutions adopted by the British Association; and as these resolutions exhibit the general outline of objects sought to be attained, they are inserted here, as pointing out clearly the causes in which the Expedition to the Antarctic regions originated.

" Resolved — 1. That the British Association views with high interest the system of simultaneous magnetic observations which has been for some time carried on in Germany and various parts of Europe, and the important results to which it has already led; and that they consider it highly desirable that similar series of observations, regularly continued in correspondence with, and in extension of these, should be instituted in various parts of the British dominions.

" 2. That this Association considers the following localities as particularly important: — Canada, Ceylon, St. Helena, Van Diemen's Land, and Mauritius, or the Cape of Good Hope; and that they are willing to supply instruments for their use.

" 3. That in these series of observations the three elements of horizontal direction, dip, and intensity, or their theoretical equivalents, be insisted on, as also their hourly changes, and, on appointed days, their momentary fluctuations.

" 4. That the Association considers it highly important that the deficiency, yet existing in our knowledge of terrestrial magnetism in the southern hemisphere, should be supplied by observations of the magnetic direction and intensity, especially in the high southern latitudes between the meridians of New Holland and Cape Horn; and they desire strongly to recommend to Her Majesty's government the appointment of a naval expedition expressly directed to that object.

" 5. That in the event of such expedition being undertaken, it would be desirable that the officers charged with its conduct should prosecute both branches of the observation alluded to in Resolution 3., so far as circumstances will permit.

" 6. That it would be most desirable that the observations so performed, both at the fixed stations and in the course of the expedition, should be communicated to Professor Lloyd.

" 7. That Sir J. Herschel, Mr. Whewell, Mr. Peacock, and Professor Lloyd, be appointed a Committee to represent to Government these recommendations."

A memorial was addressed to the Government by the Committee above named, embodying the chief arguments for taking up the cause as a national concern, and specifying more particularly the objects proposed to be accomplished, and the means of their accomplishment. This memorial, on its presentation to Lord Melbourne, was not only supported by the personal arguments of the eminent philosophers by whom it was framed, but on its being referred by the Government to the President and Council of the Royal Society, (its acknowledged advisers upon all points of scientific inquiry,) by similar and even more urgent representations on their part, " who, on this occasion, in a manner most honourable to themselves, and casting behind them every feeling but an earnest desire to render available to science the ancient and established credit of their institution, threw themselves unreservedly and with their whole weight into the scale, with immediate and decisive effect." * The

* Quarterly Review, No. CXXXI. p. 297. June, 1840.

strong interest taken in the cause by their President, the Marquis of Northampton, on all occasions a warm and zealous friend to science, contributed, without doubt, not a little to this result.

The following Report of a joint committee of physics and meteorology, adopted by the Council of the Royal Society, on the propriety of recommending the establishment of fixed magnetic observatories, and the equipment of a naval expedition for magnetic observations in the antarctic seas, to Her Majesty's Government, was presented to Lord Melbourne by the deputation named in the appended resolutions of the Council:—

" The subject of terrestrial magnetism has recently received some very important accessions which have materially affected not only the point of view in which henceforward it will be theoretically contemplated, but also the modes of observation which will require to be adopted for completing our knowledge of the actual state of the magnetic phenomena, and furnishing accurate data for the construction and verification of theoretical systems. It was for a long time supposed that the changes in the position assumed by the needle at any particular point on the earth's surface, might be conceived as resulting from regular laws of periodicity, having for their arguments, first, a great magnetic cycle of several centuries, depending on unknown, and perhaps internal movements or relations; and, secondly, on the periodic alter-

nations of heat and cold, depending on the annual
and diurnal movements of the sun. The discovery
of the affection of the needle by the aurora borealis,
and of the existence of minute and irregular movements, which might be referred either to unperceived auroras or to other local and temporary
causes, sufficed to show that the laws of terrestrial
magnetism are not so simple as to admit of this
summary form of expression; and the important
discovery, first announced, we believe, by Baron
von Humboldt, that those temporary changes take
place simultaneously at great distances in point of
locality, (a discovery which has since been remarkably confirmed and extended to very great
intervals of distance, so as to include the whole
extent of the European continent, by Gauss and
Weber, and their coadjutors of the German Magnetic Association,) has sufficed to show that the gist
of the inquiry lies deeper, and depends upon relations far more complex, while at the same time
the dominion of what might previously have been
regarded as local agency, would require, in the
new views consequent on the establishment of
these facts, to be extended far beyond what ordinary usage would authorise as a just application of
that epithet.

" For a long time in the history of terrestrial
magnetism the variation alone was attended to.
The consideration of the dip was then superadded;
but the observation of this element being more

difficult and delicate, our knowledge of the actual
and past state of the dip over the earth's surface is
lamentably deficient. It has lately appeared, however, that this element can be observed with considerable approximation, though not with nicety,
at sea, so that no reason subsists why materials for
a chart of the dip, analogous to that of variation,
should not be systematically collected. Lastly,
the intensity has come to be added to the list of
observanda; and from the great facility and exactness with which it can be determined, this branch
of magnetic knowledge has in fact made most rapid
progress.

" These three elements, the horizontal direction,
the dip, and the intensity, require to be precisely
ascertained before the magnetic state of any given
station on the globe can be said to be fully determined. Nor can either of them, theoretically
speaking, be said to be more important than the
others, though the direction, on account of its immediate use to navigators, has hitherto had the
greatest stress laid upon it, and been reduced into
elaborate charts. A chart of the lines of total
intensity has been recently constructed by Major
Sabine.

" All these elements are, at each point, now ascertained to be in a constant state of fluctuation,
and affected by those transient and irregular
changes which are above alluded to; and the investigation of the laws, extent, and mutual rela-

tions of these changes, is now become essential to
the successful prosecution of magnetic discovery,
for the following reasons : —

" 1st. That the progressive and periodical being
mixed up with the transitory changes, it is impossible to separate them so as to obtain a correct
knowledge and analysis of the former without
taking express account of and eliminating the
latter, any more than it would be practicable to
obtain measures of the sea-level available for an
inquiry into the tides, without destroying the irregular fluctuation produced by waves.

" 2ndly. That the secular magnetic changes
cannot be concluded from comparatively short
series of observation, without giving to those observations extreme nicety, so as to determine with
perfect precision the mean state of the elements at
the two extremes of the period embraced, which,
as already observed, presupposes a knowledge of
the casual deviations.

" 3rdly. It seems very probable that discord-
ances found to exist between results obtained by
different observers, or by the same at different
times, may be, in fact, *not* owing to error of observation, but may be due to the influence of these
transitory fluctuations in the elements themselves.

" 4thly and lastly, Because the theory of these
transitory changes is in itself one of the most interesting and important points to which the attention of magnetic inquirers can be turned, as they

are no doubt intimately connected with the general causes of terrestrial magnetism, and will probably lead us to a much more perfect knowledge of those causes than we now possess.

"Actuated by these impressions, on the occasion of a letter addressed by Baron von Humboldt to His Royal Highness the Duke of Sussex, P.R.S., the Council of this Society, on April 13. 1837, resolved to apply to Government for aid in prosecuting, in conjunction with the German Magnetic Association, a series of simultaneous observations; and in consequence of an application founded on such their resolution, a grant of money was obtained for the purchase of instruments for that purpose. By reason, however, of the details and manipulations of the methods then recently introduced into magnetic observations by Gauss being at that time neither completely perfected, nor their superiority over the old methods fully established by general practice, the precise apparatus to be employed in these operations was not at the time agreed upon, and was still under discussion, subject to the report of the Astronomer Royal on the performance of an instrument on Gauss's principle established at Greenwich, at the time when the subject in its present more extended form was referred by the Council to this Joint Committee, so that the grant in question has not, in point of fact, been employed or called for. The Committee consider this as in some respects fortunate, as in consequence of the delay time has been given for a much maturer consideration of the whole subject; and should it now be taken up as a matter of public concern, they consider that it will be necessary to provide for a more continuous and systematic series of observations, by observers regularly appointed for the purpose and provided with instruments and means considerably more costly than those contemplated on the occasion in question.

"On the general advisableness of calling for public assistance in the prosecution of the extensive subject of terrestrial magnetism, in both the modes referred to them for their consideration, (viz. by magnetic observatories established at several stations properly selected on land, and by a naval expedition expressly directed to such observations in the antarctic seas,) your Committee are fully agreed. They consider the subject to have now attained a degree of theoretical as well as of practical importance, and to afford a scope for the application of exact inquiry which it has never before enjoyed, and which are such as fully to justify its recommendation by the Royal Society to a revival of that national support to which we are indebted for the first chart of variations constructed by our illustrious countryman Halley in A. D. 1701, on the basis of observations collected in a voyage of discovery expressly equipped for that purpose by the British government.

"As regards the first branch of the question referred to their consideration, they are of opinion that the stations which have been suggested to them, viz. Canada, St. Helena, the Cape, Van Diemen's Land, and Ceylon (or Madras), are well selected, and perhaps as numerous as they could venture to recommend, considering the expense which would require to be incurred at each, and, that in each of these stations it would be desirable,

1st. That regular hourly observations should be made (at least during the daytime) of the fluctuations of the three elements of variation, dip, and intensity, or their equivalents, with magnetometers on the more improved construction, during a period of three years from their commencement.

" 2ndly. That on days, and on a plan appointed, agreed on in concert with one another and with European observatories, the fluctuations of the same elements should be observed during twenty-four successive hours, strictly simultaneous with one another, and at intervals of not more than five minutes.

" 3rdly. That the absolute values of the same elements shall be determined at each station, in reference to the fluctuating values above mentioned, with all possible care and precision, at several epochs comprehended within the period allowed.

" 4thly. That in the event of a naval expedition of magnetic discovery being despatched, observations be also instituted at each fixed station, in correspondence with, and on a plan concerted with the commander of, such expedition.

" As regards the second branch of the subject referred to them, viz., the proposal of an antarctic voyage of magnetic research, they are of opinion, as already generally expressed, that such a voyage would be, in the present state of the subject, productive of results of the highest importance and value; and they ground this opinion on the following reasons : —

" 1st. That great and notorious deficiencies exist in our knowledge of the course of the variation lines generally, but especially in the antarctic seas, and that the true position of the southern magnetic pole or poles can scarcely even be conjectured with any probability from the data already known.

" 2ndly. That our knowledge of the dip throughout those regions, and the whole southern hemisphere, is even yet more defective, and that even such observations of this element as could be procured at sea, still more by landing on ice, &c., would have especial value.

" 3rdly. That the intensity lines in those regions rest on observations far too few to justify any sure reliance on their courses over a large part of their extent, and over the rest are altogether conjectural. Nevertheless, that there is good reason to believe in the existence and accessibility of two points of maximum intensity in the southern as in the northern hemisphere, the attainment of which would be highly interesting and important.

4thly. That a correct knowledge of the courses of these lines, especially where they approach their respective poles, is to be regarded as a first and, indeed, indispensable preliminary step to the construction of a rigorous and complete theory of terrestrial magnetism.

" 5thly. That during the progress of such an expedition, opportunities would of necessity occur (and should be expressly sought) to observe the transitory fluctuations of the magnetic elements in simultaneous conjunction with observations at the fixed stations and in Europe, and so to furnish data for the investigation of these changes in localities very unlikely to be revisited for any purposes, except those connected with scientific inquiries.

" Your Committee, in making this Report, think it unnecessary to go into any minute details relative to the instruments or other *matériel* required for the proposed operations, still less into those of the conduct of the operations themselves. Should such be required from them, it will then be time to enter further into these and other points, when the Committee will most readily devote themselves to the fullest consideration of the subject.

" J. F. W. HERSCHEL,
" Chairman of the Joint Physical and
" Meteorological Committee."

RESOLUTIONS OF THE COUNCIL.

1. That this Report be received and approved.

2. That the Council, deeply impressed with the importance of the scientific objects which might be attained by an antarctic expedition, particularly by the institution of magnetic observations in southern regions, do earnestly recommend that Her Majesty's Government be pleased to direct the equipment of such an expedition.

3. That the imperfect state of our present knowledge of the amount and fluctuations of the magnetic elements, renders the establishment of fixed magnetical observatories, for a limited time, at various points of the earth's surface, highly desirable, particularly in Canada, St. Helena, Van Diemen's Land and Ceylon, and at the Cape of Good Hope; and that the Council do earnestly recommend Her Majesty's Government to cause such observatories to be established.

4. That a deputation, consisting of the President, Treasurer, and Secretaries of the Society, Sir John F. W. Herschel, the Chairman, and Major Sabine and Mr. Wheatstone, the Secretaries of the joint Committee of Physics and Meteorology, be requested to communicate the above Resolutions to Lord Melbourne, and to urge on the Government the adoption of the measures therein proposed.

Thus urged upon the Government by the most illustrious philosophers of our country, the request

VOL. I.　　　　a

was acceded to by Lord Melbourne; and the Lords Commissioners of the Admiralty being pleased to honour me with the command, I received my commission for Her Majesty's ship Erebus, on the 8th of April, 1839, and their Lordships' directions to proceed with the equipment of the expedition upon the most liberal scale, to be provided with all requisite means to carry into full execution the several points suggested, and observations recommended, by the two learned bodies, in the most complete manner. The Erebus, a bomb of three hundred and seventy tons, like all others of her class, was of strong build and with a capacious hold. The second vessel appointed for the service was the Terror, of three hundred and forty tons; she had been originally strengthened for contending with the ice of the arctic seas, upon the occasion of the detention of so many of our whale ships in Baffin's Bay, during the winter of 1836, and employed in the subsequent summer under the command of Sir George Back, upon his arduous but unsuccessful attempt to reach Repulse Bay. The damages she sustained during that voyage had already been repaired, and her fortification being considered perfectly sufficient, she was not commissioned until a month later, by my trusty and tried friend and messmate, Commander Francis Rawdon Moira Crozier; and from the numerous applicants for the service, the following officers were selected and appointed to the Erebus and Terror:—

	ERREBUS.		TERROR.
Captain.	James Clark Ross.	*Commander.*	Francis R. M. Crozier.
Lieutenant.	Edward Joseph Bird.	*Lieutenant.*	Archibald M'Murdo.
	John Sibbald.		Charles G. Phillips.
	James F. L. Wood.		Joseph W. Kay.
Master.	Charles T. Tucker.	*Master.*	Pownall P. Cotter
Surgeon.	Robert M'Cormick.		(acting).
Purser.	Thomas R. Hallett.	*Surgeon.*	John Robertson.
Mate.	Alexander J. Smith.	*Clerk in Charge.*	George H. Moubray.
	Henry Oakeley.		bray.
	Joseph Dayman.	*Mate.*	Peter A. Scott.
Assistant Surgeon.	Joseph D.		Thomas E. L. Moore.
Hooker.			William Molloy.
Second Master.	Henry B. Yule.	*Assistant Surgeon.*	David Lyall.
		Second Master.	John E. Davis.

The complement of each ship amounting to sixty-four persons.

Every improvement that former experience could suggest in preparing the ships for the service, and contributing to the health, comfort, and safety of their crews, was granted by the Admiralty.; and from Mr. Rice, of Chatham Dock Yard, to whom I am indebted for the memorandum of the fittings of the Erebus at Chatham Dock, inserted in the Appendix, I received that zealous and able assistance which, from his high abilities, but, I regret to say, unrewarded merits, I had reason to expect.

As opportunities might not occur of replenishing our stores and provisions, it was desirable to carry with us as much as we could possibly stow away. Preserved meats, according to Donkin's invention, in consequence of their portability and excellence, formed a large proportion of our provisions; these were chiefly furnished by John Gillon and Co., of Leith, and proved most excellent of their kind. I would, however, suggest to them and others

a 2

engaged in this branch of trade, that for voyages of several years' duration it would be better that the canisters in which the meats are preserved, should be of a much stouter tin, equal at least to those originally used by Messrs. Donkin and Co., their canisters being liable to rust through when long on board a ship and in hot climates. The following is a list of the quantities supplied by different firms : —

	Meats.	Vegetables.	Soups.	Concent. Soup.	Total Weight.
	lbs.	lbs.	pints.	¼ pints.	lbs.
Gillon - -	14,188	1512	- -	8217	Meats - - 33,484
Gamble -	4802	4300	230	1651	Vegetables 15,004¼
Cope - -	4324	1700	2000	2000	Soups (equal
Nicol - -	3480	850	482	1160	to) - - 6140
Cooper -	3732	5398½	2400	3400	Gravy - 4806½
Wells - -	2958	1244	1028	2806	Total - - 59,437
Total - -	33,484	15,004¼	6140	19,234	Tons Cwt. Qrs. Lbs. or 26 10 2 14

and the relative proportion of each of the several kinds is given in the following table, from which it will be seen that no pains or expense were spared to provide the expedition with such provisions as should be most likely not only to preserve the health of their crews, but add greatly to their comfort ; nor would the liberality with which our ships were supplied be ill bestowed, if extended to the whole of our navy ; indeed, in the end, I believe there would be a considerable saving of expense, and the subject is well deserving the attention of our rulers, if it were upon the score of humanity alone, when the great amount of suffering, disease, and death, that might be averted by furnishing our ships with a large supply of the preserved meats and vegetables is taken into consideration.

A LIST OF ARTICLES SUPPLIED FOR THE USE OF THE ANTARCTIC EXPEDITION IN THE YEAR 1839.

PRESERVED MEATS, SOUPS, AND VEGETABLES.

Mutton, boiled	-	3740 lbs.
„ roasted	-	3924 „
„ seasoned	-	12 „
„ and vegetables	-	184 „
Beef, boiled	-	4005 „
„ roasted	-	4232 „
„ seasoned	-	3937 „
„ and vegetables		4158 „
Veal, roasted	-	3000 „
„ boiled	-	986 „
„ seasoned	-	22 „
„ and vegetables		14 „
Ox-cheek	-	2872 „
„ and vegetables	-	336 „
Soup and bouilli	-	2062 „
Concentrated gravy soup	-	290 pints
Ditto	-	2898 ½ „
Ditto	-	12278 ½ „

PRESERVED, MEATS, SOUPS, AND VEGETABLES.

Vegetable soup	-	2618 pints
Ditto	-	1761 qts.
Carrots and gravy	-	528 lbs.
Turnips and gravy	-	436 „
Dressed cabbage	-	366 „
Table vegetables	-	471 „
Mixed vegetables	-	200 „
Carrots	-	10,782 „
Parsneps	-	1201 „
Beet-root	-	480 „
Onions	-	300 „
Turnips	-	180 „

MEDICAL COMFORTS.

Cranberries	-	2690 lbs.
Pickles, mixed	-	2493 „
„ walnuts		2453 „
„ onions	-	2511 „
„ cabbage	-	2398 „
Mustard	-	624 „
Pepper	-	120 „

Warm clothing of the best quality was also furnished to both ships, to be issued gratuitously to the crews whilst employed amongst the ice, to protect them from the severity of the climate, and every arrangement was made in the interior fitting of the vessels that could in any way contribute to the health or comfort of our people.

As soon as our preparations were completed, I received my final instructions from the Lords Commissioners of the Admiralty, which, in accordance with custom, are here inserted : —

By the Commissioners for executing the office of Lord
    High Admiral of the United Kingdom of Great
    Britain and Ireland, &c.

Whereas it has been represented to us that the science
of magnetism may be essentially improved by an extensive
series of observations made in high southern latitudes, and
by a comparison of such observations with others made at
certain fixed stations, and whereas practical navigation
must eventually derive important benefit from every improvement in that science; we have, in consideration of
these objects, caused Her Majesty's ships Erebus and
Terror to be in all respects prepared for a voyage for carrying into complete execution the purposes above mentioned :
and from the experience we have had of your abilities,
zeal, and good conduct, we have thought fit to entrust
you with the command of the expedition, and to direct
Commander Crozier, whom we have appointed to Her
Majesty's ship Terror, to follow your orders for his proceedings.

You are therefore required and directed, as soon as both
vessels shall be in all respects ready, to put to sea with
them, and on your way to your ulterior destination, you
will touch at the Island of Madeira, in order to obtain the
sea-rates of the several chronometers with which each
vessel has been supplied. From thence (but making a
short series of observations at the Rock of St. Paul) you
will make the best of your way to the Island of St.
Helena, where you are to land the observers and the instruments for the fixed magnetic observatory intended for
that station.

In approaching that island, and in proceeding from
thence to the Cape of Good Hope, you will endeavour to
ascertain at what point you cross the curve of least
magnetic intensity; the interest attached to the place of
which is set forth in the herewith inclosed Report of the
council of the Royal Society; and this Report having been

drawn up at our especial request, and containing the several objects of scientific inquiry recommended to your attention by that body, you will follow their suggestions, and carry out their views, as far as may be in your power, consistently with the safety of Her Majesty's ships, and with the means we have placed at your disposal.

At the Cape of Good Hope the instruments and observers for the second fixed magnetic observatory are to be carefully landed; and having completed your water, and replaced the stores which you have expended, you are to proceed to the eastward, touching at Marion and Crozet Isles for observations, if the weather and other circumstances should be favourable for that purpose.

As we have provided the expedition with invariable pendulums, and all the necessary apparatus for determining the figure of the earth; and as it is desirable that these observations should be made at several points, more especially in high southern latitudes, it is probable that Kerguelen Island will be found well suited to that purpose, as well as to an extensive series of magnetic and other observations; but the selection of these stations is freely confided to your judgment.

If the operations at Kerguelen Island, or at such other places as you may select, should be completed before the end of February, 1840, you will possibly find the sea sufficiently open to proceed directly to the southward, to examine those places where indications of land have been noticed, and to make the requisite observations on any outlying islands that you may be able to discover; but, at that advanced period of the season, you are cautiously to avoid being beset in the ice, as your early arrival at Van Diemen's Land is of far greater importance to the great object of the expedition than any results you could hope there to obtain.

Should your observations at Kerguelen Island detain you beyond the above specified period, you will have an opportunity of touching at the Islands of St. Paul and

Amsterdam, and of proceeding to Van Diemen's Land by whatever course shall appear to you best calculated for inferring the position of the magnetic pole.

At Van Diemen's Land you are to communicate with Lieutenant Governor Sir John Franklin, who will have been instructed to prepare instruments for the third magnetic observatory, which you are to establish in the most advantageous position, and to place in charge of an officer, with a sufficient number of assistants, to enable him to continue uninterruptedly the observations proposed to be made during the period of your absence, making such provision for their victualling and lodging as appears to be most convenient, and not inconsistent with the Naval Regulations.

Having brought this observatory into active operation, you will lose no time in proceeding to Sydney, which, according to the views contained in the before-mentioned Report, will be a station eminently fitted for the determination of all the magnetic elements, and which will hereafter be the centre of reference for every species of local determination.

The remaining winter months may be advantageously employed in visiting New Zealand and the adjacent islands, and in obtaining there as many series of observations as the time will allow, in order to enable you to judge with greater precision of the course to be adopted in the following summer; but taking care to return to Van Diemen's Land by the end of October, to refit Her Majesty's ships, and to prepare them for a voyage to the southward.

In the following summer, your provisions having been completed and your crews refreshed, you will proceed direct to the southward, in order to determine the position of the magnetic pole, and even to attain to it if possible, which it is hoped will be one of the remarkable and creditable results of this expedition. In the execution, however, of this arduous part of the service entrusted to your

enterprise and to your resources, you are to use your best
endeavours to withdraw from the high latitudes in time to
prevent the ships being beset with the ice; but if, notwithstanding your efforts, they should be cut off from a
timely retreat, you are to select the safest inlet you can find
for the security of Her Majesty's ships during the winter;
and you will house-in the ships, and further take every possible precaution for the health and comfort of the officers
and crews, which your former experience in the northern
expeditions may suggest to you, and for which you have
been supplied with abundant means. Having provided
for these two most important objects, you will endeavour
to turn your detention there to the best account, by sedu-
lously pursuing the different series of observations which
the fixed observatories will, at that time, be carrying on in
concert with yours.

Should the expedition have been able to avoid wintering
in a high latitude, you will return to Van Diemen's Land,
availing yourself of every opportunity you can seize of
pursuing there, or in such other places as your deliberate
judgment may prefer, those series of observations and experiments best adapted to carrying out the leading objects
of the expedition.

On the breaking up of the succeeding winter, you will
resume the examination of the antarctic seas in the
highest latitude you can reach, and proceeding to the
eastward from the point at which you had left off the
preceding year, you will seek for fresh places on which
to plant your observatory in all directions from the pole.

In the event of finding any great extent of land, you
will, as far as may be practicable, lay down the prominent
parts of its coast line; and you will endeavour not only
to correct the positions of Graham Land and Enderby
Land, and other places which have been seen only at a
distance, but to obtain some knowledge of the nature of
those yet unvisited tracts for geographical research; and
the magnetic objects of your voyage may be so conducted

as mutually to assist each other. With this view we have
directed the hydrographer to furnish you with such parts
of the instructions usually given to surveying vessels as
may lead to the more clear and satisfactory expression of
those shores which you may have to examine.

The South Shetlands, or the Orkneys, or perhaps the
Sandwich Islands, and lastly, the Falklands, will probably
terminate your magnetic labours in the antarctic seas;
and if at those latter islands you should not receive further
orders from us, you will return to England by such a
route as you may think most conducive to the ruling object of the expedition.

In an enterprise of the nature which has been briefly
stated in these orders, much must be left to the discretion,
temper, and judgment of the commanding officer; and we
fully confide in your combined energy and prudence for
the successful issue of a voyage, which will engross the attention of the scientific men of all Europe. At the same
time we desire you constantly to bear in mind our anxiety
for the health, the safety, and the comfort of the officers
and crew entrusted to your care.

We also caution you against allowing the two vessels
to separate; and we direct you to appoint, not only a
sufficient number of well-chosen rendezvous, but to keep
up the most unreserved communication with the Commander of the Terror, placing in him every proper confidence, furnishing him with a copy of these orders, and
acquainting him from time to time with all your views
and intentions for the execution of them; so that the
service may not only have the full benefit of your united
efforts in its prosecution, but that in case of unavoidable
separation, or of any accident to yourself, he may have the
advantage of knowing, up to the latest period, all your
ideas and intentions.

We also recommend that a frequent change should take
place of the observations made in the two ships, in order
that any scientific discovery made by the one, should be

quickly communicated to the other, as well for their advantage and guidance in making their future observations, as for the purpose of more certainly ensuring their preservation.

In the event of any irreparable accident happening to either ship, and the removal of the crew to the other, the officers and men are hereby authorised to perform their several duties in their respective ranks and stations, in the vessel to which they may be transferred; and should the Erebus be the one disabled, you are in that case to take command of the Terror.

In the event of any fatal accident to yourself, Commander Crozier is hereby authorised to take command of the expedition, either on board the Erebus or Terror, as he may prefer (placing the senior lieutenant in command of the other ship), to carry these instructions into execution.

In the event of England being involved in hostilities with any other power during your absence, you are clearly to understand that you are not to commit any hostile act whatever; the expedition under your command being fitted out for the sole purpose of scientific discoveries, and it being the established practice of all civilised nations to consider vessels so employed as exempt from the operations of war. Confiding in this general feeling, we trust that you would receive assistance from the ships and subjects of any foreign power with which you might fall in; but, if the case should arise, special application to that effect will be made to the respective governments.

While employed in the services stated in these orders, you will take every opportunity of acquainting our secretary, for our information, of your progress; and on your arrival in England, you are forthwith to repair to this office in order to lay before us a full account of your proceedings, taking care before you leave the ship to demand from the officers and all other persons on board, the logs and journals they had kept, and the charts, drawings,

and observations which they had made, and which are all
to be sealed up; and you will issue similar directions to
Commander Crozier and his officers, &c.; the said logs,
journals, and other documents to be thereafter disposed of
as we may think proper to determine. You will also
receive our future directions for the disposal of all such
specimens of the animal, vegetable, and mineral kingdoms
as in the course of the voyage may have been collected by
any person on board of either of the ships, and which you
are to endeavour to preserve, as far as may be done
without inconvenience.

Given under our hands, the 14th day of September,
1839.

(Signed) MINTO.

S. JOHN BROOKE PECHELL.

To James Clark Ross, Esquire,
Captain of H. M. S. Erebus, at Chatham.

By Command of their Lordships,
    (Signed)   C. WOOD.

The Report of the Council of the Royal Society
alluded to in my instructions, contained a detailed
account of every object of inquiry which the diligence and science of the several committees of that
learned body could devise. It occupies a small
volume of one hundred pages, so that it is only
possible to insert in this place their instructions
upon the subject of Terrestrial Magnetism, which
is described as the most important, and which is
considered as the great scientific object of the
expedition.

REPORT.

The president and council of the Royal Society having
recommended to Her Majesty's government the equip-

ment of an antarctic expedition for scientific objects, were informed by the Lords Commissioners of the Admiralty that it had been determined to send out Captain James Clark Ross on such an expedition, and the council were at the same time requested to communicate to them, for their information, any suggestions on those subjects, or on other points to which they might wish Captain Ross's attention to be called, in preparing the instructions to that officer.* The council, having due regard to the magnitude and importance of the question submitted to them, considered that they would best fulfil the wishes of Her Majesty's Government by a subdivision of the inquiry into different parts, and by referring the separate consideration of each part to distinct committees, consisting of those members of the society who were especially conversant with the particular branches of science to which each division of the inquiry had relation. These several committees, namely, those of physics, of meteorology, of geology and mineralogy, of botany and vegetable physiology, and of zoology and animal physiology, after bestowing much time and great attention in the investigation of the subjects brought under their notice, have each drawn up very full and complete reports of the results of their labours. These reports have been considered and adopted by the council, and have been incorporated in the following General Report, which the council present as their opinion on the matters which have been referred to them by Her Majesty's Government. They take this opportunity of declaring their satisfaction at the prospect of the benefits which are likely to accrue to science from the expedition thus liberally undertaken by the government on the representations made to them by the Royal Society and other scientific bodies in this country, and in conformity with a wise and enlightened policy. They also desire to express their grateful sense of the prompt atten-

* This request was conveyed in a letter from Sir John Barrow, addressed to the secretary of the Royal Society, and dated June 13. 1839.

tion which has been uniformly paid to their suggestions, and of the ample provision which has been made for the accomplishment of the various objects of the expedition.

Royal Society, 8th August, 1839.

Section 1. — PHYSICS AND METEOROLOGY.

The Council of the Royal Society are very strongly impressed with the number and importance of the desiderata in physical and meteorological science, which may wholly or in part be supplied by observations made under such highly favourable and encouraging circumstances as those afforded by the liberality of Her Majesty's Government on this occasion. While they wish therefore to omit nothing in their enumeration of those objects which appear to them deserving of attentive inquiry on sound scientific grounds, and from which consequences may be drawn of real importance, either for the settlement of disputed questions, or for the advancement of knowledge in any of its branches, — they deem it equally their duty to omit or pass lightly over several points which, although not without a certain degree of interest, may yet be regarded in the present state of science rather as matters of abstract curiosity than as affording data for strict reasoning; as well as others, which may be equally well or better elucidated by inquiries instituted at home and at leisure.

1. Terrestrial Magnetism.

The subject of most importance, beyond all question, to which the attention of Captain James Clark Ross and his officers can be turned, — and that which must be considered as, in an emphatic manner, the great scientific object of the Expedition, — is that of Terrestrial Magnetism; and this will be considered: 1st, as regards those accessions to our knowledge which may be supplied by observations to be made during the progress of the Expedition, independently of any concert with or co-operation of other observers; and 2ndly, as regards those which depend on and require such concert; and are therefore to be considered with reference to the observations about to be carried on simultaneously in the fixed magnetic observatories, ordered to be established by Her Majesty's Government with this especial view, and in the other similar observatories, both public and private, in Europe, India, and elsewhere, with which it is intended to open and maintain a correspondence.

Now it may be observed, that these two classes of observations naturally refer themselves to two chief branches into which the science of terrestrial magnetism in its present state subdivides itself, and which bear a certain analogy to the theories of the elliptic movements of the planets, and of their periodical and secular perturbations. The first comprehends the actual distribution of the magnetic influence over the globe, at the present epoch, in its mean or average state, when the effects of temporary fluctuations are either neglected or eliminated by extending the observations over a sufficient time to neutralise their effects. The other comprises the history of all that is not permanent in the phenomena, whether it appear in the form of momentary, daily, monthly, or annual change and restoration, or in progressive changes not compensated by counter changes, but going on continually accumulating in one direction, so as in the course of many years to alter the mean amount of the quantities observed. These last-mentioned changes hold the same place, in the analogy above alluded to, with respect to the mean quantities and temporary fluctuations, that the secular variations in the planetary movements must be regarded as holding, with respect to their mean orbits on the one hand, and their perturbations of brief period on the other.

There is, however, this difference, that in the planetary theory all these varieties of effect have been satisfactorily traced up to a single cause, whereas in that of terrestrial magnetism this is so far from being demonstrably the case, that the contrary is not destitute of considerable probability. In fact, the great features of the magnetic curves, and their general displacements and changes of form over the whole surface of the earth, would seem to be the result of causes acting in the interior of the earth, and pervading its whole mass; while the annual and diurnal variations of the needle, with their train of subordinate periodical movements, may, and very probably do, arise from, and correspond to electric currents produced by periodical variations of temperature at its surface, due to the sun's position above the horizon, or in the ecliptic, modified by local causes; while local or temporary electric discharges, due to thermic, chemical, or mechanical causes, acting in the higher regions of the atmosphere, and relieving themselves irregularly or at intervals, may serve to render account of those unceasing, and as they seem to us casual movements, which recent observations have placed in so conspicuous and interesting a light. The electrodynamic theory, which refers all magnetism to electric currents, is silent as to the causes of those currents, which may be various, and which only the analysis of their effects can teach us to regard as internal, superficial, or atmospheric.

It is not merely for the use of the navigator that charts, giving a general view of the lines of Magnetic Declination, Inclination, and Intensity, are necessary. Such charts, could they really be depended on, and were they in any degree complete, would be of the most eminent use to the theoretical inquirer, not only as general directions in the choice of empirical formulæ, but as powerful instruments for facilitating numerical investigation, by the choice they afford of data favourably arranged ; and above all, as affording decidedly the best means of comparing any given theory with observation. In fact, upon the whole, the readiest, and beyond comparison the fairest and most effectual mode of testing the numerical applicability of a theory of terrestrial magnetism, would be, not servilely to calculate its results for given localities, however numerous, and thereby load its apparent errors with the real errors, both of observation and of local magnetism ; but to compare the totality of the lines in our charts with the corresponding lines, as they result from the formulæ to be tested, when their general agreement or disagreement will not only show how far the latter truly represents the facts, but will furnish distinct indications of the modifications they require.

Unfortunately for the progress of our theories, however, we are yet very far from possessing charts even of that one element, the Declination, most useful to the navigator, which satisfy these requisites ; while as respects the others (the Inclination and Intensity) the most lamentable deficiencies occur, especially in the Antarctic regions. To make good these deficiencies by the continual practice of every mode of observation appropriate to the circumstances in which the observer is placed throughout the voyage, will be one of the great objects to which attention must be directed. And first —

At sea. — We are not to expect from magnetic observations

made at sea the precision of which they are susceptible on land. Nevertheless, it has been ascertained that not only the Declination, but the Inclination and Intensity, can be observed, in moderate circumstances of weather and sea, with sufficient correctness, to afford most useful and valuable information, if patience be bestowed, and proper precautions adopted. The total intensity, it is ascertained, can be measured with some considerable degree of certainty by the adoption of a statical method of observation recently devised by Mr. Fox, whose instrument will be a part of the apparatus provided. And when it is recollected that but for such observations the whole of that portion of the globe which is covered by the ocean must remain for ever a blank in our charts, it will be needless further to insist on the necessity of making a daily series of magnetic observations, in all the three particulars above-mentioned, whenever weather and sea will permit, an essential feature in the business of the voyage, in both ships. Magnetic observations at sea will, of course, be affected by the ship's magnetism, and this must be eliminated to obtain results of any service. To this end,

First. Every series of observations made on board should be accompanied with a notice of the direction by compass of the ship's head at the time.

Secondly. Previous to sailing, a very careful series of the apparent deviations, as shown by two compasses permanently fixed, (the one as usual, the other in a convenient position, considerably more forward in the ship,) in every position of the ship's head, as compared with the real position of the ship, should be made and recorded, with a view to attempt procuring the constants of the ship's action according to M. Poisson's theory; and this process should be repeated on one or more convenient occasions during the voyage ; and, generally, while at anchor, every opportunity should be taken of swinging round the ship's head to the four cardinal points, and executing in each position a complete series of the usual observations.

Thirdly. Wherever magnetic instruments are landed and observations made on *terra firma*, or on ice, the opportunity should be seized of going through the regular series on shipboard with more than usual diligence and care, so as to establish by actual experiment in the only unexceptionable manner the nature and amount of the corrections due to the ship's action for that particular geographical position, and by the assemblage of all such observations to afford data for concluding them in general.

Fourthly. No change possible to be avoided should be made in the disposition of considerable masses of iron in the ships during the whole voyage; but if such change be necessary, it should be noted.

Fifthly. When crossing the magnetic line of no dip it would be desirable to go through the observation for the dip with the instrument successively placed in a series of different magnetic azimuths, by which the influence of the ship's magnetism in a vertical direction will be placed in evidence.

On land, or on ice. — As the completeness and excellence of the instruments with which the expedition will be furnished will authorise the utmost confidence in the results obtained by Captain Ross's well-known scrupulosity and exactness in their use, the redetermination of the magnetic elements at points where they are already considered as ascertained, will be scarcely less desirable than their original determination at stations where they have never before been observed. This is the more to be insisted on, as lapse of time changes these elements in some cases with considerable rapidity; and it is therefore of great consequence that observations to be compared should be as nearly cotemporary as possible, and that data should be obtained for eliminating the effects of secular variations during short intervals of time, so as to enable us to reduce the observations of a series to a common epoch.

On the other hand it cannot be too strongly recommended, studiously to seek every opportunity of landing on points (magnetically speaking) unknown, and determining the elements of those points with all possible precision. Nor should it be neglected, whenever the slightest room for doubt subsists, to determine at the same time the geographical position of the stations of observation in latitude and longitude. When the observations are made on ice, it is needless to remark that this will be universally necessary.

With this general recommendation it will be unnecessary to enumerate particular localities. In fact it is impossible to accumulate too many. Nor can it be doubted that in the course of antarctic exploration, many hitherto undiscovered points of land will be encountered, each of which will, of course, become available as a magnetic station, according to its accessibility and convenience.

There are certain points in the regions about to be traversed in this voyage which offer great and especial interest in a magnetic point of view. These are, first, the south magnetic pole (or poles), intending thereby the point or points in which the horizontal intensity vanishes and the needle tends vertically downwards; and secondly, the points of maximum intensity, which, to prevent the confusion arising from a double use of the word poles, we may provisionally term magnetic *foci*.

It is not to be supposed that Captain Ross, having already signalised himself by attaining the northern magnetic pole, should require any exhortation to induce him to use his endeavours to reach the southern. On the contrary, it might better become us to suggest for his consideration, that no scientific datum of this description, nor any attempt to attain very high southern latitudes, can be deemed important enough to be made a ground for exposing to *extraordinary* risk the lives of brave and valuable men. The magnetic pole, though not attained, will yet be pointed to by distinct and unequivocal indications; viz. by the approximation of the dip to 90°; and by the convergence of the magnetic meridians on all sides towards it. If such convergence be observed over any considerable region, the place of the pole may thence be deduced, though its locality may be inaccessible.

M. Gauss, from theoretical considerations, has recently assigned a probable position in lon. 146° E., lat. 66° S. to the southern magnetic pole, denying the existence of two poles of the same name, in either hemisphere, which, as he justly remarks, would entail the necessity of admitting also a third point, having some of the chief characters of such a pole intermediate between them. That this is so may be made obvious without following out his somewhat intricate demonstration, by simply considering, that if a needle be transported from one such pole to another of the same name, it will *begin* to deviate from perpendicularity *towards* the pole it has quitted, and will end in attaining perpendicularity again, after pointing in the latter part of its progress obliquely *towards the pole to which it*

is moving, a sequence of things impossible without an intermediate passage through the perpendicular direction.

It is not improbable that the point indicated by M. Gauss
will prove accessible; at all events it cannot but be approachable
sufficiently near to test by the convergence of meridians the
truth of the indication; and as his theory gives within very
moderate limits of error the true place of the northern pole,
and otherwise represents the magnetic elements in every explored region with considerable approximation, it is but
reasonable to recommend this as a distinct point to be decided
in Captain Ross's voyages. Should the decision be in the
negative, *i. e.* should none of the indications characterising the
near vicinity of the magnetic pole occur in that region, it will
be to be sought; and a knowledge of its real locality will be
one of the distinct scientific results which may be confidently
hoped from this expedition, and which can only be attained
by circumnavigating the antarctic pole compass in hand.

The actual attainment of a *focus* of maximum intensity is
rendered difficult by the want of some distinct character by
which it can be known, previous to trial, in which direction to
proceed, when after increasing to a certain point the intensity
begins again to diminish. The best rule to be given, would be
(supposing circumstances would permit it) on perceiving the
intensity to have become nearly stationary in its amount, to
turn short and pursue a course at right angles to that just
before followed, when a change could not fail to occur, and
indicate by its direction towards which side the focus in question were situated.

Another, and as it would appear, a better mode of conducting
such a research, would be, when in the presumed neighbourhood of a focus of maximum intensity, to run down two parallels
of latitude or two arcs of meridians separated by an interval
of moderate extent, observing all the way in each, by which
observations when compared, the concavities of the isodynamic
lines would become apparent, and perpendiculars to the chords,
intersecting in or near the foci, might be drawn.

Two foci or points of maximum *total* intensity are indicated
by the general course of the lines in Major Sabine's chart in
the southern hemisphere, one about long. 140° E., lat. 47° S.,
the other more obscurely in long. 235° E., lat. 60° S. or there-

abouts. Both these points are certainly accessible; and as the course of the expedition will lead not far from each of them, they might be visited with advantage by a course calculated to lead directly across the isodynamic ovals surrounding them.

Pursuing the course of the isodynamic lines in the chart above mentioned, it appears that one of the two points of *minimum* total intensity, which must exist, if that chart be correct, may be looked for nearly about lat. 25° S., long. 12° W., and that the intensity at that point is probably the least which occurs over the whole globe. Now this point does not lie much out of the direct course usually pursued by vessels going to the Cape. It would therefore appear desirable to pass directly over it, were it only for the sake of determining by direct measure the least magnetic intensity at present existing on the earth, an element not unlikely to prove of importance in the further progress of theoretical investigation. Excellent opportunities will be afforded for the investigation of all these points, and for making out the true form of the isodynamic ovals of the South Atlantic, both in beating up for St. Helena, and in the passage from thence to the Cape; in the course of which, the point of least intensity will, almost of necessity, have to be crossed, or at least approached very near.

Nor is the theoretical line indicated by Gauss as dividing the northern and southern regions, in which free magnetism may be regarded as superficially distributed, undeserving of attention. That line cuts the equator in 6° east longitude, being inclined thereto (supposing it a great circle) 15°, by which quantity it recedes from the equator northward in going towards the west of the point of intersection. Observations made at points lying in the course of this line may hereafter prove to possess a value not at present contemplated.

As a theoretical datum, the horizontal intensity has been recommended by Gauss, in preference to the total, not only as being concluded from observations susceptible of great precision, but as affording immediate facilities for calculation. As it cannot now be long before the desideratum of a chart of the horizontal intensity is supplied, the maxima and minima of this element may also deserve especial inquiry, and may be ascertained in the manner above pointed out.

The maxima of horizontal intensity are at present undetermined by any direct observation. They must of necessity however, lie in lower magnetic latitudes than those of the total intensity, as its minima must in higher, and from such imperfect means as we have of judging, the conjectural situations of the maxima may be stated as occurring in

20° N.	80° E.	I.
7 N.	260 E.	II.
3 S.	130 E.	III.
10 S.	180 E.	IV.

Observations have been made of the horizontal intensity in the vicinities of II. and III., and are decidedly the highest which have been observed anywhere.

In general, in the choice of stations for determining the absolute values of the three magnetic elements, it should be borne in mind, that the value of each new station is directly proportional to its remoteness from those already known. Should any doubt arise, therefore, as to the greater or less eligibility of particular points, a reference to the existing magnetic maps and charts, by showing where the known points of observation are most sparingly distributed, will decide it.

For such magnetic determinations as those above contemplated, the instruments hitherto in ordinary use, with the addition of Mr. Fox's apparatus for the statical determination of the intensity, will suffice ; the number of the sea observations compensating for their possible want of exactness. The determinations which belong to the second branch of our subject, — viz. those of the diurnal and other periodical variations, and of the momentary fluctuations of the magnetic forces, — require, in the present state of our knowledge, the use of those more refined instruments recently introduced. Being comparative rather than absolute, they depend in great measure (and as regards the momentary changes, wholly) on combined and simultaneous observation.

The variations to which the earth's magnetic force is subject, at a given place, may be classed under three heads, namely, 1. the *irregular* variations, or those which *apparently* observe no law ; 2. the *periodical* variations, whose amount is a function of the *hour* of the day, or of the *season* of the year ; and 3. the *secular* variations, which are either slowly progressive, or else

return to their former values in periods of very great and
unknown magnitude.

The recent discoveries connected with the *irregular* variations of the magnetic declination, have given to this class of
changes a prominent interest. In the year 1818, M. Arago
made, at the Observatory of Paris, a valuable and extensive
series of observations on the declination changes; and M.
Kupffer having about the same time undertaken a similar
research at Cazan, a comparison of the results led to the discovery that the perturbations of the needle were *synchronous*
at the two places, although these places differed from one
another by more than forty-seven degrees of longitude. This
seems to have been the first recognition of a phenomenon, which
now, in the hands of Gauss and those who are labouring with
him, appears likely to receive a full elucidation.

To pursue this phenomenon successfully, and to promote in
other directions the theory of terrestrial magnetism, it was
necessary to extend and vary the stations of observation, and to
adopt at all a common plan. Such a system of simultaneous
observations was organized by Von Humboldt in the year 1827.
Magnetic stations were established at Berlin and Freyberg:
and the Imperial Academy of Russia entering with zeal into
the project, the chain of stations was carried over the whole of
that colossal empire. Magnetic *houses* were erected at Peters-
burgh and at Cazan; and magnetic instruments were placed,
and regular observations commenced, at Moscow, at Sitka, at
Nicolajeff in the Crimea, at Barnaoul and Nertschinsk in
Siberia, and even at Pekin. The plan of observation was defi-
nitely organized in 1830; and simultaneous observations were
made seven times in the year, at intervals of an hour for the
space of forty-four hours.

In 1834, the illustrious Gauss turned his attention to the
subject of terrestrial magnetism; and having contrived instruments which were capable of yielding results of an accuracy
before unthought of in magnetic researches, he proceeded to
inquire into the simultaneous movements of the horizontal
needle at distant places. At the very outset of his inquiry he
discovered the fact, that the synchronism of the perturbations
was not confined (as had been hitherto imagined) to the larger
and extraordinary changes; but that even the minutest devi-

ation at one place of observation had its counterpart at the other. Gauss was thus led to organize a plan of simultaneous observations, not at intervals of an hour, but at the short intervals of five minutes. These were carried on through twenty-four hours six * times in the year; and magnetic stations taking part in the system were established at Altona, Augsburg, Berlin, Bonn, Brunswick, Breda, Breslau, Cassel, Copenhagen, Dublin, Freyberg, Göttingen, Greenwich, Halle, Kazan, Cracow, Leipsic, Milan, Marburg, Munich, Naples, St. Petersburg, and Upsala.

Extensive as this plan appears, there is much yet remaining to be accomplished. The stations, numerous as they are, embrace but a small portion of the earth's surface; and what is of yet more importance, none of them are situated in the neighbourhood of those *singular points* or curves on the earth's surface, where the *magnitude* of the changes may be expected to be excessive, and perhaps even their *direction* inverted. In short, a wider system of observation is required to determine whether the amount of the changes (which is found to be very different in different places) is dependent simply on the *geographical* or on the *magnetic* co-ordinates of the place; whether, in fact, the variation in that amount be due to the greater or less distance of a disturbing centre, or to the modifying effect of the mean magnetic force of the place, or to both causes acting conjointly. In another respect also, the plan of the simultaneous observations admits of a greater extension. Until lately the movements observed have been only those of the magnetic *declination*, although there can be no doubt that the *inclination* and the *intensity* are subject to similar perturbations. Recently, at many of the German stations, the *horizontal component* of the intensity has been observed, as well as the declination; but the determination of another element is yet required, before we are possessed of all the data necessary in this most interesting research.

The magnetic observations about to be established in the British colonies, by the liberality of the government, will (it is hoped) supply in a great measure these desiderata. The stations are widely scattered over the earth's surface, and are situated at

* Recently reduced to *four*.

points of prominent interest with regard to the Isodynamic and
Isoclinal lines. The point of maximum intensity in the northern
hemisphere is *in* Canada; the corresponding maximum in the
southern hemisphere is *near* Van Diemen's Land; St. Helena
is close to the line of *minimum intensity;* and the Cape of Good
Hope is of importance on account of its southern latitude. At
each observatory the changes of the *vertical component* of the
magnetic force will be observed, as well as those of the *horizontal component* and *declination;* and the variations of the two
components of the force being known, those of the *inclination*
and of the *force* itself are readily deduced. The simultaneous
observations of these three elements will be made at numerous
and stated periods, and we have every reason to hope that the
directors of the various European observatories will take part
in the combined system.

But interesting as these phenomena are, they form but a
small part of the proper business of an observatory. The *regular* changes (both periodic and secular) are no less important
than the irregular; and they are certainly those by which a
patient inductive inquirer would seek to ascend to general laws.
Even the empirical expression of those laws cannot fail to be of
the utmost value, as furnishing a correction to the absolute
values of the magnetic elements, and thereby reducing them to
their mean amount.

The hourly changes of the *declination* have been frequently
and attentively observed; but with respect to the periodical
variations of the other two elements, our information is as yet
very scanty. The determination of these variations will form
an important part of the duty of the magnetic observatories;
and from the accuracy of which the observations are susceptible,
and the extent which it is proposed to give them, there can be
no doubt that a very exact knowledge of the empirical laws will
be the result.

With respect to the *secular* variations, it might perhaps be
doubted whether the limited time during which the observatories
will be in operation is adequate to their determination. But it
should be kept in mind that the monthly mean corresponding to
each hour of observation will furnish a separate result; and that
the number and accuracy of the results thus obtained may be
such as fully to compensate for the shortness of the interval

through which they are followed. A beautiful example of such a result, deduced from three years' observation of the declination, is to be found in the first volume of Gauss's magnetical work, of which a translation is published in the fifth number of Taylor's Scientific Memoirs.

It remains to say a few words of the instrumental means which have been adopted for the attainment of these ends.

The magnetic instruments belonging to each observatory and in constant use, are, 1. a declination instrument; 2. a horizontal force magnetometer; 3. a vertical force magnetometer. These instruments are constructed after the plan adopted by Professor Lloyd in the Magnetic Observatory of Dublin. The magnet, in the two former, is a heavy bar, fifteen inches long, and upwards of a pound in weight. In the declination instrument the magnet rests in the magnetic meridian, being suspended by fibres of silk without torsion. In the horizontal force magnetometer, the magnet is supported by two parallel wires, and maintained in a position at right angles to the magnetic meridian by the torsion of their upper extremities. In both instruments the changes of position of the magnet are read off by means of an attached collimater having a divided scale in its focus. The magnetometer for the vertical force is a bar resting by knife edges on agate planes, and capable of motion therefore in the vertical plane only. This bar is loaded so as to rest in the horizontal position in the mean state of the force; and the deviations from that position are read off by micrometers near the two extremities of the bar.

In addition to these instruments, each observatory is furnished with a dip circle, a transit with an azimuth circle, and two chronometers. Each vessel also is supplied with a similar equipment. Should therefore the ships be under the necessity of wintering in the ice, — and generally, on every occasion when the nature of the service may render it necessary to pass a considerable interval of time in any port or anchorage, — the magnetometers should be established, and observations made with all the regularity of one of the fixed observatories, and with strict attention to all the same details.

The selection of proper stations for the erection of the magnetometers, and the extent of time which can be bestowed upon each, must in a great measure depend on circumstances which can only be appreciated after the expedition shall have sailed. The observatory at St. Helena (the officers and instruments for which will be landed by Captain Ross) will in all probability, — and that at the Cape (similarly circumstanced in this respect) may possibly, — be in activity by the time the ships arrive at Kerguelen's Land, which we would recommend as a very interesting station for procuring a complete and as extensive a series of corresponding observations as the necessity of a speedy arrival at Van Diemen's Land for the establishment of the fixed observatory at that point will allow; taking into consideration the possibility of obtaining during the intermediate voyage a similar series at some point of the coast discovered by Kemp and Biscoe. In the ulterior prosecution of the voyage, a point of especial interest for the performance of similar observations will be found in New Zealand, which, according to the sketch of the voyage laid before us by Captain Ross, will probably be visited shortly after the establishment of the Van Diemen's Land observatory. The observations there will have especial interest, since, taken in conjunction with those simultaneously making in Van Diemen's Land, they will decide the important question, how far that exact correspondence of the momentary magnetic perturbations which has been observed in Europe, obtains in so remote a region, between places separated by a distance equal to that between the most widely distant European stations.

In the interval between quitting Van Diemen's Land and returning to it again, opportunities will no doubt occur of performing more than one other series of magnetometer observations, the locality of which may be conveniently left to the judgment of Captain Ross, bearing in mind the advantage of observing at stations as remote as possible from both Van Diemen's Land and New Zealand.

The research for the southern magnetic pole and the exploration of the antarctic seas will afford, it may be presumed, many opportunities of instituting on land hitherto unknown, or on firm ice when the vessel may be for a time blockaded, observations of this description; and in the progress of the circumnavigation, the line of coast observed or supposed to exist under the name of Graham's Land, or those of the islands in that vicinity, South Shetland, Sandwich Land, and finally on the homeward voyage the Island of Tristan d'Acunha, will afford stations each of its own particular interest.

. A programme will be furnished of the days selected for simultaneous observations at the fixed observatories, and of the details to be attended to in the observations themselves as above alluded to. These days will include the *terms* or stated days of the German Magnetic Association, in which, by arrangements already existing, every European magnetic observatory is sure to be in full activity. These latter days, which occur four times in the year, will be especially interesting, as periods of magnetometrical observations by the expedition, when the circumstances of the voyage will permit. For the determination of the existence and progress of the diurnal oscillation, in so far as that important element can be ascertained in periods of brief duration, it will be necessary to continue the observations hourly during the twenty-four for not less than one complete week. At every station where the magnetometers are observed, the absolute values of the dip, horizontal direction, and intensity will require to be ascertained.

Sydney, for a station of absolute determinations, would be with great propriety selected, as there can be no doubt of its becoming at no distant period a centre of reference for every species of local determination.

The meteorological particulars to be chiefly attended to, as a part of the magnetic observations, are those of the barometer, thermometer, wind, and especially auroras, if any. In case of the occurrence of the latter indeed, the hourly should at once be exchanged for uninterrupted observation, should that not be actually in operation. The affections of the magnetometers during thunder-storms, if any, should be noticed, though it is at present believed that they have no influence.

During an earthquake in Siberia in 1829, the direction of the horizontal needle, carefully watched by M. Erman, was uninfluenced; should a similar opportunity occur, and circumstances permit, it should not be neglected.

Should land or secure ice be found in the neighbourhood of the magnetic pole, every attention will of course be paid to the procuring a complete and extensive series of magnetometric observations, which in such a locality would form one of the most remarkable results of the Expedition.

The other objects of inquiry recommended by the Committee of Physics and Meteorology are enumerated in the following summary of the Report: —

1. Magnetic observations of the inclination, declination, and intensity at sea, throughout the voyage, daily in both ships, whenever the motion of the vessel will permit.

2. Precise determinations of the same particulars wherever the expedition may land, or disembark on ice.

3. Most careful series of magnetometric observations, in correspondence with those to be made at the fixed observatories, according to a plan concerted with the officers of those observatories, and with Professor Lloyd, the particulars of which will be furnished to each party concerned, and distributed to all the European and other observatories.

4. A circumnavigation of the Antarctic Pole, with a view to affording opportunities and proper stations for magnetic and other observations.

5. An inquiry into the actual position of the southern magnetic pole or poles, and the points or foci of greatest and least total and horizontal intensity, and into the course and figure of the isodynamic ovals presumed to occupy the area of the South Atlantic.

6. The determination of the length of the invariable pendulum at several stations in high south latitudes.

7. Observations of the tides, i. e. of the heights and times of high water, made at such stations at which the ships may remain long enough, and at which the correct establishment is unknown.

8. The keeping of a regular meteorological register in both ships during the whole voyage, and the paying attention to the phenomena of solar and terrestrial radiation, and generally to all phenomena bearing on the subject of meteorology.

9. The temperature of the sea at the surface and at stated moderate depths should be observed as frequently as possible, and whenever opportunity may occur, also at the greatest depths attainable ; and attention should be directed to the temperature of currents and shoals, as well as to its variation on approaching land. The temperature of the soil at various depths should be taken on landing, as well as that of springs, wells, &c.

10. Soundings should be attempted in deep seas, and specimens of the water brought up be preserved for future examination.

11. Observations should be collected of the aurora in high south latitudes; and attention directed to meteors and shooting stars on those occasions when experience has shown that they occur periodically in great abundance; as well as to the appearance of the zodiacal light, and other phenomena of a similar occasional nature.

12. Observations of the comparative brightness of southern stars should be procured, and especially of the variable stars α Hydræ and η Argûs.

13. The amount and laws of horizontal refraction, both celestial and terrestrial, in high south latitudes, should be investigated.

14. The phenomena of eclipses should be attended to.

The Geological, Zoological, and Botanical Committees also drew up catalogues of desiderata, with full instructions for the collection and preservation of specimens of the animal, vegetable, and mineral kingdoms; and the Admiralty furnished us with ample means for carrying out their several recommendations.

The two former collections were undertaken by Mr. M'Cormick and Mr. Robertson, in addition to their duties as chief medical officer of each ship; and for the diligence and zeal with which they performed their task, my thanks are especially due; as also to Dr. Joseph D. Hooker and Mr. Lyall, whose unceasing exertions in the botanical department have contributed several thousand new genera and species to the catalogues of the Southern Flora.

To Mr. M'Cormick and Dr. Hooker I am besides indebted for several very interesting notices of the geology and botany of the places visited by the Expedition, which are inserted either in the narrative or the Appendix.

The drawings and vignettes contained in these volumes were principally furnished by Mr. Davis; those of Christmas Harbour, Nine Pin Rock, and deep soundings, by Lieutenant Dayman; and some, which bear his name, by Dr. Hooker.

I have also to express my deep obligations to Dr. Sir John Richardson, of Haslar Hospital, and J. E. Gray, Esq., of the British Museum, for undertaking, gratuitously, the publication of an account of the zoological collection formed during the course of our voyage; and to those gentlemen of the British Museum who have assisted them in the laborious task; and to Dr. Hooker, for the elaborate manner in which he is describing the extensive botanical collection in the beautifully executed " Flora Antarctica."

For the illustration of these two great works, which are now advancing towards completion, the government, at the recommendation of the Lords Commissioners of the Admiralty, granted the sum of two thousand pounds; and I hope that naturalists will at once appreciate the liberality of this measure, and acknowledge that the money has been advantageously employed.

It has been impossible, in the course of the narrative, to do more than glance at some of the important scientific results of the expedition ; but the whole of the observations are in course of publication, chiefly in the Philosophical Transactions of the Royal Society.   Under the able supervision of Colonel Sabine, nearly all relating to terrestrial magnetism, which were transmitted by me, as opportunities offered, to England, have already appeared ; and the magnetometric portion of them, in a separate volume, is in a forward state of preparation.   The expense of these publications has been also defrayed by the government.

I am also indebted to Admiral Beaufort for the kind assistance he has given me in the construction of the plans and charts contained in these volumes; to Mr. Davis, of the Terror, by whom they were drawn from my original documents ; and to the Messrs. Walker, for the accuracy and beauty with which they have been engraved.

Indeed, I am unable to express the gratitude I feel to those gentlemen who have so generously come forward to afford their gratuitous assistance in the publication of the accumulated labours of the Expedition : in their hands I feel assured that full justice will be done to the several subjects under their discussion, and that when all shall have been completed, I think it will be acknowledged that the Expedition has accomplished the more important objects for which it was sent forth.

JAMES C. ROSS.

Aston House, Aylesbury,
June 1. 1847.

CONTENTS

OF

THE FIRST VOLUME.

CHAPTER I.

CHAPTER II.

CHAPTER IX.

CHAPTER X.

LIST OF PLATES AND MAPS

IN

THE FIRST VOLUME.

VOYAGE

OF

H. M. S. EREBUS AND TERROR

TO THE

ANTARCTIC OCEAN,

1839—43.

CHAPTER I.

THE fortification of the Erebus being at length
complete, she was warped out of dock on the 15th
of August, and, by the united efforts of both ships'
crews, her equipment proceeded rapidly.

1839.

Aug. 15.

On the 2d of September, the Right Hon. the Earl Sept. 2.
Minto, Vice-Admiral Sir Charles Adam, and Rear-
Admiral Sir William Parker, the three Senior Lords
Commissioners of the Admiralty, inspected the
Erebus, and were pleased to express their satis-
faction at the complete manner in which she had
been fitted for the intended service.

On the 16th I received their lordships' final Sept. 16.
instructions, and on the 19th the Erebus and
Terror moved down the river to the moorings off
Gillingham. Here the remainder of our stores and

B

provisions was taken on board, and observations
for the determination of the effect produced on the
compasses by the iron of the ship were obtained.
This operation, so simple and desirable at all times,
became more important and essential in ships
destined to navigate the more interesting regions
of magnetic power, and to penetrate to the highest
attainable magnetic latitude.

The Commander in Chief, Sir Robert Waller
Otway, and his family, from whom, during the
period of our fitting out under his immediate command, we had experienced many instances of kind
consideration and assistance, honoured our ships
by a visit on the 24th. On the morning of the
25th Captain Superintendent Clavell and the pay
clerks came on board, and paid the crews three
months' advance, in addition to the wages then
due to them; soon after noon the moorings were
slipped, and we sailed down the river, followed by
the Terror. As we passed Sheerness a pilot came
on board, but not having sufficient depth of water
over the flats, we were obliged to anchor near the
buoy off the Mouse until the next morning, when,
towed by her Majesty's steam vessel Hecate, we
proceeded to Margate Roads, where we anchored
at 2h. 20m. P.M. The Terror joined us the following evening, and many people from Margate visited
the ships during their stay at this anchorage. We
were here supplied with a bower anchor from the
dock-yard at Deal, to replace a damaged or defective
one that had broken whilst we were in the act of

heaving it up, fortunately at a time that no harm 1839.
could result from the gross negligence of those
whose duty it was to ascertain the soundness of
that on which, under different circumstances, the
ship, and lives of all on board, might have mainly
depended.

A prevalence of westerly wind detained us in Sept. 30.
Margate Roads until the evening of the 30th September. It suddenly shifted to the eastward at
six P.M., when we weighed, and beat round the
Foreland; before midnight, we hove to for a few
minutes in the Downs, to discharge our pilot, and
to enable the Terror to join company.

We made good way down Channel until after Oct. 3.
noon of the 3d October, when, abreast of the Start
Point, we encountered a strong south-westerly gale;
but, being unwilling to lose more time by entering
any of the Channel ports, we kept the sea, and were
gratified to find our ships behave well throughout
the gale, although much deeper laden than we considered desirable. During the night of the gale
the Terror parted company; but, as our run to
Madeira, the first appointed rendezvous, was so
short a distance, we proceeded without delay on
our voyage alone.

On the morning of the 5th we were off the Oct 5.
Lizard, the last point of the coast of England seen
by us, and from which therefore we took our departure. It is not easy to describe the joy and
lightheartedness we all felt as we passed the entrance of the Channel, bounding before a favourable

breeze over the blue waves of the ocean, fairly
embarked in the enterprise we had all so long desired to commence, and freed from the anxious and
tedious operations of our protracted but requisite
preparation.

The daily, almost hourly, observations of various
kinds, from which so large a measure of useful
and important results were expected, were now
reduced into a practical system, and immediately
entered upon with eager zeal and diligence by the
officers of the Expedition.

During our passage across the Bay of Biscay we
had no favourable opportunity of determining the
height of its waves, as we experienced no violent
storm: we had, however, a very rough and awkward
sea, occasioned by a strong south-westerly breeze,
and mixing confusedly with the long rolling north-
westerly swell peculiar to this bay. The highest
waves we measured scarcely exceeded thirty-six feet
from their base to their summit; the velocity of their
motion and their distance apart could not be determined without the presence of another vessel.

We availed ourselves of every opportunity of trying for soundings, but without finding the bottom
with from three to six hundred fathoms of line. The
specific gravity of the water we found to be 1·0278
at the surface, and the same to the depth of three
hundred fathoms, although it was from ten to fifteen
degrees colder than at the surface. In lat. 48° 20′ N.
and long. 8° 0′ W. we passed through one of those
very remarkable luminous patches that have been

frequently before observed. It was about sixty or
seventy feet in diameter, and much brighter in the
centre than at the edges. It consisted of aggre-
gated myriads of animalculæ, which emit a beautiful
phosphorescent light when agitated by the vessel
passing through their mass.

In the evening of the 19th, having reached the
assigned position of the shoal called " the Eight
Stones," we hove to, and tried for, but could not
obtain, soundings with three hundred fathoms of
line, adding another to the many proofs of the non-
existence of that supposed danger.

At daylight the next morning Madeira island
was seen, and we anchored in Funchal Roads in
the afternoon. By the kind and prompt attention
of Mr. Stothard, the English consul, we were enabled at once to commence the necessary observations for rating our chronometers, and for the
magnetic desiderata of dip, variation, and intensity,
— the principal objects of our visit to this delightful spot. Some uncertainty still existing as to the
exact altitude of Pico Ruivo, the highest mountain
of the island, above the level of the sea, a party of
officers was despatched to its summit, with two
mountain barometers, for the purpose of its determination: this service was entrusted to Lieutenants
Wilmot and Lefroy of the Royal Artillery, and
corresponding observations were made with the
standard barometers of the Erebus and Terror,
near high-water mark, by the officers of the ships.

The result of these operations gave, for the height

of Pico Ruivo, 6097·08 or 6102·90 English feet, according as Gay Lussac's or Rudberg's measure be taken for the expansion of air by heat. The result is computed by Bessel's tables[*], in which the hygrometric state of the atmosphere at the two stations is taken into the account. This elevation is some hundred feet greater than the height which was assigned by Lt.-Colonel Sabine from barometrical observations made by the late Captain Clavering, R. N., and himself, in the winter of 1821–22. It is probable that this difference has been occasioned by the frequently practised deception of the guides: when fog conceals the highest peak from view, they halt at a station they call the " *Homme à pied*," which, under such circumstances, may be easily mistaken for the summit, having a steep descent on every side. By this artifice the guides save themselves and the travellers the trouble and fatigue of descending into a deep ravine, and of thence ascending the most toilsome portion of the journey to the peak.

Since this was written, the result of Lieutenant Wilkes's observations has been published in his Narrative of the United States' Exploring Expedition. His computations assign an elevation to Pico Ruivo above half-tide of six thousand two hundred and thirty-seven feet: a difference of nearly one hundred and forty feet from our observations, and much greater than we should expect

* Scientific Memoirs, vol. ii. art. xvi.

from the perfect and accurate instruments employed on both occasions.

The details of our observations are given in the Appendix, together with a letter I have received on the subject from Colonel Sabine, as it contains a useful caution and suggestion on barometrical measures.

The pile of stones erected by Lieutenant Wilkes's officers was pointed out to our party by the guides; but the notice left there by the Americans of their visit had been removed by some persons last year, and used by them, as the guides informed our officers, to light their fire. We did not learn the names of those who had been guilty of this un-gracious act.

The day was splendidly beautiful, and our officers obtained a most magnificent view from their elevated position, overlooking the whole of the island: a circumstance of but rare occurrence, owing to the almost constant mist which encompasses the higher parts of the mountain, occasioned by the condensation of the vapour with which the atmosphere of this island is so fully charged.

On the evening of the 22d a remarkable phenome- non was witnessed by us from the anchorage. We observed a very faint appearance of a pale rose colour rising behind the hills, to the left of Loo island, and twenty degrees west of the polar star: it increased in brightness and extent, until in twenty minutes it attained the altitude of thirty-three degrees, and bearing from N.W. to N. by E. by compass.

At 7h. 45m. P.M., when it had risen to forty-three degrees, the colour became generally more deeply red, but much fainter near the edges, and by a few minutes after eight entirely disappeared. At half-past nine the same portion of the heavens was again illumined in a similar manner. Two coruscations, of a paler colour and yellowish tinge, were at this time distinctly visible, radiating from the point of first appearance; they were what might be termed about one foot broad, and ten feet apart at the altitude of twenty-five degrees, where they blended with the other light. At half-past ten the whole gradually passed away.

The wind was N. by W.; the compass was not at all affected during its continuance; the stars were seen through it, and the moon, which was for some time behind a cloud, seemed to produce only a comparatively slight change, when she afterwards shone forth with great brilliancy.

Much anxiety was expressed by the inhabitants of the island at this unusual phenomenon: various and absurd were their conjectures as to the cause. The more prevalent were, either that a new volcano had burst forth, or that some very large vessel had been destroyed by fire. Both these suppositions were proved erroneous on the arrival of the Terror at 8 A. M. on the 24th. She was about two hundred miles to the northward of Madeira at the time of its occurrence, and the description given of it by Commander Crozier and the officers of that ship agreed so exactly with our own observations, that no doubt could remain of its identity.

From the circumstance of the Terror being so many miles nearer to it than we were, and from its being observed still to the northward of her, without any material difference in its altitude, there can be no doubt that its region must be considered far beyond the limits of our atmosphere; but I must leave it to those more conversant with these matters to assign its cause.

During our stay at this island we were much in-debted to Mr. Stothard for the liberal hospitality with which he placed his residence in Funchal entirely at the service of Commander Crozier and myself, and for affording us every facility in there making our observations: and also to the friend-ship and kind attentions of Mr. Veitch, late Consul-general; particularly for the gratification and ad-vantage we derived from inspecting with him his celebrated "Jardin" of the mountain, where he has successfully cultivated several kinds of the tea, and other Chinese plants.   The garden, or tea planta-tion, contained three or four hundred shrubs, and all our party considered the infusion of some of the species which we tasted to have such an excellent flavour as, in our opinion, to justify his expectations of eventually making it an article of commercial importance; provided the cost of labour in its preparation would not here, as at Rio, be found an obstacle.

Bananas, dates, figs, spices, and all the choice tropical fruits, grow abundantly in the gardens about
the town: and the quantity of coffee raised in the
island, and which is of a very good quality, is sufficient to supply the wants of the whole population.

Our magnetic and other observations were only
just completed, when a strong westerly breeze and
heavy south-westerly swell, attended with such
indications as to the experienced islanders predicted
a coming storm, obliged us hurriedly to depart at
4h. P. M. on the 31st. At daylight on the 2d of
November we saw the lofty peak of Teneriffe, distant about sixty miles: our object being to land our
letters, we steered for Santa Cruz, the chief town of
the Canary Islands; but, baffled by calms and light
winds, it was not until the evening of the 4th that
we were enabled to accomplish our purpose, and to
bear away for the Cape de Verd Islands.

We got the N. E. trade wind on the 6th, in latitude 27° N., and passed the tropic of Cancer on the
evening of the 8th. We met with large numbers
of flying-fish, attended by their persecutors, the
bonito and dolphin; and thus early on our voyage
we began the collection of natural history, by pre-
serving as many different kinds of these creatures
as we could procure, and by means of towing nets
and other devices, gathered numerous curious and
entirely new species of animalculæ, which, like the
grass of the meadows to land animals, constitute
the foundation of marine animal subsistence; and
by their emitting a phosphorescent light upon dis-

turbance, render the path of the ship through the
waters on a dark night surprisingly brilliant.

On the 13th St. Jago Island was seen, and the
next morning, at ten o'clock, we anchored in Port
Praya.

By permission of the Governor we landed our
tents and instruments on Quail Island, and our
observations were immediately commenced. The
island, being of volcanic origin, is by no means a
desirable position for magnetic determinations; but
we had by this time learned to place more reliance
on those taken on board our ships than on any
made on shore, even under the most favourable circumstances. Our observations were here confined
to the rating of our chronometers, and the spot
selected for this purpose is close to a small beach
on the west side of the island, and quite convenient
to the anchorage.

Some of our officers, whose time and duties admitted of their making excursions to a distance
from the shore, described the country, particularly
the valley of St. Domingo, where was the ancient
capital of the islands, as far more beautiful and
fertile than they could have supposed from the
desolate aspect its coasts present. Not far from the
town we saw a fine specimen of the giant tropical
tree of Africa, the Baobab (*Adansonia digitata*) : its
short, pear-shaped trunk, not more than ten feet
high, exceeded thirty-eight feet in circumference,
and at this period its fruit was forming.

The heat was most oppressive, and the sickly

1839.

season being scarcely over, I was glad to leave as soon as possible. A few days were sufficient to complete our observations, and procure a supply of live stock, fresh fruit, vegetables, and water; all of which, except water, are of excellent quality and moderate price.

Nov. 20.

We sailed from Port Praya on the morning of the 20th, and on that day the hourly register of the height of the barometer, and the temperature of the air and surface of the ocean, was substituted for the three-hourly observations hitherto recorded, chiefly for the purpose of marking the progress of barometric depression in approaching, and re-ascension in receding from, the equator, a pheno-menon represented as being of the greatest and most universal influence, as it is in fact no other than a direct measure of the moving force by which the great currents of the trade winds are produced; so that the measure of its amount and the laws of its geographical distribution lie at the root of the theory of these winds.

In lat. 8° N., and long. 26° W., we entered the Variables, as the space between the N.E. and S.E. trades is called: here violent gusts of wind and torrents of rain alternate with calms and light baffling breezes, which, with the suffocating heat of the electrically-charged atmosphere, render this part of the voyage both disagreeable and unhealthy, especially in a flush-decked vessel, where the ne-cessity of keeping the hatchways covered prevents the free circulation of air.

As opportunities offered, experiments were made
to determine the height of the plane of vapour,
a desideratum of great meteorological importance,
connected with all the most interesting questions
regarding the distribution of aqueous vapour over
the globe and the irrigation of the continents. The
results of these experiments differed so widely from
each other, owing chiefly to the great difficulty of
any thing like exact determination in observations
of this nature, and probably in some degree from
an actual difference of its altitude, under various
conditions of the atmosphere, ranging from one
thousand two hundred to nearly three thousand
feet, barely entitle them to be esteemed more than
a rough approximation, giving an elevation of about
two thousand feet as its mean height in the tropical
regions.

On the 27th, the sky being very clear, the planet
Venus was seen near the zenith, notwithstanding
the brightness of the meridian sun, and was an
object of much admiration to us all. It enabled us
to observe the higher stratum of clouds to be
moving in an exactly opposite direction to that of the
wind, a circumstance which is frequently recorded
in our meteorological journal, both in the N. E. and
S. E. trades, and has also been observed by former
voyagers. Captain Basil Hall witnessed it from
the summit of the Peak of Teneriffe ; and Count
Strzelecki, on ascending the volcanic mountain of
Kirauea, in Owhyhee, reached, at 4,000 feet, an
elevation above that of the trade wind, and ex-

perienced the influence of an opposite current of air, of a different hygrometric and thermometric condition ; facts which tend in some degree to explain the means by which the equilibrium of the atmosphere under certain conditions is maintained in those regions. Count Strzelecki further informed me of the following seemingly anomalous circumstance,—that at the height of 6,000 feet he found the current of air blowing at right angles to both the lower strata, also of a different hygrometric and thermometric condition, but *warmer* than the interstratum.

Our approach to St. Paul's Rocks, for which we were steering, was indicated by the appearance of the sea-birds which inhabit them, and at nine the next morning their two higher points were seen like specks on the horizon, at a distance of three or four leagues: the lower and smaller rocks gradually rose into view on nearing them, but our ships having been carried during the night so far to leeward, by a strong westerly current which we found to prevail here, we could not fetch them until late in the evening.

Nov. 29.   We landed early the next morning, but not without difficulty, owing to the surf and swell which broke through the several channels into the central basin. We found the steep north-eastern side of the cove the most practicable point, and near it we obtained our observations.

These remarkable rocks, which lie in lat. 0° 56′ N. and long. 29° 20′ W., and more than five hundred miles distant from any continent, appear to have been raised from the bed of the ocean by volcanic agency, and not in any part exceeding seventy feet above its surface, present the form of an oblong crater, the longer axis lying in a N. E. and S. W. direction. Mr. Darwin, however, considers them not to be of igneous origin, and, in this particular, unlike all the other detached islands of the Atlantic.

The following geological remarks upon them are by Mr. M'Cormick, surgeon of the Erebus, who attended to that branch of natural knowledge:—

" Situated nearly on the equator, in latitude 0° 56′ N., and longitude 29° 20′ W. ; they consist of a group of rocks, altogether scarcely exceeding half a mile in circumference. The four largest form a kind of bay on the N. W. side, in which there is a considerable swell, from the surf breaking heavily through the three channels by which these rocks are separated from each other. The highest rock is on the N. E. side of the bay, rather sharply peaked, seventy feet above the level of the sea. The next in height, and the most remarkable, from its uniform white colour, is sixty-one feet, and situated on the S. W. or opposite side. This rock is composed of a very hard kind of hornstone, readily affording sparks under a blow of the hammer, and coated over with a thin layer of calcareous matter, evidently produced from the excrement of the numerous birds which have selected this spot as a breeding-place.

" The *Pelecanus Sula*, and *Sterna stolida*, are the only species inhabiting these rocks, together with a fierce and active crab, which appears to be a destructive enemy to their eggs.

" Not a vestige of vegetation of any kind is to be found, excepting a solitary species of *Conferva*, scantily distributed on the rocks, near the surface of the sea, and with which the noddies and boobies build their nests.

" The hornstone rests upon a very singular-looking rock, of a white colour, and meagre earthy feel; adhering slightly to the tongue, resembling *kaolin*, or decomposed felspar, beautifully streaked with thin veins of what appears to be serpentine, hard and vitreous as glassy felspar.

" These are the two prevailing rocks, occurring in various states of decomposition; where they are exposed to the spray of the sea, in many places much honey-combed, and intersected by masses of conglomerate, and very curious veins, from half an inch to half a foot in diameter, formed of two thin black plates of rock, much hardened and brittle, with a ringing sound, bearing all the marks of having been subjected to intense heat: frequently the space between the plates, or sides of the veins, is filled by a deposit of carbonate of lime; in others, by a calcareous-looking substance, which does not effervesce with acids, while some are empty.

" At low water, the sea-face of the rocks presents a band of pale red, the work of the coral insects, against which the surf is continually breaking. These rocks having been considered remarkable, as not being of a volcanic nature, I made a full collection of specimens*; and although, certainly, no lava or igneous rocks have made their way to the surface, in evidence of their true origin, yet the whole group presents, at a single glance, the most striking effects of the agency by which they have been forced upwards. The confused mass is mingled together without the slightest approach to stratification; in many places, the altered appearance of the rocks, from the effects of heat, prove them to have been volcanic, differing from other volcanic islands in the Atlantic, only from the melted matter not having reached the surface, but remaining as it were capped by the bed of the ocean."

Our observations here gave for the magnetic dip 27° 8' N., and the variation 13° 20' W.

We judged it to be low water this afternoon at three o'clock, and to have fallen between five and six feet; but owing to the surf we were unable to determine these points with the desired accuracy. The annexed sketch by Mr. Dayman will serve to convey a good idea of the size and arrangement of these rocks.

One of our party, in attempting to wade across a narrow channel, was taken off his feet by a heavy wave, and was for some time in imminent peril. Frequently he regained the margin of the shore, and

---

* A list of these specimens is given in the Appendix.

C

˅struggled to maintain his hold, but was as frequently carried back by the retiring wave; whilst,
unable to afford him the least assistance, we could
only look on from the opposite side with the most
painful apprehensions of seeing him taken away
by one of the numerous sharks that were playing
about the cove; however, being an expert swimmer,
he at length succeeded in crawling up the rocks,
greatly weakened by his long-continued exertions,
though fortunately without other injury than a few
bruises.

As we pulled off to the ships in the afternoon,
we were led to believe, from the discoloration of the
water, that it is probably shallow to the distance of
a quarter of a mile from the shore. During our
absence soundings had been obtained with three
hundred fathoms on a rocky ground, and some
small black stones came up with the lead, the islets
bearing then S. 57 E., distant two-thirds of a mile;
but they failed to reach the bottom with five
hundred fathoms, when they bore S. 67 E. at twice
that distance, so that the ascent of the submarine
mountain of which these peaks form the summit
must be very steep.

Dec. 3.   We crossed the equator about midnight, the 3d
of December, in long. 30 W., and the ceremony of
shaving those who had not done so before was
perpetrated the next morning with as much amuse-
ment and good-natured fun as usual on such occasions. Some difference of opinion prevails as to
the proper meridian in which to cross the line; but

having to visit St. Paul's Rocks, we were obliged to run thus far to leeward, or I would have preferred the longitude of about 26° or 27° W., for the strong westerly current is liable to carry ships with a scant trade too near to the coast of Brazil.

This current we found to diminish in strength as we proceeded to the southward, and in the 8th or 9th degree of latitude it gives place to a feeble northerly set.

The Magellhanic clouds and the beautiful constellation of the Southern Cross now became apparent; and although in my estimation the latter is inferior in beauty to several of our northern constellations, yet marking, night after night, by its gradually increasing altitude in the heavens, our advance upon our course, and becoming henceforward the pole-star that was to guide us throughout our researches, even as we hoped, to the utmost navigable limits of the Antarctic Ocean, we could not behold it without sanguine anticipations of the future.

In this part of the tropics we observed large patches of the splendid *Pyrosoma*, exhibiting a beautiful pale silvery light as we sailed past them: when taken out of the water the light is discontinued, until on irritating any particular part of the creature it again shows itself at that point, and soon pervades the whole animal mass.

As we approached the magnetic equator, or line of no dip, our observations relative to this interesting question were more frequent; and in order to secure a faithful record of those of each ship, as well as to detect the cause of any differences in either, it became our practice every day at 1 p. m. to communicate by signal the results of all that had been obtained up to that time. So much advantage was derived from this measure, that I would strongly recommend its adoption by any expedition that may be employed on a service of this nature. We had watched the progressive diminution of the dip of the needle, and steering a course as nearly south as the wind permitted, in order to cross the line of no dip at right angles, we found the change so rapid as to be ascertained with great precision; so much so that the signal for our being on the exact point of no dip, where the needles, being equally poised between the northern and southern magnetic systems, assumed a perfectly horizontal position, was being hoisted from both ships at the same instant of time. Nothing could be more satisfactory than the perfect accordance of our observations in a determination of so much importance: nor could it fail to be of more than ordinary interest to me to witness the needle thus affected; having some years previously, when at the north magnetic pole, seen it in a directly *vertical* position: nor was it unnatural, when we saw the south pole of the needle beginning to point below the horizon, to indulge the hope that ere long we might be permitted again to see it in a similar position at the south magnetic pole of the earth.

The regularity, as well as the rapidity, with which

the alterations of dip occur, is also worthy of notice. At two hundred and eighty miles north of the magnetic equator, the dip was 9° 36', showing about 2·05 minutes of change for every mile of latitude; at two hundred and ninety-two miles to the south, the dip was 9° 52', or about 2·03 minutes for every mile of latitude. It is to be remembered that this large amount of change is limited to the region of the magnetic equator; near the poles, it requires an approach of about two miles to produce an alteration of a single minute of dip.

The geographical position of the magnetic equator where we crossed it was lat. 13° 45' S, long. 30° 41' W. Here we again felt the influence of a westerly current of nearly a mile an hour.

The next matter of " great and especial interest in a magnetic point of view, " to which my attention was directed in the instructions drawn up for my guidance, at the request of the Lords Commissioners of the Admiralty, by the Committee of Physics of the Royal Society, was that of the situation of the point of minimum total intensity, or that point where the intensity is the least which occurs over the whole surface of the globe. It may be proper first to explain that, in passing from the north to the south magnetic hemisphere, there is upon every meridian a point at which the intensity, after having gradually diminished, again begins to increase as you advance to the higher magnetic latitudes.

These several points united form a circle round

the earth similar to the magnetic equator, or circle of no dip, like it dividing its circumference into two nearly equal portions, and with which it was until lately erroneously considered to be identical. Upon this circle there is a spot where the intensity is at a minimum, now to be the particular object of our investigation, together with the direction of that circle, and the form and extent of the lines and ovals of isodynamic or equal intensity.

In order to accomplish these several objects, it became necessary to pursue a course widely different from that usually followed by vessels bound to St. Helena, and imposed upon us the tedious operation of beating up to that island against the trade wind, an experiment seldom, if ever, attempted, and in our dull-sailing ships could only be effected by the sacrifice of a considerable portion of time. As we stood

Dec. 16. to the southward we crossed the circle, or equator of less intensity, in lat. 19° S. and long. 29° 15′ W., two hundred miles more to the northward than previous observations had led us to expect.

Dec. 17. On the morning of the 17th December, the island of Trinidad was seen; and at 7h. 30m. A. M. Commander Crozier and I, accompanied by several officers, left the ships. After pulling along the lee-side of the island, we at length landed in a small cove, a short distance to the northward of the Nine Pin Rock, of Halley, the surf on all other parts being too great to admit of it without hazarding the destruction of our boats. The island is a mass of volcanic matter, and rises abruptly on its leeward side to an elevation of about two thousand feet in some parts. The trap rocks of which it is composed assume most extraordinary shapes: the more remarkable of these are the Sugar Loaf Hill, near the southern, and the Nine Pin Rock, at the north-western part of the island. This latter projected to the height of eight hundred and fifty feet, almost perpendicularly from the sea, in the form of a beautifully proportioned column, is attached at its inner side to a ridge of hills two or three hundred feet high, which, like the mountains that present an insuperable barrier between the short beach of large rounded pebbles on which we landed, and the interior of the island, is chiefly composed of greenstone.

As a magnetic station, our observations here were utterly valueless, but the results may be useful by pointing out, in a striking manner, the great amount of error to which those made on shore are liable. Three dipping needles placed at only just sufficient distance apart to ensure their not influencing each other, indicated as much as three degrees difference of the dip, and all of them considerably less than that corresponding to the geographical position. To as large an amount also were the observations of variation vitiated by the local disturbing magnetic influence; whilst those taken on board our ships were perfectly free from these errors.

Horsburgh mentions that the island abounds with wild pigs and goats; one of the latter was seen.

c 4

1839.   With the view to add somewhat to the stock of useful creatures, a cock and two hens were put on shore; they seemed greatly to enjoy the change, and, I have no doubt, in so unfrequented a situation, and so delightful a climate, will quickly increase in numbers. We returned to our ships at 7 P.M., and made all sail to the southward. Trinidad was still in sight the next morning, at a distance of nearly fifty miles, and might be seen still further under more favourable circumstances.

CHAPTER II.

On each side of the tropic of Capricorn, which we crossed on the evening of the 19th, we experienced sharp squalls regularly between 8 A.M. and noon, and sometimes they occurred about 3 A. M. The cumulostratus clouds, of which Sir John Herschel has given so admirable a description, were in all cases the origin of these sudden gusts of wind. The cumuli, like beautiful rolls of wool, were first seen to windward, at the height of 3° 46', resting upon an ill-defined misty-looking cloud, about one degree high. They formed an irregular arch as they rose; and driven towards us by the wind, we could see the rain falling abundantly. When it had attained 35° of altitude, the squall struck the ship, and compelled us to lower the topsails, and take in all the sails but the foresail. They generally occurred three or four times in the forenoon. During their continuance the wind always veered more to the northward, and they were always preceded by a very perceptible increase of the short sea that obtains in this part of the ocean.

A curious phenomenon was witnessed by many of the officers at 8h. 30m. this evening. It was a beautiful clear night, not a cloud to be seen in any part of the heavens, yet we had a light shower of rain of more than an hour's continuance. The temperature of the dew-point by Daniell's hygrometer being 72°, that of the air 74°.

In addition to our almost daily experiments on the temperature of the ocean to the depth of six hundred fathoms, we had made several fruitless attempts to obtain soundings as we passed through the tropics. These repeated failures were principally occasioned by the want of a proper kind of line, but they served to point out to us that which was most suitable. I accordingly directed one to be made on board, three thousand six hundred fathoms, or rather more than four miles in length, fitted with swivels to prevent it unlaying in its descent, and strong enough to support a weight of seventy-six pounds.

On the 3d of January, in latitude 27° 26′ S., longitude 17° 29′ W., the weather and all other circumstances being propitious, we succeeded in obtaining soundings with two thousand four hundred and twenty-five fathoms of line, a depression of the bed of the ocean beneath its surface very little short of the elevation of Mount Blanc above it.

As I shall have occasion hereafter to enter more fully into the general question of the maximum depth of the sea, I shall take that opportunity of describing the method by which the soundings were obtained, and the accuracy with which the several depths were determined. We were at this

time only forty-five miles to the north-west of a
spot where a shoal is marked on the chart as having
been discovered in 1701. The great depth of water
would seem to throw some doubt on the reality of
this supposed danger, but being exactly to leeward
of the assigned position we were unable to ascertain the fact.

In latitude 21° S., and longitude 15° 30′ W., we   Jan. 8.
recrossed the line of least magnetic intensity. By
taking advantage of every change of the wind,
which we found to vary from S.S.E. to E.S.E.
at different periods of the day, we advanced on an
average between twenty-three and twenty-four
miles each day, and eventually anchored in St.
Helena Roads at 3° 30′ P. M. on the 31st January.   Jan. 31.

The chief purpose of our visit being to establish
a permanent magnetic observatory, and to land
Lieutenant Lefroy of the Royal Artillery, and the
party under his command, together with all the
instruments intended for their use, I obtained permission from His Excellency Lieutenant-General
Middlemore to make an examination of the lands   Feb. 2.
belonging to the crown; and having selected a
spot near the house that had been erected for the
residence of the Emperor Napoleon, but which had
never been occupied by him, as a site for the
observatory, it was immediately granted by the
governor. All the arrangements for the lease of the
premises, and the contracts for the necessary buildings, were completed in a few days by the diligent

and ready co-operation of the Board of respective Officers, consisting chiefly of Lieut.-Col. Trelawny of the Royal Artillery, and Captain Alexander of the Royal Engineers, to whom I am more especially desirous to express thus publicly my thanks for the prompt and effectual means they adopted to forward the service with which I was charged.

Here as invariably on all volcanic islands, it was found quite impossible to obtain correct measures of the magnetic elements, by reason of the large amount of the disturbing influence of the rock itself. So powerful indeed was it in this particular instance, that even at the distance at which our ships were anchored it produced such anomalies in the results of our observations for the deviation of dip, variation, and intensity, as to mask the ordinary effects of the ship's iron. The comparisons of our magnetic instruments were just as unsatisfactory, for no two places could be found, however near to or distant from each other, where accordant results could be obtained even with the

same instrument. The importance, therefore, of St. Helena as a magnetic station will be manifested more by the detection of the momentary, irregular, and secular changes than by absolute determinations; and for meteorological purposes it cannot fail to be of essential advantage. Taking leave of our kind friend the governor, Col. Trelawney, Capt. Blackwell, and the officers of the 91st regiment, to whom we are all indebted for their attentions and many acts of friendship, we weighed on the morning of the ninth, after sending our letters and despatches on board the "Bombay" for conveyance to England, and proceeded on our voyage.

The trade wind prevented our fetching so far to the eastward as I wished, so that we crossed for a third time the line of least magnetic intensity in lat. 21° S. and long. 8° W. Our slow progress through this, magnetically speaking, very interesting region afforded us the opportunity of obtaining a vast number of observations, which having been transmitted to England from the Cape of Good Hope were placed in the hands of Lieut.-Colonel Sabine of the Royal Artillery, and published, under his supervision, in the Philosophical Transactions * of the Royal Society, to which I must refer the scientific inquirer for the observations themselves, and also for a more detailed account of the results. It is enough to state here, in the words of Col. Sabine, " that the determination of the position of the line of least intensity is easier, and in some respects more sure, than that of an isodynamic line, because it is independent of the correctness of an assumed intensity at a base station. It is therefore to be expected that the position of this line will become in future years the subject of frequent examination, seeming to mark, from time to time, the progress of the secular change in its position. This may be done with the more interest and ad-

* Part I. for 1842.

1840.

vantage, because there is reason to believe that its position is changing rapidly in the space referred to, particularly in the eastern meridians ; and that the southern magnetic hemisphere, in so far as its boundary may be indicated by this line, is in that quarter of the globe gaining rapidly on the northern."

He further states, that whilst the general direc-rection of the line of least intensity, drawn from observations * of Dunlop, Erman, and Sulivan, corresponding nearly to the epoch of 1825, is consistent with that deduced from our observations in 1840, yet its earlier position is every where three or four degrees south of that which would be inferred from the later determinations. Its average northerly movement therefore, during the last fifteen years, appears to have rather exceeded annually thirteen miles.

Feb. 15.

A water-spout of small size, seen on the morning of the fifteenth, was followed by a heavy shower in the afternoon of an hour's continuance. The rain which fell at a temperature of 67°, in a few minutes reduced that of the air from 79° to 73.°

In lat. 26° 10' S. and long. 12° 50' W. we made another attempt at deep sounding, but failed, owing to the line being accidentally checked and breaking at twelve hundred and sixty fathoms.

Feb. 22.

This evening, soon after dark, a number of cuttle fish sprang on board over the weather bulwark, fif-

* See Phil. Trans. 1840. Plate V.

teen or sixteen feet high; several passed entirely across the ship, and altogether not less than fifty were found upon the decks. We could not on this, as on a former occasion, ascribe their visit to the sea washing them into the vessel, the water at the time being quite smooth, and only a moderate breeze blowing.

Whilst running before a strong northerly breeze, we observed heavy clouds gathering to the S. W., and could scarcely reduce our sails before we experienced a most violent squall from that quarter, which was almost immediately succeeded by a calm of short duration. These sudden gusts of wind are not at all indicated by the barometer and are not unfrequently the cause of the loss of masts, when not prepared for in time. The northerly wind resumed its power until about noon, when it again shifted suddenly to the southward, so that we seemed to have got into another region of the variables. Before and during the heavy torrents of rain, which poured down for the next twenty hours with but little intermission, we were surprised that both the barometer and sympiesometer rose steadily. The temperature of the rain (as noticed also on the fifteenth) being 67°, again reduced that of the air from 74°5 to 69°.

In lat. 31° 20′ S. we crossed the meridian of Greenwich on our eastward course.

Although the south-westerly breeze of the pre- ceding day hardly amounted to a moderate gale, we found that this morning we had run into a heavy

1840. swell from that direction. The result of several experiments gave only twenty-two feet for the entire height of the waves, or eleven feet above and below the general level of the ocean; the velocity of the undulations eighty-nine miles per hour, and the interval between each wave nineteen hundred and ten feet.

Steering for the shoal, called Kattendyk on our charts, in lat. 33° S. and long. 4° 52′ E, we kept the lead constantly going, but could not get soundings with from one hundred and twenty to one hundred and fifty fathoms, although we passed exactly over its presumed position; and the next day, in

March 1. lat. 33° 10′ S. and long. 5° 50′ E., we could not reach the bottom with five hundred and eighty fathoms.

March 3. At 9h. 30m. A.M., when in lat. 33° 21′S. and long. 9° E., being perfectly calm, we lowered the boats down and again succeeded in obtaining deep soundings: on this occasion, in two thousand six hundred and seventy-seven fathoms, and at a distance of about four hundred and fifty miles west of the Cape of Good Hope. The current was setting to the westward, at the rate of a mile per hour; and for several days previously we had experienced its influence fully to that amount.

March 7. This evening we observed a gradual diminution of the temperature of the air and the sea, as we approached the coast of Africa; and before midnight we entered a cold mist, which prevented our seeing to any considerable distance: the water appearing discoloured, we tried for, but did not obtain, sound-ings, with one hundred and thirty fathoms of line.

By 1 P. M., the next day, the temperature of the sea had fallen from 70° to 56°5, that of the air being 65°, and the mist unpleasantly cold to our feelings. We were at this time in lat. 32° 21′ S. long. 17° 6′ E., therefore about forty-five miles from Paternoster Point, when we struck soundings in one hundred and twenty-seven fathoms, on a bed of fine dark sand. We had expected to have found an *elevation* in the temperature both of the air and sea on our approach to the African coast, by reason of the radiation of heat from its shores; but the cause of the depression became evident on the morning of the 9th, when, having sighted Cape Paternoster at daylight, we found we had to con-tend against a current increasing in strength and coldness of temperature as we neared the land. The existence of a body of cold water rushing from the eastward, round the Cape of Good Hope, has long been suspected; but, its extension so far to the northward has not, I believe, been before noticed. As we were several days beating up to the Cape we collected the following curious facts respecting it. Thus on the 7th, when distant one hundred and twenty miles from the coast, and be-fore we perceived the effects of the current, the temperature of the air was 71°, that of the sea 70°, and the depth of water more than four hundred

D

fathoms; which being placed in order will serve to explain the arrangement of the following table.

No.	Date.	Distance off Shore.	Temperature.		Depth of Water.	Remarks.
			Air.	Sea.		
		Miles.			Fms.	
1	7	120	71°	70°	400	No soundings.
2	8	90	65	63	130	No soundings.
3	—	45	65	56	127	Temp. at that depth, 45°.
4	—	10	59	54	65	
5	9	10	59	54	47	
6	10	60	64	61	200	Temp. at that depth, 43°.5.
7	—	20	61	55	130	
8	11	52	67	64	203	
9	—	32	60	54	142	
10	12	51	69	66·5	313	
11	—	36	67	67	202	
12	—	27	58	54·5	72	
13	13	7	63	55	58	
14	—	4	59	51·5	48	
15	14	27	62	57·5	115	
16	15	6	55	51	76	W. N. W. from Cape.
17	16	11	66	62	190	W. S. W. from Cape.
18	17	4	65	60	37	In False Bay, S. E. from Cape.

By a careful examination of the above experiments it will be manifest that the distance to which the cold water extends from the coast depends materially upon the depth of the soundings. It barely reaches forty miles from the shore, where the sea is more than three hundred fathoms deep, but spreads over double that distance in the shallower parts. At forty-five miles from the land, and at a depth of one hundred and twenty fathoms, the temperature was found to be 45°, that of the surface being 56°; and at sixty miles off the land, at two hundred fathoms, it was 43°.5, the surface being 61°.

All these circumstances combine to show that a northerly current of very limited extent, but of considerable force, exists from the Cape of Good Hope, along the western coast of Africa; which, in general terms, may be represented by a volume of water sixty miles wide and two hundred fathoms deep, averaging a velocity of about a mile an hour, and of the mean temperature of the ocean, running between the shores of Africa and the waters of the adjacent sea.   The cloud of mist which hangs over this stream of cold water is occasioned, of course, by the condensation of the vapour of the superincumbent atmosphere, whose temperature is generally so many degrees higher than that of the sea.   It is sufficiently well defined to afford useful notice to seamen of their near approach to the land.

We anchored on the evening of the 17th in Simon's Bay, and immediately commenced the necessary comparisons of our magnetic and other instruments, the sandstone formation of the country being more favourable for the purpose than that of any other place we had touched at since leaving England. Observations for the effect of the ship's iron on the various instruments employed were made in both ships, as also, by the kind and ready assistance of Captain Puget, on board of the "Melville," the first two-decker on which I had ever had an

March 17.

opportunity of experimenting, and in which it proved to be of very small amount.

We here found no difficulty in replenishing our stores and provisions, for by an especial order to that effect from the Commander-in-Chief, Rear-Admiral the Honourable George Elliot, C. B., and the active exertions in our favour of J. Deas Thompson, Esquire, the naval storekeeper, every want was promptly and liberally supplied, and every thing done for us that a cordial interest in our undertaking could suggest.

To His Excellency Lieutenant-General Sir George Napier I am also much indebted for offering me any portion of the crown lands that might be required for the site of the Magnetic Observatory, which I was directed to establish here, and leave under the superintendence of Lieutenant Eardley Wilmot, of the Royal Artillery, who, with his party of three assistants, and all the necessary instruments, were now disembarked from the Erebus. In making a selection of so much importance I gladly availed myself of the judgment and local knowledge of Mr. M'Lear, at present and for several years past the resident astronomer, and by his advice decided on a spot adjoining the Cape Observatory; thereby securing to Mr. Wilmot the co-operation of practised observers when long continued series of observations should render their aid desirable, and at all times relieving him from a considerable amount of labour, by rendering the

astronomical observations of the observatory available for his purposes. I am truly obliged to Mr.
M'Lear for his kindness on that occasion, and for
the alacrity with which he offered and has given
every assistance in his power to promote the erection of the necessary buildings, and forward the
views and wishes of Mr. Wilmot in the discharge
of his arduous and responsible duties.

CHAPTER III.

WE weighed on the morning of the 6th, and as we
stood out of Simon's Bay the "Melville" manned
her rigging, and gave us three encouraging cheers,
which we as cordially returned. Light baffling
airs from the S. E. delayed us, but just before
dark we succeeded in clearing the breakers of the
"Bellows" rock, by about a quarter of a mile.

The Terror was obliged to make another tack, so
we shortened sail to wait for her; but, soon after
midnight, the wind changed suddenly, and the weather became so dark and thick, with violent squalls
and much thunder and lightning, that we parted
company, and at daylight, not seeing her, we pursued
our course alone towards Prince Edward Islands,
where I was desirous of landing to obtain observations.

We found the temperature of the surface of the
sea to increase rapidly after leaving Cape Point,
where, as well as in Simon's Bay, it was at 58°;
half a mile from the Cape it was at 58°.5; at 8h.
P. M., within a quarter of a mile of the "Bellows,"
it was 59°; at 9h. P. M., only two miles and a half
further to the south, it was up to 64°; at which time
we were probably in much deeper water: at midnight it was 66°, as was also that of the air; and
from which it did not afterwards differ materially,

showing that we had got to the southward of the
cold water current that runs along the west, and
perhaps the south, coast of Africa.

It is evident, therefore, that this current does not
come down directly from the south, as it only extends to seven or eight miles from the Cape, and beyond that distance we have to descend to more than
six hundred fathoms before we can find water of so
low a temperature as 43°.5.   It may be that if the
whole body of the sea is moving from east to west, as
some suppose, that in passing over the shoal bank
off Cape Aguilhas, the waters belonging to a greater
depth, and of consequently a colder temperature, may
thus be brought near to the surface; but at ninety
and one hundred and twenty miles to the S. E.
of the Cape, and near the edge of the bank, we
found the temperature at seventy-seven fathoms
55°.2, and at one hundred fathoms 54°; so that the
current which runs close along the shore must be
of a much lower temperature if that of the west
coast is supplied from this source.   I will continue
to notice in detail all that came within our observation bearing upon this question, or that may assist
the further investigation of these strange and un-
explained currents.   The frequent changes in their
direction, their various velocities, and the broad
belts of cold water we passed through, are all separ-
ately deserving of more attention of the navigator
than we had time to bestow on them; and a more
strict inquiry into their causes might prove highly
advantageous to ships passing the Cape, by point-

ing out the best parallel in which to profit most by them, or, in stormy weather, how to avoid them.

After blowing from almost every point of the compass the wind settled in the north, and in order to get clear of the Aguilhas bank, on which we found a harassing jobble of a sea, we ran before it to the southward until midnight, when a calm of several hours' continuance was succeeded by a light southerly wind. At 1 P. M., when eighty-four miles S. by E. from the Cape, we had no soundings with six hundred fathoms. In trying the temperature of the sea, at various depths, we unfortunately lost two of our self-registering thermometers by the line breaking, which is the reason that these experiments were afterwards less frequently made than might have been desirable in the course of our voyage to Van Diemen's Land.

The southerly wind obliged us to stand to the eastward, and the whole of this and the following day we experienced a heavy swell, indicative of a past gale; but this, about midnight of the 9th, was changed into a short, irregular, breaking sea, which we considered to be probably occasioned by our falling down upon the western edge of the Aguilhas bank, for it continued throughout the night, and the next day we found ourselves in seventy-seven fathoms; some pieces of dead coral and broken shells came up with the lead. Both yesterday and to-day we passed through many long lines of brown-coloured animalculæ: they were about five or six feet broad and several miles in

length, lying in the direction of the wind: on examination they proved to consist of a species of gre-
garious mollusca, the animals having no organic
connection together; but there were always two
fixed points of contact, and they moved simultaneously in wavy lines.

Besides these we found many kinds of curious
marine animals amongst the long leaves of the
floating sea-weed (*Macrocystis pyrifera*) that
abounds in every part of this ocean. The gigantic
albatross (*Diomedea exulans*) was seen in great
numbers, and many of them taken by means of a
fishing-line, as were also some of the prettily
speckled Cape pigeon (*Procellaria capensis*), and
several other kinds of petrel, which in these regions
seem to take the place of the beautiful varieties of
gulls which inhabit our northern seas.

April 11.   This morning the wind shifting to the S. E. we
wore and stood to the southward, being still on the
Aguilhas bank. In the afternoon we obtained
soundings in one hundred and twenty-five fathoms,
dark sand and shells; but after sailing seven
miles on that course we could not reach the
ground with three hundred and twenty fathoms of
line: thus marking the southern limits of this
extraordinary and extensive bank in the longitude
of 21° 20′ E. to be between the latitudes of 36° 37′
and 36° 44′ S., and about a hundred and thirty
miles from the Cape whose name it bears.

April 12.   To-day the température of the air was up to 74°,
that of the sea was 69°.

Although we were not above forty miles from yesterday's position, we had no soundings with six hundred fathoms, so suddenly does the depth of water increase, to the south, upon leaving the bank.

The variation of the compass was observed to have increased to 30° W. It fell calm towards midnight, and by our observations at noon we found that we had been carried away by a current above thirty miles to the southward of our supposed position, and the following day, to the south-westward, above fifty miles. We had some rain during the night, and flashes of lightning were seen to the south-eastward. Steering in that direction we approached the storm, and shortly got into the midst of the heaviest rain I ever witnessed. It came down literally in sheets of water, accompanied by very violent squalls from various quarters, alternately with perfect, but almost momentary, calms. The temperature of the rain which fell being 61° brought down that of the air from 67° to 64°, whilst the surface of the sea *rose* to 73°.5 from 71°.

Heavy thunder and the most vivid lightning occurred during this great fall of water, which lasted without intermission for more than ten hours, and it required the utmost vigilance in the officers and crew to manœuvre the ship during the rapid changes both in the strength and direction of the wind, and the extraordinary bubbling of the sea produced by these fierce contending gusts. But before noon it blew fresh from the eastward, gra-

1840.

dually veering round to the northward, and in the evening increased to a strong north-westerly breeze, with so heavy and irregular a sea that we spent the night in great anxiety, and in momentary expectation that our boats would be washed away by some of the broken waves that fell on board, or, that from the frequent shocks the ship sustained when the seas struck her, we should lose some of the masts, although we had taken every precaution to secure them. This dangerous commotion we attributed to the current by which for several days we had been carried to the south-westward, but which had during the last day changed its course to the north-westward, and which was running at the extraordinary rate of sixty-eight miles per diem, or nearly three miles an hour, in direct opposition to the wind.

April 15.

The temperature of the surface of the sea fell so rapidly from 73° to 61°, that I concluded we were approaching a body of ice, and some indications in the sky favoured this belief. We did not however see any, and before midnight the temperature had again risen to 67°, so that, if its fall were occasioned by ice, we had probably passed it in the dark.

April 16.

At noon we were in lat. 41° 24′ S. and long. 25° E., and detected another change in the current, it having carried us N. 75 E., twenty-two miles during the last twenty-four hours; and again we found a gradual depression in the temperature of the sea from 68° at 1h. A. M. to 58° at noon, without any other cause than that of the air falling to 52° as the wind shifted to the southward.

We were now south of that stream, which, taking the direction of the Natal coast, is known to extend far out to sea; and had got into a counter current, setting to the eastward at the rate, on an average of several days, of about a mile an hour. We had no soundings to-day with six-hundred fathoms, the temperature at that depth being 43°.8.

In the course of the past week a change of thirty degrees of temperature, both of the air and of the sea, took place, which, to those who had passed the previous months in a tropical climate, was likely to be productive of serious injury to their health, unless carefully guarded against. This alteration of climate in so short a time was at first very sensibly felt, and it was necessary to issue positive regulations about the clothing of our people, amongst whom severe colds were beginning to make their appearance.

Running before a strong westerly wind, and rapidly nearing Prince Edward's Island, from which at noon we were distant only about twenty miles, we were not surprised to see many penguins; but the weather was so hazy, that we could not perceive the land until we found ourselves within two or three miles of its southern point. Sailing close along its south-eastern side, and at about one mile south of the East Cape, we sounded in eighty-six fathoms, fine sand, coral, and corallines. This line of coast is composed of black, perpendicular, volcanic cliffs, much worn away by the action of the waves. We observed two or three conical hillocks, like the small craters of a volcano, of a deep red colour, whether arising from an oxide of iron, or vegetable matter, we could not discern. The South Cape has a perpendicular face, the termination of a long terrace-like projection from the foot of the hills. The mountains in the centre of the island rise to a considerable height; but their summits being enveloped in mist, we could not determine their elevation, although we could see they were partially covered with snow. We imagined we could distinguish small trees, still of this there is considerable doubt: Captain Cook, although at a much greater distance, asserts that he saw trees and shrubs, but he was assuredly mistaken. Long lines of sea-weed extended two or three miles from the shore beyond the East Cape, whilst strong eddies of tide, occasioned probably by their meeting at this point, seeming to indicate concealed dangers, and darkness now coming on, we hauled off for the night, having first seen a small cove a short distance to the northward, where we hoped to be able to land the next morning. This part of the coast was populated by vast numbers of penguins, in groups of many thousands each, and other kinds of sea-birds were abundant. Some seals that were playing in the surf about the small detached rocks were pronounced to be of the fur species (*Arctocephalus Falklandicus*), by those well acquainted with them: it is not improbable that on the western coast some of their haunts, or, as the sealers term them, "rookeries," might be found.

The soundings during the night were very irregular. A dredge put overboard for a short time in ninety-five fathoms, at about five or six miles east of the island, came up quite full of a small white coral, and between thirty and forty different kinds of marine animals, corallines, flustræ, and sponges. At daylight in the morning we found that we had been carried so far to leeward by a strong tide, or more probably a current, and so heavy a swell prevailed from the westward, the forerunner of the coming gale, that I reluctantly gave up my intention of landing, rather than lose any more time in hopeless endeavours, and bore away for the Crozets. There did not seem to be any bay along the north-eastern or south-eastern coast where a ship could find anchorage, unless it be just to the northward of the East Cape, where we supposed we saw a small sandy beach between two extensive patches of sea-weed; nor did Commander Crozier see any as he passed along the north shore the next day, in the Terror. He mentioned a remarkable detached tower-shaped rock, at some distance off the North Cape. This promontory he found by good observation to be in lat. 46° 53′ S. and long. 37° 33′ E., agreeing very nearly with Cook in the latitude, but differing considerably in the longitude. In the Erebus we were unfortunate in not getting observations near the southern part of the island: nor could we approach the smaller north-eastern island suffi-

1840. ciently near to see any creeks or bays; but I was afterwards told that sealers sometimes anchor at a place called Cave Bay, on its east side, in lat. 46° 40′ S. with the N. E. point bearing N. E. by E.; the Cave, W. N. W; and Mary's Point, S. W. ½ S. in eight to ten fathoms water. The larger island, though discovered by a French navigator in 1772, was named by Captain Cook, some years afterwards, Prince Edward's Island, in honour of the late Duke of Kent, the father of our most gracious Queen.

April 22. The westerly gale continued throughout the 22d and 23d, but early on the 24th it veered to the north, and increased to a violent storm, with its usual accompaniment of heavy rain, fortunately of only a few hours' duration, for the heavy cross sea the change of wind occasioned washed away our hammock nettings, and swept several things off our decks: towards evening the wind moderated, and backed round to the westward. During this run we passed many large patches of sea-weed, which had probably been torn from the shores of Prince Edward's Island, and as we did not see any as we approached it from the westward, it would seem to show that a westerly current prevails in these parts of the ocean, although, from the accordance of the dead reckoning with our observations, it is probably of inconsiderable strength.

April 25. A comparatively fine day: we continued to pass many large patches of sea-weed, and although arrived near the position on our charts of Crozet's group of islands, we could see nothing of them, and

I should have lost much time in the search,
had I not, fortunately, before leaving the Cape of
Good Hope, obtained a more accurate account of
their situation from a merchant of Cape Town, at
whose request I undertook to convey some provisions to Possession, or to East Island, for a party
of seamen employed there in the capture of the
sea elephant (*Morunga Elephantina*).

Land was seen at daylight this morning, bearing
E. by S. at the distance of ten miles. It proved to
be Penguin, or Inaccessible Island, and well deserves either of the names it bears, for it was
literally covered with penguins on all the ledges
of its rugged shores, nor could we any where see a
point on which it would be possible to land. Like
all other volcanic islands, its summits terminate in
curiously shaped pinnacles, and not the smallest
appearance of vegetation was perceptible. The
great quantities of sea-weed and numerous water-
fowl we met with would have given us timely notice
of our approach to land.

"Pig Island" of the sealers was soon afterwards
seen to the northward. It is the westernmost
island of the group, and presented a much more
agreeable aspect, but the weather being unfavourable, and its eastern, or lee side, having many dangerous reefs and detached rocks off it, we did not
venture nearer than two or three leagues; but after
passing close to Inaccessible Island, we shaped a
course for the southern extreme of Possession

E

1840.   Island, which we had been informed extended as
far as the 47th degree of latitude.

During the night the wind increased to a strong
breeze from the westward, with thick weather, and
we were obliged to carry a heavy press of sail to
clear the land under our lee, which we had scarcely
accomplished when a south-westerly gale came on.

April 27.   Although still very foggy at times, we were enabled to bear away at 10 A. M., and having passed
over the assigned position of Possession Island, we
saw the land at 5 P. M. through the haze, five or
six miles distant, but daylight was now almost gone;
we nevertheless stood towards it, until darkness
closed the scene, when the ship was hauled off for
the night.

April 28.   The morning was more clear, when, as the day
broke, between six and seven o'clock, we perceived
the lofty mountains of East Island four or five
leagues directly to windward of us, so much had we
been carried to the eastward during the night.
The whole day was spent in beating up against the
current and strong westerly breeze, and at sunset
we were still several miles from the shore.

I could not but regret this serious loss of time,
but having appointed Possession Island our first
rendezvous, until the end of this month, in case of
parting from the Terror, I wished to communicate
with one or other of the sealing parties, to ascertain
whether they had seen her off the islands. I was
still more anxious to land the provisions which I
had on board for the winter stock of those people

who might have been in much want of them. We therefore continued beating to windward all night, and at daylight, the fog having cleared away, we had a good view of this perfect mountain mass of volcanic land; its shores bold and precipitous with many projecting rocks, which seem to have been formed by the unceasing action of the waves cutting away the softer parts, and with the exception of a single beach of some extent, on the north-east part of the island, affording no place where either a habitation could be built, or a boat land.

This beach appearing to us the only favourable spot for the sealing party, we fired several guns as we stood close in to the shore, and by these means attracted their notice, for we soon afterwards observed with our glasses a large fire on the east side of the bay, which the people had made to point out to us their location. We were still too far to leeward for them to venture off to us, and after beating to windward until 2 P. M., when just as we could have fetched into the bay, the wind suddenly increased to a strong gale, and the violent gusts that rushed along the almost perpendicular coast line, raising the spoondrift in clouds over us, reduced us to a close-reefed main-topsail and storm staysails, under which, when within half a mile of the shore, we wore and stood off again, seeing the utter hopelessness of communicating with the party until the return of more moderate weather.

We were greatly disappointed at being thus defeated; but these frequent repulses only made us more determined to do our utmost to effect the objects we had in view: and although we were driven by the gale and current far away to leeward, yet, towards evening, when it abated, we began to maintain our ground, and, by carrying a heavy press of sail throughout the night, we found ourselves the April 30. next morning several miles to windward of East Island, and had Possession Island distinctly in sight on our weather bow. Knowing the greater facility of communicating with this land by reason of the shelter its extent affords from the strong westerly gales that blow almost continually except at this period of the year, and as the larger establishment of sealers was on this island, I preferred beating up to it as the weather was fine and we were making good way, rather than run down to the leeward party at the risk of being again unable to land at their station.

Soon after noon it fell quite calm; and, after firing a few guns, we observed a white flag hoisted on a pole by the party in America Bay: we were, at this time, about five miles from the shore and directly between Possession and East Islands; the weather was still too unsettled for a boat to come off to us. While lying becalmed in this passage we obtained soundings in eighty-five fathoms, on a bank of sand, shells, and corallines. At dusk, on a breeze springing up from the north-west, we stood off to sea for the night.

May 1.   It blew hard from the north-westward with so dense a haze that it was only during a partial clearing, and when within four miles of Dark Head we had a glimpse of the high perforated rock that stands out more than a mile from the coast to the westward, and is an unerring mark, by which the Cape may always be distinguished:— as we bore away close along the shore we got into smooth water, but, passing " Windy Bay," the squalls that came down the valley compelled us to lower our topsails and keep them down until we had passed the opening.

The remarkable " Red Crag," near which the flag had been displayed yesterday, came in sight and guided us to America Bay, where we saw the party on the beach launching their boat. Mr. Hickley, their leader, came on board, and he, as well as his boat's crew, looked more like Esquimaux than civilized beings, but filthier far in their dress and persons than any I had ever before seen. Their clothes were lite-rally soaked in oil and smelt most offensively ; they wore boots of penguins' skins with the feathers turned inwards. They told us that the weather had been so tempestuous that until yesterday they had not been able to launch a boat for five weeks ; they had therefore been very unsuccessful at the Sea Elephant fishery, and were disappointed to find that they were not to be removed to " Pig Island " for the winter ; which they describe as being so overrun with these animals, that, to use their own words, " you can hardly land for them." The breed was left there by Captain Distance, in 1834, and in less than six years have increased in an almost incredible manner, although great numbers are every year killed by the sealers, not only for present subsistence, but salted down for supplies on their voyages to and from the Cape. Some goats had been landed from an American ship some years ago on Possession Island, and were also thriving on the long coarse grass with which it abounds, but still maintained their domestic state, under the protection of the sealers. The party consisted in all of eleven men, one of whom had been on the island for three years: they seemed to have no wish to return to the Cape of Good Hope and were quite contented, having plenty of food. The tongue, flippers, and part of the carcase of the Sea Elephant are eaten by them, and they get a great abundance of a species of rock-fish (probably a *Cottus* or *Notothenia*), about the size of a small haddock, with a very large head, which they preserve by drying upon the rocks. The eggs of sea-birds in the breeding season may be collected by boat loads, and are said to be excellent food, particularly that of the albatross, which averages above a pound in weight, and the young birds, when first taken from the nest, are described by them as being quite delicious: it is possible, however, they may have acquired the Esquimaux taste as well as their habits. They described the soil as being good, but they have never planted potatoes or other vegetable, although they have no doubt of their thriving here as the temperature is never very low. Wild ducks are so numerous in a lake on the top of the Red Crag that dogs, trained for the purpose, get them any number whenever they are wanted.

They had no plan of the island, and their information on this subject was vague and unsatisfactory; they stated it to be twenty miles long and ten broad; having three bays on its east side, in which ships may anchor, but the western coast is quite unapproachable by ships of any size, on account of the heavy swell that constantly rolls in upon its shores: a boat belonging to this party and all the crew were lately lost there, whilst in search of sea elephants.

In America Bay, Lively Bay, and Ship Bay, vessels at anchor are well protected from the prevailing winds, but must leave the two latter immediately on the springing up of an easterly breeze, as America Bay is the only one where there is room for a ship to beat out. These winds are said to be of rare occurrence, so much so that the French frigate Heroine, which was sent in 1834 to survey this group of islands, remained the whole period of her stay, above five weeks, moored in Ship Bay; since then, however, two English whalers were wrecked in the same bay, by trying to ride out an easterly gale.

Mr. Hickley told us that there was every indication of an easterly wind, which is more frequent just at this time of the year, and the height of the barometer seemed to confirm his opinion, or I should have anchored for a few hours to have examined the bay; but convinced from the nature of its formation that it could be of no use as a magnetic station, and, being anxious to rejoin the Terror as soon as possible at our next rendezvous, we bore away with the intention of laying down as much of the coast line of the island as we could before dark.

Like the rest of the group it is evidently of igneous origin; near the tops of some of the hills we could perceive short basaltic columns, and two or three appearances of extinct craters: the coast is high and precipitous at the north end and singularly stratified; along its eastern shore it is more broken into small bays, and we observed several cataracts issuing from the more extensive green patches upon the hill-sides, and dashing over the black cliffs into the sea beneath.

The remarkable "Dark Head," at the northern extreme of the island, is in lat. 46° 19′ S., long. 51° 53′ E.; the southern point is in lat. 46° 28′ S., and long. 51° 56′ E.; the variation of the compass 35° 13′ W. The centre of East Island is in lat. 46° 27′ S., and long. 52° 14′ E.

These results, though sufficient for all the purposes of navigation, were not obtained with exactness, owing to the unfavourable state of the weather for observations.

Leaving the south end of Possession Island at 4 P. M. we steered close along the southern coast of East Island. Though not more than three or four miles in diameter its loftiest pinnacles attain a height of at least four thousand feet, and the precipices of its shores in some places rise several hundred feet perpendicularly from the sea. Nearly every cape has its detached rock extending off it,

from half a mile to two miles: one of these near
Bull Bay lies still further off, and being considerably inclined, in one point of view, resembles a ship
under a press of sail; hence its appellation, "Ship
Rock." Another, near the south-eastern extreme,
is called "Church Rock," from another fancied
similarity; but the most remarkable of them all is
the perforated rock to the westward of the North
Cape of Possession Island, through which we were
told a small vessel might sail.

Favoured by a strong north-westerly breeze we
advanced rapidly towards Kerguelen Island. On
the morning of the 3d, when in lat. 47° 17′ S.,
long. 58° 50′ E., the first piece of Antarctic ice was
seen by us, though so small as scarcely to deserve
the name of an ice-berg, being not more than
twenty feet high and evidently fast dissolving, yet
it was sufficiently solid to injure seriously any
vessel that might run against it. We passed several
beds of floating sea-weed, and were accompanied
on our course by many of the great albatross, and
the large dark petrel, and still more numerously by
the speckled Cape pigeon and stormy petrel, of two
· or three different kinds. These birds added a degree of cheerfulness to our solitary wanderings,
which contrasted strongly with the dreary and
unvarying stillness of the tropical region, where
not a sea-bird is to be seen, except only in the vicinity of its few scattered islets, which is the more
remarkable where the ocean abounds so plentifully
with creatures fit for their food.

A sperm whale, a seal, and a shoal of porpoises were seen. Blowing a strong breeze, almost a gale, from the north-west, with thick weather, and at 5 p. m., being within twenty miles of an islet called "Bligh's Cap" by Cook, we rounded-to, under close-reefed topsails, to wait for daylight and clearer weather to make the land. At 7h. 30m. p. m. we struck soundings in one hundred and fifteen fathoms, on a bank of fine black sand and small stones; and, during the night, the depth varied from one hundred and twenty to one hundred and forty-five fathoms.

It was nearly nine o'clock the next morning before the weather cleared up so as to admit of our running for the islet, and before noon it again became so thick that we could not see more than two or three miles; yet such was our confidence in the accuracy of the positions assigned by our great navigator to all the places he discovered or visited, that we unhesitatingly pursued our course, and at a quarter past twelve the high and apparently inaccessible little rock was seen directly ahead of us; we passed very close by it, steering for Cape François of Kerguelen Island. When we had run the distance to within half a mile, the fog was so dense that we could scarcely see twice the length of the ship, and darkness coming on, we were obliged to haul off for the night, under easy sail. The soundings were in from seventy to eighty fathoms, rocky bottom; and in the morning Cape François was in sight five or six miles on our

weather bow, but the wind had by that time freshened considerably, and the sea running high, we
were unable to maintain our ground; so that,
although we carried a heavy press of sail throughout
the day and night, we found that we were drifted
away twenty miles to leeward of the Cape when
day broke the next morning.

We beat back in the course of the day, and at
11 P. M. hove to, within two miles of our port,
awaiting daylight to enter it : again we were disappointed. It was beautiful weather at midnight, with
very little wind, and a perfectly smooth sea; so
suddenly, however, do gales come on in these stormy
regions, that in less than three hours it blew so
hard as to reduce us to close-reefed topsails, and a
heavy sea arising, we were driven away from the
land. The storm, which increased in fury, continued to blow violently the next day, and until nine
the following morning, when it began to moderate,
and we again made sail as the wind gradually
abated. The remainder of this, and the whole of
the next day, were occupied in regaining the land,
and in obtaining a connected series of soundings on
a bank of black sand and rock, which we found to
extend above a hundred miles from the Cape. The
discovery of this great bank, so likely to be of
important advantage to the numerous vessels that
occasionally visit the dangerous shores of this
island, by warning them of their approach to the
land, could not fail to remove every feeling of
regret at the delay and fatigue to which we had

been exposed. I have called it on the chart the "Erebus Bank;" and a dangerous reef of rocks, E. by S. from Cape François, distant between fifteen and sixteen miles, upon which the sea broke violently, received the name of "Terror Reef." The position and extent of this reef were accurately determined by Captain Crozier and the officers of the Terror; and together with such surveys as we were able to make during our stay in this neighbourhood, and such information as I have been able to obtain from the Hydrographic Office, by the permission of Captain Beaufort, serve as the foundation of a general plan of the island; but much remains yet to be done, and carefully minute examination will be necessary before any thing like an accurate map of the numerous harbours, reefs, rocks, and other dangers, can be accomplished.

Many sperm whales were seen during the several days we were beating about upon the Erebus Bank, and large flocks of sea-birds hovered over the patches of sea-weed we met with, whether floating detached, or still fixed to the rocks.

This morning being close in with the remarkable "Arched Rock" which forms the south cape of Christmas Harbour, and favoured with moderate weather we got fairly between the heads soon after noon; the wind, however, was directly against us, and rapidly increasing in strength, threatened to drive us out once more to sea. As we reached the narrows, which form the inner harbour, so

violent were the squalls, and so contracted the
channel (not quite one third of a mile), that we
were beating for three hours without losing or
gaining a ship's length; darkness coming on put
an end to the laborious struggle, and compelled us,
at six o'clock, to anchor in twenty-three fathoms,
fine sand and stones. Although not exactly where
we desired to be, we were thankful to have found
so good an anchorage, for it almost immediately
began to blow a complete gale, which lasted the
whole night.

The Terror arrived the next morning, but, owing
to the unsettled state of the weather, it was not
until the 15th that we could warp up to the head of
the harbour, and secure the ships in positions convenient for easy and frequent communication with
the shore. The remainder of this and the whole of
the following day were occupied in getting the ship
to rights, and landing the observatories.

The 17th, being Sunday, our people had a day of
rest after their labours. I may here mention that
it was our invariable practice every Sunday to read
the Church service, and generally a short sermon
afterwards; and it is remarkable how very seldom
during the whole period of our voyage, that either
the severity of the weather, or the circumstances of
the expedition, were such as to interfere with the
performance of this duty. Few could have had
more convincing assurances of the providential
interpositions of a merciful God, and I do believe

1840.

there was not an individual in either of the ships, who did not regret when we were unavoidably prevented assembling for the purpose of offering up our prayers and thanksgivings to our Almighty Guide and Protector.

CHAPTER IV.

KERGUELEN Islands were discovered in 1772 by
M. Kerguelen, a lieutenant of the French navy.
He first observed two small islands on the 13th of
January, which he named the " Isles of Fortune,"
after the ship he commanded, and afterwards came
in sight of the main island, but being driven off by
tempestuous weather he was unable to approach
its shores and returned to the Mauritius.

From the exaggerated account he gave of the
extent of this new discovery, it was very generally
believed that the great southern continent which the
philosophers of that time considered necessary to
maintain the balance of our earth was at length
found: and M. de Kerguelen, in command of the
Rolland of 64 guns, accompanied by L'Oiseau frigate, was sent again to examine more fully this
interesting land.

His second expedition was hardly more fortunate than the former. In December, 1773, he
again came in sight of the principal island, and
gave the name of Cape François to a fine bold promontory, which forms at once the northern headland of one of its best harbours, and the north
extreme point of the main island. His ship was
driven off the coast by strong westerly gales, and

was unable to regain it: but on the 6th of January, 1774, M. de Rosnevet, in the frigate L'Oiseau arrived off the harbour, near the head of which one of his officers landed, and "took possession of the bay and of all the country, in the name of the King of France, with all requisite formalities," but it does not appear that any further knowledge of the extent and capabilities of this land was obtained.

Captain Cook was preparing for his third and last voyage, when the news of this discovery reached England, and he was directed in his instructions from the Admiralty to search for it on his way to Van Diemen's Land. Accordingly, on the 24th of December, whilst sailing along the parallel of its latitude, he observed, through the fog, two islands of considerable height, and eight or nine miles in circumference; these he named Cloudy Islands. A remarkable elevated rock which he recognized as that named the Isle of Re-union by M. Kerguelen, was soon afterwards seen, and by him called Bligh's Cap, by which name it is now distinguished. And on Christmas day the Resolution and Discovery anchored in the Baie de L'Oiseau, and although not the discoverers of this extensive island they were the first ships that ever anchored in any of its numerous harbours. Captain Cook named it Christmas Harbour, not knowing at the time that it had been previously named by its French discoverer.

An accurate survey of the harbour and a general

examination of the eastern coast of the island from
Cape François to Cape George, near its southern
extremity, resulted from the visit of this great
navigator; and the illusion which had taken possession of men's minds of its being a part of the
great southern continent was dispelled by a reference to the log-book of the Adventure, in which
ship Captain Furneaux, the companion of Cook on
his second voyage, crossed the meridian of this land
about fifty miles to the southward of Cape George
in February, 1773, after separating from the Resolution, thus proving that no part of this land
extends to the southward beyond the fiftieth
degree of latitude.

In March, 1799, many of its numerous and
secure harbours were examined and surveyed by
Captain Robert Rhodes, when in command of the
Hillsborough, employed in killing sea-elephants,
seals, and whales, in the southern hemisphere; and
the following extracts relating to some of the more
accessible and convenient anchorages for vessels
employed in the southern fishery are taken from a
manuscript memoir written by him, and will serve
to elucidate the chart of these islands, which I have
constructed from the best materials I could collect,
in addition to the surveys of the several harbours
at the northern part of the island that were made
by the officers of the Expedition.

Captain Rhodes states, that "after our arrival in
the Great South West Bay, I found the season had
expired for killing sea elephants and seals, but in

F

the course of the same month we perceived the
right or black whale to set into the different bays
and harbours in great quantities. Our success was
commensurate to my most sanguine expectations,
and we remained here until October following."

During the time (nearly eight months) they were
at Winter Harbour, in lat. 49° 20′ S., and long.
69° 24′ E., he explored not less than fifty inlets
or coves in the boats of the Hillsborough, where
ships of any tonnage might ride in perfect safety
in the most tempestuous seasons.   He gave names
to these several harbours, and intended to have
published a chart of his labours, " as " (he writes)
" an unerring guide to future navigators, and to
have thus discharged a duty, which is as pleasing
to my own feelings as I trust it will be found important to the commercial interests of the British
Empire ; " but it does not appear that either the
chart or the memoir was ever published.

" If bound into Hillsborough Bay, leave the
islands off Christmas Harbour on the port hand,
and steer S. E. by S. by compass along the land
at a distance of about three or four leagues.
This course will carry you between the beds of
kelp and sea-weed that lie off the coast, and when
you have run the distance of seventeen miles from
Cape François, Howe's Foreland will bear S.W. by
compass, distant seven or eight miles : at the same
time a ledge of rocks may be seen from the deck
bearing N.E. distant five or six miles. You
may then steer South to S. by W. by compass
until you have run about fifteen miles, leaving se-

veral small islands on your port hand; you will then open the Bay in which Port Palliser is situated, which may be known by a small round island off Penguin Cove, which forms the harbour. Leave this island on the port hand, and the course in is W. by N. by compass, where there is good anchorage in from seven to nine fathoms water.

" Between Port Palliser and Howe's Foreland is an extensive bay, with two branches that run in W.S.W. and W.N.W. at a distance of fifteen or sixteen miles. This bay is separated from Whale Bay by a narrow isthmus not exceeding three quarters of a mile in breadth, where a boat may be occasionally hauled across, and this will save a distance of upwards of fifty miles if going into Hillsborough Bay." There are also several good harbours in this bay, which I have called Rhode Bay in compliment to this diligent investigator.

" From Port Palliser to Cape Henry, the north head of Hillsborough Bay, the course is S. by W. and the distance twelve or thirteen miles. On leaving Port Palliser steer E.S.E. until you are beyond all the beds of kelp, and then the above course will carry you clear of all dangers until you arrive off Cape Henry. This Cape is on an island, and forms a high bluff headland, and there are several smaller islands and rocks both north and south of the Cape. Between Port Palliser and Cape Henry there are seven different bays of considerable extent with coves that form good harbours, all tending in from West to W.N.W.

" From Howe's Foreland or any of the projecting points or headlands that form the several bays and inlets between it and Cape Henry, Mount Campbell may be seen, as also the low land of Cape Digby. The mountain has a round top, is of a moderate elevation, and may be seen, in clear weather, at fifteen or sixteen leagues' distance. In running down the coast Mount Campbell will be discovered some time before you raise the low land of the Cape, which forms its termination at a mile and a half from it; it is distant from any other mountain seven or eight miles, and bears from Howe's Foreland S. E. by compass. Mount Campbell and Cape Digby are the best guides into Hillsborough Bay.

" When arrived off Cape Henry, you will open Whale Bay, so named from the great numbers of whales that frequent the place at a certain season of the year. In the mouth of this bay is a small reef, which always shows itself, and lies about six miles S. by W. from Cape Henry. You may go on either side of the reef; but if intending to enter Hillsborough Bay steer for the group of islands which lies to the S. S. W. of the reef, and about three miles from it. You may anchor within those islands, in any depth from twenty to seven fathoms, on good holding ground. There are here several inlets and coves, which afford good harbours. Keep those islands on the starboard hand, and you will soon shut in Mount Campbell, and Seal Island will be on with Cape Daniel and the south head of Hillsborough Bay: then steer S. W. until you raise a small reef which lies in the middle of the bay, near the entrance of Hunter's Sound. Here you will have from thirty-six to forty-two fathoms on a soft muddy bottom.

" Leave this reef on the port hand, and steer W. by N. by compass; this course will carry you to Winter Harbour, which is distant from the group of islands fourteen miles. You will here find a safe and good harbour, where you may anchor in from seven to nine fathoms."

" When the western extreme of the islands bears north by compass, you will then be shut in and entirely land-locked; here you will have from fifteen to twenty-five fathoms on a soft muddy bottom; but when you advance four or five miles further up the sound, you will find from seventy to one hundred fathoms near the Raven and Duck islands.

" Whale Bay, to the northward of Hunter Sound, affords several good harbours.

" Irish Bay lies to the southward of Winter Harbour, and likewise affords some very good harbours.

" Foundery Branch, so named from the great quantity of iron ore and limestone found there, contains many inlets and coves, in which ships may anchor protected from all winds and weather. This branch lies S.E., about thirteen miles from Winter Harbour.

" Elizabeth Harbour bears E. by S. from Winter Harbour; there is good anchorage in it, in from four to nine fathoms water. There is a reef in the mouth of it, which you may pass on either side in perfect safety, and will not find less than nine or ten fathoms until well within the reef.

"Betsy Cove, which lies in the head of Accessible Bay, is an excellent harbour, and has from five to seven fathoms water over a tough blue clay. It is the southernmost harbour in the coast north of Cape Digby, and is about eight miles from it.

"In passing Cape Digby, it will be necessary to give it a birth of three miles, to clear the spit of land that runs out from it to nearly that distance."

Christmas Harbour, situated at the northern extremity of the island, has an entrance of nearly a mile wide, between Cape François on the north and the "*Arched*" Point on the south, on which side is a small bay that somewhat increases the breadth for nearly half the depth of the inlet, when it suddenly contracts to less than one-third of a mile, and thence gradually diminishes to the head of the bay, which terminates in a level beach of fine dark sand, extending quite across, and of about four hundred yards in length.

The shores on each side are steep, and rise in a succession of terraces to the height of more than a thousand feet. The highest hill, which is on the north side of the harbour, attains an elevation of thirteen hundred and fifty feet: from its form it received the name of Table Mount. Its summit is a very distinctly formed oval-shaped crater, about one hundred feet across its major axis. On the north side of this hill are some perfect basaltic columns, very beautifully arranged, and numerous fragments of the same prismatic structure are

strewed about and piled around the sides of the
cone. From this point we obtained a most commanding and extensive view of the neighbouring
country, of a considerable portion of its north-
western coast, and of the adjacent islands.

On the south side of the harbour is the extraordinary rock noticed by Cook, and which forms
so conspicuous an object in his accurate drawing
of this place. It is a huge mass of basalt much
more recent than the rock on which it rests, and
through which it seems to have burst in a semi-
fluid state. It is upwards of five hundred feet
thick, and rests upon the older rock at an elevation
of six hundred feet above the level of the sea; and
it was between these rocks of different ages that
the fossil trees were chiefly found, and one exceeding seven feet in circumference was dug out and
sent to England. Some of the pieces appeared so
recent that it was necessary to take it in your hand
to be convinced of its fossil state, and it was most
curious to find it in every stage, from that of char-
coal lighting and burning freely when put in the
fire, to so high a degree of silicification as to scratch
glass. A bed of shale, several feet in thickness,
which was found overlaying some of the fossil trees
had probably prevented their carbonization when
the fluid lava poured over them. A still more extraordinary feature in the geology of this island is
the numerous seams of coal, varying in thickness
from a few inches to four feet, which we found
imbedded in the trap rock; the positions of two of

1840. the larger of these seams are marked on the annexed plan.   Whether the coal is in sufficient abundance ever to be of commercial importance we had not the opportunity of ascertaining: but at the present day, when steam vessels are traversing every portion of the ocean, it may not be unworthy a more extended examination, for in no situation would it be more desirable to have a coal depôt than at this island, lying, as it does, immediately in the high road to all our Indian and Australasian colonies, abounding with excellent harbours, and at a convenient distance from the Cape of Good Hope.   For many interesting geological details respecting the formation of the land in the vicinity of Christmas Harbour I must refer to the following report of Mr. M'Cormick, who was most indefatigable in its examination:—

" The northern extremity of the island, visited by the expedition, is entirely of volcanic origin: the bold headlands of Capes Cumberland and François present a striking appearance from the sea; the trap rocks, of which they are composed, form a succession of terraces nearly horizontal, which, on first making the land, have a very striking resemblance to stratified sandstone or limestone.

" Basalt is the prevailing rock, assuming the prismatic form, and passing into greenstone, and the various modifications of amygdaloid and porphyry. The general direction of the mountain ranges inclines to the S.W. and N.E., varying in height generally from 500 to 2500 feet.   Many of the hills are intersected by trap dykes; these dykes are of very frequent occurrence, and are usually of basalt.

" Several conical hills, with crater-shaped summits, have evidently once been volcanic vents. Three or four very singular isolated hills, composed of an igneous kind of arenaceous rock which occur in Cumberland Bay, present a very smooth outline; they consist of pieces of broken fragments, through which the mass protrudes in places in prismatic columns.

" The vast quantities of debris which have accumulated at the base of the hills, in many places to the height of 200 or 300 feet and upwards, afford strong evidence of the rapid disintegration which this land is undergoing from the sudden atmospheric vicissitudes to which it is exposed.

" The whole island appears to be deeply indented by bays and inlets, the surface intersected by numerous small lakes and watercourses. These becoming swollen by the heavy rains which alternate with the frost and snow, accompanied by violent gusts of wind, rush down the sides of the mountains and along the ravines in countless impetuous torrents, forming in many places beautiful foaming cascades, wearing away the rocks, and strewing the platforms and valleys below with vast fragments, and slopes of a rich alluvium, the result of their decomposition.

" Quartz, in beautiful crystals, forming drusy cavities in the trap rocks in Cumberland Bay, occurs in great abundance, whilst zeolites predominate in the rocks about Christmas Harbour.

" The most remarkable geological feature in the island is the occurrence of fossil wood and coal, and, what is still more extraordinary, imbedded in the igneous rocks. The wood, which for the most part is highly silicified, is found enclosed in the basalt, whilst the coal crops out in ravines, in close contact with the overlying porphyritic and amygdaloidal greenstone.

CHRISTMAS HARBOUR,

" In which the ships were moored during the period the expedition remained at the island, is bounded on the south side by a ridge of basaltic rocks, disposed in terraces and platforms, dipping slightly to the N. W., and surmounted by a remarkable block of basalt, rising to about 1000 feet above the harbour. It has in some places a conglomerate structure, the enclosed fragments being excessively hard and ponderous. It is beneath this rock that the fossil wood is found, I having discovered the first fragment whilst ascending the hill on the day after the ships were secured in the harbour, and on a further search it was found in considerable abundance, both imbedded in the basalt and in the debris below, or scattered on the surface amongst the fragments of rock. A portion of the trunk of a large tree, seven feet in circumference, and much silicified, was dug out of the soil immediately below the rock. About 400 feet from the summit is a bed of shale, nearly horizontal, averaging six feet in thickness; but in some places it is exposed to a much greater extent. No remains of leaves could be discovered in it, although the wood occurs in the basalt near it.

" The ' Arched Rock' at the entrance to the harbour terminates this ridge to the southward. It is about 150 feet high, the base of the arch 100 feet across, and is composed of the same kind of basaltic rock. Several fragments of wood, much twisted, softer, and more recent in appearance than the hard silicified wood above described, occur enclosed in the basalt in the inside of the ' arch.'

" In the small bay inside of ' Arched Point,' a bed of coal, four feet thick and forty feet in length, appears above the debris, thirty feet above the sea, and covered by basalt, which rises about 500 feet above it. The coal is slaty, of a brownish-black colour, and the fracture like wood coal: the bed takes a northerly direction.

" On the north side of the harbour, near the centre of the small bay formed by Cape François, a thin vein of coal, not more than two or three inches in thickness, again makes its appearance in a cave excavated in the shale. The coal is covered by a kind of ' slag,' and underlies the shale, above which the basalt rises to about the same height as on the south side of the harbour. The cave is thirty feet wide at the entrance, twenty feet deep, and twelve feet in height.

" From the centre of the terraced ridge terminating in Cape François rises a conical hill, its *crater*-shaped summit being 1200 feet above the level of the sea. A shallow lake (covered with ice at the time), thirty yards in length from N. to S., and contracted in the centre to six yards, occupies the depression at the summit, round which piles of fragments of prismatic basalt arise on the east and west to about fifty feet, sloping towards the north and south, where gaps are left. Perfect basaltic columns, some of them ten and twelve feet between the joints, being generally five or six angled prisms, are inclined round the acclivity of the cone, inter-mixed with piles of broken fragments, exhibiting the same prismatic structure. At a deep gorge, six feet wide, on the north side of the mountain, these columns are beautifully arranged. The narrow isthmus between the head of Christmas Harbour and the N. W. coast, scarcely a mile across, consists of low ridges, with intervening swampy ground, and two lakes: the rocks are amygdaloid, with superincumbent basalt.

CUMBERLAND BAY AND THE N. W. COAST, ETC.

" The primary objects of the two expeditions up this bay in boats having been to explore the N. W. or weather shore by an overland journey across the Isthmus, at the head of Cumberland Bay, the rapid movements of the party, amidst the most unfavourable weather, seldom afforded an oppor-tunity for more than general remarks on the geo-logical structure of the country passed through.

" On leaving Christmas Harbour two bays were passed, — ' Foul Haven,' and ' Mussel Bay ;' the headland dividing these presents a perpendicular escarpment of basalt. Approaching Cape Cumberland, the sea breaks upon a low black rugged ledge of basalt, backed by a swampy green bog, two miles in length, and half a mile in breadth, beyond which rises a range of trap hills.

" A remarkable rock, called the ' Sentry Box,' faces the entrance to Cumberland Bay ; it was not landed upon, but the succession of terraces, nearly horizontal to its summit, sufficiently indicated its basaltic structure to be the same as the main land.

" The range of mountains flanking Cumberland Bay on each side generally present the same trap terraces as in Christmas Harbour. Six miles and a half up the bay are two inlets nearly opposite to each other; the one on the south side is a mile and half deep, a mile broad at its widest part, and one-third of a mile at the entrance. The trap rocks surrounding this bay differ from the others in containing drusy cavities of beautiful quartz crystals, many fine fragments of which were scattered about the surface of the rocky ledges.

" At the top of the bay is a remarkable hill, between 300 and 400 feet in height, constituted of an igneous arenaceous slate, confusedly intermingled with greenstone and basalt, having a crater-shaped summit, filled by a lake 200 yards long, and 150 broad, three feet deep near the margin, and the centre covered with thin ice. It is surrounded by an irregular wall of greenstone, from five to twenty feet in height.

"The water finds an outlet by a watercourse down the S. E. side of the hill, forming a small cascade in its first descent from the lake.

"The ascent of the hill on the S. E. side is by a narrow gorge, three feet wide, nearly perpendicular, and through a mass of hard arenaceous rock, having a tendency to the prismatic form. On attaining the summit, a quantity of loose fragments of slate strew the surface. Near the centre, a basaltic dyke, three feet wide, and having a direction S. E. and N. W., divides an amorphous mass of arenaceous slate from the greenstone on the north side; the latter rock contains much hornblende, with a ferruginous-coloured surface. The base and sides are scattered over with loose pieces of slate, intermingled with masses of trap. There are three other gorges by which the hill may be ascended. The irregular structure of this hill, with its large 'crater-shaped' summit, and the confused intermingling of the trap and singular slate rock, which latter seem to be of an 'arenaceous' composition, indicate vast disturbance at the period it was thrown up from below.

"A little to the southward of this hill a bed of coal, one foot in thickness, and ten feet in length, breaks out in a cleft at the base of a hill along a watercourse having a S. E. and N. W. direction. The coal is very light and friable, with a beautiful black glossy fracture, and, like cannel coal, does not soil the fingers. It is covered by a porphyritic amygdaloid and greenstone rock, and not a vestige of shale or slate is to be found in the same hill.

In the adjacent hill, south of this, another bed of coal appears at the surface for about twenty feet, also in a deep cleft in the mountain, about twenty yards up a watercourse, and fifty feet above the sea: the direction the same as the last. The coal, however, is very different, having a slaty fracture, and dull brownish-black colour: it burnt very well, the boat's crew having cooked their provisions with it. The bed is two feet in thickness, and appears again on the opposite side of the watercourse, which is twelve feet across, and traversed by a small dyke of basalt three inches in breadth. The superincumbent rock, as in the last instance, is amygdaloidal greenstone.

"In a S. E. direction from the head of the bay is an opening between the mountain ranges, found to terminate in a part of 'White Bay;' the Isthmus, five miles across, consisting of a few low ridges, and a valley of the usual trap formation. A large dyke of basalt crosses the latter in an E. N. E. ½ E. direction, forming a wall from three to four feet in height.

"At the S.W. end of the bay a creek runs up, beyond which is a swampy valley; and two miles from the head of the creek is a lake one mile and a half long, and nearly half a mile broad, filling up a pass in the mountains, which rise above it to the height of about 2500 feet, the highest land met with. This range presents the same trap formation of basalt, greenstone, and amygdaloid. Veins of hornstone, and an indurated claystone, were, however, first found in situ here, about a foot in thick-

ness, although numerous fragments frequently occurred scattered about the watercourses. I found
a solitary piece of fossil wood, highly silicified, at
the upper margin of the lake—the only vestige met
with in Cumberland Bay and its vicinity. A small
lump of coal was also found near the lower end of
the lake, but neither could be found in situ. The
valley continued in a S. S. W. direction, between
the same range, for four miles above the lake.

" In the small bay on the N. side of Cumberland
Bay is a smooth undulating hill, covered with loose
fragments of slate, piled up to 150 feet in height,
and completely insulated from the greenstone range
at the back. Some of the fragments of this remarkable looking ' *arenaceous slate*,' with red mark-
ings, bore a striking resemblance to the impressions
of sea-weed. On the opposite or west side of the
bay another ' *slate hill*' forms a kind of belt in the
trap range, 600 feet high, covered with loose fragments from the summit to the base, through which
amorphous masses protrude in places. At the line
of junction with the basalt, where a watercourse
runs down, it assumes a prismatic tendency. About
two thirds up is a vein of friable slaty kind of slag,
a foot deep, and ten feet in length, covered by the
basalt, and in all probability a bed of coal exists
beneath. The slaty fragments were not marked
with the sea-weed-like impressions, as in the hill on
the opposite side. On the south side of Cumberland Bay, near the upper end, is another of these
remarkable hills, having a smooth marbled appearance at a distance, the light colour forming a great

contrast with the dark trap ranges. The southern extremity rises to nearly 300 feet, gradually sloping down towards the north. Prismatic columns, mostly five and six angled, appear in places through the pile of loose fragments with which the hill is covered. The fragments of slate on this hill are much marked by red concentric lines, apparently caused by oxide of iron. In crossing over the Isthmus from the head of Cumberland Bay to the N.W. coast, several pieces of coal occurred scattered about a watercourse, but none *in situ*, although, had circumstances permitted its being followed up, a bed would no doubt have been discovered not far distant.

" On this coast, being the weather shore, the quantity of debris at the base of the hills is enormous, forming a steep slope of 300 to 500 feet, down to the black ledge of basalt on which the sea breaks. The whole is covered by a carpet of vegetation, intersected by numerous watercourses and cascades, rushing down from the trap range of mountains above, rendering it an almost impassable bog, in which the party sank knee-deep at every step. A bay was found to bound it, and all further progress to the westward."

The vegetable productions of this island cannot fail to be of more than ordinary interest to the botanist. So remote from any shores from which birds of passage might convey the seeds of their

G

productions, it seems to have but a small number
of plants, and some of these peculiar to the island;
showing that since the successive overflowings of
volcanic matter destroyed the forests which at one
period clothed this land, of which the fossil trees
and numerous beds of coal afford abundant proof,
it appears to have remained in a state of almost
vegetable desolation, and well deserves the name
bestowed on it by Captain Cook. When he visited
it in the height of summer, the land was covered
with snow, and only five plants in flower were
collected. In the depth of winter the climate
seemed to be but little different — the thermometer
during our stay seldom descending below the
freezing point, and the snow never remaining on
the lower grounds beyond two or three days at a
time.

The following observations are by Dr. Hooker,
the Assistant Surgeon of the Erebus, an able and
zealous botanist, and to whom science is indebted
for the very important and valuable work he is
now publishing, under the title of " Flora Antarctica," of which several numbers have already
appeared, and which, when complete, will comprise
an account of all the plants collected during the
expedition. The liberal grant of 1000l. from the
Government will enable him to give drawings and
dissections of all the hitherto undescribed plants,
amounting to upwards of five hundred. To this
work I must refer the scientific botanist for any
further information he may require.

" Though Kerguelen Island is situated in comparatively a low latitude, the vegetation is decidedly antarctic both because the majority of its
native plants are peculiarly abundant in the same
or higher parallels of the southern hemisphere,
and from the mass of its vegetation being composed
of comparatively few species.

" At a little distance, the island presents the appearance of absolute sterility, and when the voyager
draws nearer the land, the scenery scarcely im-
proves.   A narrow belt of green grass runs along
the quiet shores of the harbour, mixed with, and
succeeded by, large rounded masses of a dirty
green or rusty brown colour, due to the predo-
minance of a curious umbelliferous plant, allied
to the *Bolax*, or " Balsam Bog" of the Falkland
Islands.   Higher on the hills vegetation only exists in scattered tufts, the plants being the same as
inhabit a lower level, and it almost ceases at an
elevation of 1000—1200 feet.

"Even the description given in Captain Cook's
voyage falls short of the cheerless truth, when,
quoting Mr. Anderson's journal, he says, ' Perhaps
no place hitherto discovered in either hemisphere,
under the same parallel of latitude, affords so scanty
a field for the naturalist as this barren spot;' for he
might assuredly have added ten degrees to its own
latitude in southern regions, and upwards of
twenty in the north, as the limits upon which such
a paucity of species exists; for even in Spitzbergen

there are nearly three times as many flowering plants as here.

" The number of species detected during Cook's stay in the island was eighteen, including *Crypto-gamia;* these, with the exception of one *Lichen,* were refound during the visit of the antarctic expedition, when the flora was increased to about 150 in all; namely, eighteen of flowering plants, three ferns, twenty-five mosses, ten *Jungermanniæ,* one fungus, the rest lichens and seaweeds.

" Of the flowering plants, the two great Classes were in the proportion of 1 to 2, the lowest ratio which has yet been recorded; the nearest approach to it being seen in Melville Island, where Mr. Brown (in his remarks on the plants collected there by the officers of Captain Parry's first voyage) states the proportion to be as 2 to 5. The large proportion of monocotyledonous plants here arises, as in Melville Island, from the increased ratio which the grasses bear to the other phænogamic plants. In the latter island, according to Mr. Brown's list, it is as 1 to 3·7, or, as that botanist remarks, ' nearly double what has been found in any other part of the world.' In Kerguelen Island the disproportion is further increased, being as 1 to 2·6, a third greater than that of Melville Island, and the maximum hitherto observed, except in the South Shetlands, where a solitary grass composes all the flowering vegetation.

" Two phænogamic plants, out of the eighteen, belong to genera apparently peculiar to the island;

one of them, the curious Cabbage-plant (*Pringlea*
antiscorbutica), and the other a Portulaceous plant.
Of the remaining sixteen, four are probably new
species of antarctic American genera; ten are
species actually inhabiting the latter country;
six of these, also inhabitants of Auckland and
Campbell Islands, and two are common throughout the whole southern and northern temperate
and cooler zones. Of the cryptogamic plants, most
are abundant in the higher southern latitudes,
though many are hitherto undescribed, and, perhaps, twenty peculiar to this island. Many are
natives of the European Alps, and more particularly
of the north polar regions.

  " Though Kerguelen Island is remote and comparatively bare of vegetation, there are several peculiarly interesting points connected with its Botany.
Though now destitute of even a shrub, the abundance of fossil remains proves that many parts were
for successive ages clothed with trees. The proportion of the surface that is covered with plants is
about equal to that in Spitzbergen and Melville
Island, yet the relative number of species to indivi-
duals falls strikingly short; for whilst the Flora of
Melville Island boasts of sixty-seven species of
flowering plants, and Spitzbergen of forty-five, Kerguelen Island contains but eighteen, and of these
only eight cover any considerable amount of surface.
The climate of the island is such, that, though rigorous, it supports a perennial vegetation; and scarcely

any of the plants, even the grasses, can be called annuals. Of the five plants found blossoming during December by Captain Cook, four were observed in the same state in May, and three of them continued so until the twentieth of July ; and in the month of June twelve out of the eighteen species were collected in flower. The repeated snow-storms had little influence in checking the verdure, and the umbelliferous plant was the only one actually frost-bitten by severe weather of three days' continuance.

" The more general features of the vegetation being thus cursorily noticed, there remains one plant which demands particular attention, the famous Cabbage of Kerguelen Island, hitherto unpublished, first discovered during Captain Cook's voyage. Specimens, together with a manuscript description, under the name of *Pringlea*, were deposited, in the collection formed by Mr. Anderson, in the British Museum, where they still exist. To a crew long confined to salt provisions, or indeed to human beings under any circumstances, this is a most important vegetable, for it possesses all the essentially good qualities of its English namesake, whilst from its containing a great abundance of essential oil, it never produces heartburn or any of those disagreeable sensations which our pot-herbs are apt to do. It abounds near the sea, and ascends the hills to their summits. The leaves form heads of the size of a good cabbage-lettuce, generally terminating an ascending or prostrate

stalk, and the spike of flowers, borne on a leafy
stem, rises from below the head, and is often two
feet high.   The root tastes like horse-radish, and
the young leaves or hearts resemble in flavor coarse
mustard and cress.   For one hundred and thirty
days our crews required no fresh vegetable but
this, which was for nine weeks regularly served
out with the salt beef or pork, during which time
there was no sickness on board.

" Two species of grass may also be mentioned,
as affording a nutritious fodder for goats, sheep,
and pigs."

Of land animals we saw none; and the only
traces we could discover of there being any on this
island were the singular footsteps of a pony or ass,
found by the party detached for surveying purposes, under the command of Lieutenant Bird, and
described by Dr. Robertson " as being three inches
in length and two and a half in breadth, having a
small and deeper depression on each side, and
shaped like a horse shoe."   It is by no means improbable that the animal has been cast on shore
from some wrecked vessel.   They traced its footsteps
for some distance in the recently fallen snow, in
hopes of getting sight of it, but lost the tracks on
reaching a large space of rocky ground which was
free from snow.

There is, however, abundance of food for cattle.
The sheep we landed from our ships throve won-
derfully on the grass, and soon got into good condition; they also became so very shy that we were

obliged to shoot them when wanted for our tables; one of mine managed to evade our most active sportsmen, and was left there when we took our departure. I regretted I had not brought with me some useful animals from the Cape of Good Hope, to have stocked the land.

Of marine animals, the sea elephant and several species of seals were formerly in great abundance, and annually drew a number of vessels to these shores in pursuit of them. They have now, after so many years of persecution, quite deserted the place, or have been most completely annihilated. One very fine specimen of the sea elephant was shot at Christmas Harbour during our stay, as also were a few seals. These are described in the " Zoology of the Voyage," now in progress of publication, by Dr. Richardson and I. E. Gray, Esq., of the British Museum, with the assistance of 1000*l.*, granted by the Government, at the recommendation of the Lords Commissioners of the Admiralty, for the necessary illustrations and dawings of the unknown animals that were collected during the voyage.

Some whales were seen at the entrance of the harbour, and by the parties employed in surveying the coast. These creatures appear still to be found in great numbers, so that in 1843, when we returned to the Cape of Good Hope, we heard that there were between five and six hundred whale ships fishing along the shores or in the immediate neighbourhood of this land; that most of them were nearly full; that from their great numbers constant accidents were happening in the thick fogs which prevail, by running foul of each other; and several vessels arrived at the Cape in a very shattered state. This fishery might be most successfully pursued from the Cape of Good Hope, but it is now chiefly carried on by American.vessels.

Several kinds of fish were seen, and a large collection was made, amongst them were many new species. In the account now publishing by Dr. Richardson, he has described two new genera, under the names *Notothenia*, of which three species were found here, and *Chœmethys*, of which there is yet only one known species, *Rhinoceratus*; it has a general resemblance to the *gurnards* and *prionotes*: all the species of these two genera inhabit the kelp weed of the shores of the harbour; they were taken by the hook, and proved acceptable to the table, being some of them a foot and a half long; they feed on Entomostraca, and small shell-fish that live amongst the weed.

Fifteen different species of sea-fowl were shot in the harbour, or found along its shores; amongst these, several species of petrel, three kinds of penguin, two species of gull, a duck, a cormorant, a tern, and a curious "*chionis*," different in some particulars from that first described by Forster, and probably a new species.

Of the sooty albatross (*Diomedea fuliginosa*), which appeared to have selected this as a breeding station, several young birds were still to be met with, although so late in the season, fully fledged, and ready to commence their long flight over the Antarctic seas.

The duck was obtained in abundance, and formed a delicious addition to our table. It is like the teal of England, and lives chiefly on the seeds of the cabbage, before mentioned, which is profusely scattered over all parts of the island.

The penguins, notwithstanding the disagreeable dark colour of its flesh and extreme fatness, were found to make excellent soup, which from its colour and flavour so much resembled hare soup, that it was always called by that name.

Of insects, only three or four specimens were found, viz. a *curculio*, amongst the umbelliferous plants; a small brownish moth, and two flies; but probably in the summer time many others would make their appearance.

The level beach at the head of the harbour afforded us convenient sites for our observatories, which were immediately erected; that for magnetic purposes being placed at the north extreme, under the protection of the hill to the north, which effectually prevented the sun's rays deranging the temperature, and within a few feet of high-water mark; that for the astronomical and pendulum observations on nearly the same level, at more than a hundred yards distant from it towards the centre of the beach; and close by this two small huts were erected for the convenience of the officers and men employed at the observatories.

The ships were warped up to the head of the harbour, and moored in a situation convenient for ready intercourse with the observatories; and although our operations were much impeded by frequent violent gales, we were enabled to get all the magnetometers placed and adjusted in time to take our part in the simultaneous observations made on the previously agreed on term-days of the 29th and 30th May in all the foreign and British observatories that constitute the great system of magnetic co-operation. It happened most fortunately to be a time of unusual magnetic disturbance, so that our first day's simultaneous observations proved the vast extent and instantaneous effect of the disturbing power, whatever it might be, affecting the magnetometers at Toronto in Canada and at Kerguelen Island, nearly antipodal to each other, simultaneously and similarly in all their strange oscillations and irregular movements, and thus immediately afforded one of the most important facts that the still-hidden cause of magnetic phenomena has yet presented.

A most interesting and valuable series of hourly magnetometric observations was continued night and day throughout the whole period of our stay at this island, with such exactness to time, and so much zeal and unwearying perseverance, by the officers of the Erebus and Terror, under the more immediate direction of Commander Crozier, that not a single break occurred, nor was a single hour's observation lost.

The astronomical, tidal, and pendulum observations occupied my attention exclusively; and in these I was also assisted by Commander Crozier, both of us living in one of the compartments of the observatory, only going off to the ships on Sunday to read the church service and inspect the vessels.

The senior lieutenants had charge of the ships, and occupied the crews in refitting the rigging, and the more toilsome operation of frequently resetting the anchors; for although these and the cables were of a weight and size usually supplied to ships of double our tonnage, they were unable to withstand the almost hurricane violence of the gales that prevail at this season of the year, sometimes laying the ships over nearly on their beam ends, and the sheet anchor was constantly resorted to. On one occasion the whole body of the astronomical observatory was moved nearly a foot; and had not the lower framework fortunately been sunk to a good depth below the level of the ground, it would have doubtless been blown into the sea.

The gusts occur so suddenly that I have frequently been obliged to throw myself down on the beach to prevent being carried into the water, and one of our men, whose duty it was to register the tide-gauge, was actually driven in by one of the squalls, and very nearly drowned.

During forty-five of the sixty-eight days the ships were in Christmas Harbour it blew a gale of wind, and there were only three days on which neither rain nor snow fell.

It was this extremely tempestuous weather which prevented a more extensive survey of the island. Lieutenant Bird, with two boats under his command, examined White's Bay, and with the assistance of Mr. Tucker and Mr. Davis surveyed several of its harbours. Lieutenant Philips examined Cumberland Bay, and crossed from the head of it over to the west coast, but was unable to trace it beyond a few miles, owing to the swampy nature of the land. Mr. M'Cormick and Mr. Robertson accompanied these expeditions to examine the geological and zoological productions of the country. But the severe weather they experienced kept us all in a state of anxiety about them the whole time of their absence, and the little they could accomplish was but too dearly purchased by so much suffering and exposure, and deterred me from permitting any further prosecution of their labours.

The anchorages in Cumberland Bay are much superior to those of Christmas Harbour, and are not exposed to such violent winds; they are, however, not of so ready access, and could only be entered in clear and moderate weather.

There are also several good harbours in White's Bay, of which accurate plans were made by Mr. Davis, and will be published by the Admiralty, with the chart of Kerguelen Island.

The rise and fall of tide in Christmas Harbour is remarkably small, not on any occasion amounting to more than thirty inches, and the usual spring tides are generally less than two feet; the neap tide varies from four to twelve inches, and the diurnal inequality is, comparatively, very considerable. The height of the tide was registered every quarter of an hour between the 3d of June and 4th of July; and the time of high water at full and change of the moon was exactly at two o'clock.

Our observations gave the latitude of the observatory 48° 41′ S., and its longitude 69° 3′ 35″ E. The mean dip of the magnetic needle 69° 59′ 4″ S., and the variation 30° 33′ 35″ E.

The term-day observations for the month of June being completed, and the absolute determinations obtained, the instruments and houses were embarked, and the ships got ready for sea by the middle of July, but adverse weather detained us still a few days longer, and we were not able to leave this most dreary and disagreeable harbour until the 20th July.

CHAPTER V.

F<small>RESH</small> breeze, N. W.; unmoored at daylight, weighed at 8h. 15m. A. M., and stood out to sea, passing close along Terror Reef, over which the sea was breaking, sufficiently indicating the danger, although, owing to the haziness of the weather, we had lost sight of the land, and at two or three miles from it we could not get soundings with fifty fathoms of line.

In the afternoon the freshening breeze reduced us to close-reefed topsails, and the Terror falling far astern about the same time, obliged us to haul the foresail up. We were before night well clear of the land, and the numerous rocky patches that lie a considerable distance from its shores. Upon some of these there is not less than thirty or forty fathoms, but in others the rocks are very near the surface, and unless there be a high sea running, so that it may break over these treacherous shallows, the navigation amongst them is hazardous, more especially as there is usually no anchorage near them, owing to the great depth of water.

A shoal of porpoises was seen, and we passed many floating beds of sea-weed, some of them more than a mile in breadth. The wind had increased to a gale, which continued to blow with frequent snow-squalls throughout the 21st, 22d, and 23d, which, together with the long dark nights of this season of the year, rendered it difficult, notwithstanding the constant firing of guns and burning of blue lights, to keep the ships in company with each other.

During the snow-squalls the temperature of the air invariably fell several degrees, and on one occasion was as low as 27°, although the sea maintained an uniform heat of about 36°; the vapour which rose from water of that temperature almost as speedily froze before it attained any considerable altitude, and kept us continually enveloped in haze and snow. We should have felt some alarm at meeting such large quantities of sea-weed had we not before observed that the masses which had been torn away from the shores of Prince Edward's and the Marion and Crozet's groups were met with only to the eastward of those islands, whilst scarcely any were seen as we approached them from the westward. Meeting with it now in such abundance confirmed me in the belief that there is a general tendency of the surface water in these parts to the eastward, most probably occasioned by the westerly winds, which, at this season, at any rate, prevail almost as steadily as do the trade winds in the equatorial regions.

We also found ourselves every day from twelve to sixteen miles by observation in advance of our reckoning, as may be seen by referring to the table in the Appendix, where our daily position is given; and the effect of the current is noted whenever observations for both latitude and longitude were obtained.

Several kinds of petrel were the only birds seen; but these, particularly the Cape pigeon, were very abundant.

Wind more moderate, still from the westward. The temperature of the sea rose from 37° at 1 P.M. to 46° at 11 P.M., that of the air at the same time having *fallen* from 33° to 31°. This unaccountable increase of temperature of the sea, which had for several previous days averaged about 35°.5, continued until 7 P.M. the next day, extending over a space of eighty-six miles; it then fell to 40°, the air being at 29°, with a strong south-westerly gale blowing, and frequent snow showers.

By our observations at noon we found ourselves fifty-eight miles to the eastward of our reckoning, showing the greatest amount of current during the last two days that we had experienced since leaving Kerguelen Island.

The rise of the barometer to thirty inches, remarkably high for these latitudes, was followed, at 8 P.M., by a gale from the north-west of twelve hours' duration. We continued to see many patches of sea-weed, and again at night the north wind freshened to a gale: the Terror had dropped far astern, so that at daylight we could scarcely see

H

her, although we had purposely kept under moderate sail, to our great inconvenience, the ship
rolling heavily in consequence of not having sufficient sail to steady her. Towards noon she closed
with us, and continued to keep better company
until the increasing gale reduced our sails to the
close-reefed main topsail and foresail, which had
now become necessary to keep the ship before
the high following sea, when, owing to the great
difficulty they had in steering her, we passed
ahead, and her light was only dimly seen during
the early part of the afternoon. The gale continued
all night with a heavy cross sea: there was much
lightning to the eastward; meteors in great numbers were seen darting about in all directions, and
the whole aspect of the sky proclaimed a convulsion
or disturbance of the atmosphere of an unusual
character; the barometer descended rapidly, and
at 4 A.M. stood 28·88.

July 29.   For several hours the Terror had ceased to answer our night signals, and when day broke we
could not see any thing of her. At this time, the
sea having become more regular, we hauled the
fore-sail up, and rounded to under a close-reefed
main-topsail, to enable her to rejoin, supposing
that she had broached to during the night, or that
they had found it impossible or imprudent to scud
before the gale. We remained hove to as long as
daylight lasted, when we gave up all expectation
of again meeting her until our arrival at the next

rendezvous. The barometer continued to fall until
3 P. M., when, at its lowest (28·29.), there was
nothing in the sky to indicate more than an ordinary storm, indeed the gale had abated considerably; but so great was our reliance on the barometer, that we kept the ship under snug sail, and
every way prepared for whatever might happen;
and soon the dense accumulating clouds gave
notice of the tempest which shortly followed. We,
however, escaped it with but little damage, by the
steadiness of our men that were steering, and by
keeping the vessel directly before the wind; although
the seas broke into our ship over both quarters,
flooding our decks to a depth of more than two feet,
and obliged us to knock out the ports to let the
water run off and relieve her of its weight. The
mountainous sea, before which we had been scud-
ding was quelled, for the time, by the force of the
wind, whilst the tops of the waves were driven
completely over us in sheets of water; but the
violence of the hurricane was such as soon to ex-
pend itself. Beginning at N.N.W., in an hour and
three quarters the storm had abated to the strength
of a common gale from the west, and in that short
space of time the mercury in the barometer rose
nearly half an inch.

During the night the wind and sea subsided, July 30.
and we had a comparatively fine morning. We
were all anxiously looking out for the Terror,
and wondering how she had weathered the breeze,

when a wooden hoop of a cask was seen close to us. By this we felt certain that she had run past us during the time that we were hove-to for her, and was now probably far ahead ; we therefore pressed all sail on the ship to endeavour to overtake her. The day being very favourable, we seized the opportunity of drying our sails and clothes, which had been most thoroughly drenched, and of repairing the damages we had sustained.

In this and many other respects we felt the fine weather to be a great advantage to us : but this afternoon it pleased God to visit us by an unlooked-for calamity, — Mr. Roberts, the boatswain, whilst engaged about the rigging, fell overboard and was drowned. The life-buoy was instantly let go, and two boats lowered down; they reached the spot where we saw him sink only a few seconds too late ! The gloom which the loss of one of our small party, at the outset of our voyage, occasioned, was for a time merged in feelings of painful anxiety, and afterwards of heartfelt gratitude, for the merciful preservation of the whole crew of one of the boats, who, in their humane endeavours to save the life of our unfortunate shipmate, very nearly sacrificed their own. Mr. Oakley, mate, and Mr. Abernethy, the gunner, had returned to the ship with one boat, when the other, still at a considerable distance from us, was struck by a sea, which washed four of the crew out of her. Mr. Abernethy immediately again pushed off from the ship, and succeeded in

saving them from their perilous situation, completely benumbed and stupified with the cold. The
boats were, with much difficulty, owing to the sea
that was running, hoisted up, and not until after
one of them had been again swamped alongside.

We resumed our course under all sail, although
this calamitous detention of some hours frustrated
all our expectations of overtaking the Terror. A
small iceberg, seen at a considerable distance just
before dark, warned us to be vigilant during the
night, which at this season being fifteen hours
long obliged us to run at all hazards, or to delay
our voyage to a ruinous extent. It has at all times
a good effect upon those whose duty it is to look
out, and an advantageous stimulus even to the
most diligent, occasionally to see real dangers; but
they were, in this instance, the cause of several false
alarms, from the impression left upon our minds.

The weather continued fine all night and the
greater part of the next day. Numerous birds of
the petrel kind, which were flying about, seemed
to enjoy the short-lived tranquillity, and were
eagerly employed searching the patches of floating
sea-weed for small fish and marine insects, which
find a precarious security amongst its densely in-
terwoven branches from the persecutions of their
enemies.

Barnacles, and a beautiful species of *Serpula*,
were found attached to the stems of some weed
that was hooked up as we sailed along.

Two small icebergs were seen in the course of the day; and from the low temperature of the air and sea these last two days, we were in constant expectation of meeting a large body of ice. We found also that we had been carried forward thirty miles to-day by the easterly current.

Gale followed gale in quick succession for several days, and indeed with only brief intervals of more moderate weather. Whenever the wind veered to the northward of west it was invariably accompanied by thick weather and snow showers; cold weather and a clear sky as certainly prevailed with the south-westerly gales, — the barometer also always rising with the latter, and descending with
Aug. 4. the former. On the fourth, at 8 P. M., it was down to 28·433, with only a fresh breeze; but a gale,
Aug. 5. which followed throughout the next day from the south-west, raised it more than an inch before it
Aug. 6. abated, at 8 A. M. of the sixth, when we were again favoured with a few hours of pleasant weather.

At every opportunity we continued our magnetic observations, notwithstanding the general inclemency of the weather: we were the more anxious to obtain them, owing to the utter deficiency of all such knowledge in these parts. We had been led to expect that one of the magnetic foci of greatest intensity would be found in about the latitude of 47° S. and longitude 140° E. We therefore pursued that parallel of latitude as nearly as possible; and by means of the admirable contrivance of Mr. R. W. Fox were able, in tolerably moderate weather, to determine the three magnetic elements with even more precision on board our ships than they are susceptible of on shore, on account of the unknown and indeterminable amount of local attraction; and even in the heaviest gales, after a little practice with his instrument, they may be observed with sufficient exactness to afford very useful and important information. Throughout the whole distance of between three and four thousand miles, from Kerguelen Island to Van Diemen Land, we could not have derived a single satisfactory result with the instruments in common use; and this portion of the ocean, at least, must for the present have remained a blank upon our charts. But, with Mr. Fox's apparatus, the dip and intensity observations were accomplished in an almost uninterrupted series of daily experiments.

By reference to the annexed table, the progressive increase of intensity, after leaving Kerguelen Island, and the points at which we successively crossed the isodynamic lines of 1·5, 1·6, 1·7, &c., until, on the sixth of August, in lat. 46° 44′ S., and long. 128° 26′ E., we found it to attain its greatest amount in this parallel of latitude, being there 2·034, and thence again as gradually diminishing to 1·824 at Van Diemen Land. The weather did not admit of our attempting to determine the actual position of the focus of maximum intensity, which, from our observations, we considered to be far to the southward of the course

1840. we had pursued, and beyond what it was possible
to follow at this time of the year.

Observations on the Magnetic Force, Dip, and Variation, on
board H. M. S. Erebus, during her Passage from Christmas
Harbour, Kerguelen Island, to Hobart-town, Van Diemen
Land.

Date.	Lat.	Log.	Intensity.	Dip.	Variation.	Remarks.
June	48·41	68·54	1·465	69·596	30·34 W.	Christmas Harbour.
July 22	48·29	76·55	1·539	70·55	—	
23	48·17	80·15	1·574	71·50	—	
24	47·55	83·31	1·601	72·34	—	
25	47·46	86·18	1·575	73·33	—	
26	47·12	89·45	1·565	73·35	—	
27	47·3	93·0	1·712	74·37	27·39 W.	
28	47·13	97·7	1·712	too much	motion	
30	47·39	102·42	1·855	74·28	—	
31	47·35	106·26	1·863	74·31	21·39 W.	
Aug. 1	47·45	110·39	1·815	75·8	—	
2	47·34	114·15	1·970	75·26	14·47 W.	
4	47·41	121·30	1·992	76·4	12·50	
5	47·34	124·43	1·996	76·40	—	
6	46·44	128·26	2·034	75·41	—	
7	46·13	132·0	1·980	75·17	2·41 W.	
8	45·59	135·38	1·989	73·48	0·55 E.	
9	45·17	139·19	2·005	73·23	4·26	
10	44·24	141·39	1·976	72·37	5·56	
11	44·16	142·38	1·934	73·3	11·38	
Hobart-town, Van Diemen's Land.						
	42·52	147·27	1·824	70·40	10·24	

The observations of the variation of the compass
during this run were also of more than ordinary
interest; the westerly variation gradually diminishing in amount until the eighth of August, when, in
Aug. 8. lat. 46° S. and long. 134½° E., we crossed the line
of no variation, and then as rapidly increased the
easterly variation. This position of the line of no

variation is rather further to the eastward than former observations would have placed it, and in opposition to the generally assumed progressive movement of the isogonal lines, from east to west in the southern hemisphere. It is, however, re-marked by Professor Barlow, in his laborious in-vestigation of this matter, in the Philosophical Transactions (for 1837, p. 671.), that this line of no variation, which passes through Australasia, has undergone very little change of position during these last sixty years; and it seems probable that the variation about this spot is as fixed as that on the coast of America. It would, however, be de-sirable, under favourable circumstances of weather, to repeat experiments on the variation at regular intervals of time, in order to ascertain whether a retrograde movement of the isogonal lines in these parts may not have begun, as our observations would seem to show; and as is well known to have occurred with those in England between twenty and thirty years ago.

We have also full reason to believe that at the Cape of Good Hope, where the westerly variation had been regularly increasing ever since about the year 1600, when the line of no variation passed through it, at the average rate of between seven and eight minutes annually, attained its maximum in 1840. By our observations in April of that year it amounted to 29° 14′ W., and those made at the Magnetic Observatory, since its establishment there by me at that time, and afterwards by myself, on revisiting it in April, 1843, concur to show that it has diminished to 28° 58′.

The perfection to which the making of chronometers has attained has rendered general magnetic charts almost unnecessary for nautical purposes; but there are some meridians where the change of variation is so rapid, that in cases where chronometers cannot be depended upon, or are altogether wanting, the longitude may be determined with a considerable degree of exactness by such means; especially to the southward of Australasia, on the usual track of all vessels going from England to her colonies, as also on the meridian of the Cape of Good Hope, and is well worthy the attention of those in charge of our merchant ships.

Aug. 10. The 10th was a beautiful moderate day, and afforded us an opportunity, during the afternoon, of trying the temperature of the ocean in various parts, to the depth of six hundred fathoms, but without striking ground. At 10 h. 50 m. P. M. a burr was observed round the moon, the inner circle being 0° 53′, and the outer 1° 50′ distant from her disc, exhibiting brilliant prismatic colours.

Aug. 12. At noon the south-west cape of New Holland was observed, bearing N. E. by N., distant nine or ten leagues, and some other parts of the coast soon afterwards became visible. But just at this time the wind increased so suddenly and violently, that we could hardly take in our sails quickly enough, and in a few minutes were reduced to a close-reefed main-topsail: at 8 P. M., when blowing

a perfect hurricane, the lee main-topsail sheet
gave way, and in an instant the sail was rent
into numberless ribands, and soon entirely disappeared. The only sail then left on the ship, a new
main-staysail, was soon afterwards blown away, —
no canvass could stand against such a storm. At
10 P. M. the barometer stood at 28·16; and although it then began to rise, we could not perceive
the slightest abatement of the hurricane until after
midnight, when it gradually moderated, and, at the
same time, shifted from north to west. It continued to blow a storm of ordinary violence, with
only occasional furious squalls, throughout the
13th, 14th, and 15th; when, having been driven a
great distance to the southward, we again stood in
shore, and struck soundings at 11 P. M. in ninety
fathoms. By the assistance of a bright full moon,
we saw the land of Tasmania directly ahead of us
at 3 A. M.; and after beating up into Storm Bay,
we anchored at eleven o'clock the same night, off
the light at the entrance of the Derwent, in thirteen fathoms, to wait for daylight, and get a pilot
for the river.

As soon as the tide suited we weighed the next
morning, and with a strong breeze beat up into the
river, where a pilot came on board, and gave us the
gratifying news of the arrival of the Terror the
day before us, and bringing with him a number of
newspapers, which, although of not very recent ·
date, contained much that was new to us.

It was a very fine day, and we all greatly en-

joyed the rich and beautiful scenery on both sides
of the expansive and placid waters of the Derwent;
perhaps making a more powerful impression on our
minds from the contrast which they presented to
the desolate land and turbulent ocean we had so
recently left.

We anchored at five in the afternoon off Fort
Mulgrave, when Captain Crozier came on board
with satisfactory accounts from the Terror. I
immediately proceeded to Government-house, and
received the most kind welcome from our warm-
hearted friends Sir John and Lady Franklin.

Anxious to get the permanent observatory at
work as speedily as possible, I was rejoiced to learn
from the Lieutenant-Governor that the materials of
which it was to be constructed had been prepared
several months, according to a plan sent from
England, and ready to be put together as soon as
the site should be determined upon; I therefore accompanied Sir John Franklin the next morning to
examine several places which he thought likely;
and having selected that which appeared to me the
most unexceptionable for the purpose, a party of
two hundred convicts were the same afternoon set
to work to dig the foundation, prepare the blocks
of freestone which were to form its base, and the
solid pillars of the same materials, which were to
be the supports for the instruments, and bring the
prepared timbers from the government store.

The spot selected for the building is in the go-

vernment demesne, near the site of the proposed
new Government-house, and commands a delightful
view of the beautiful river Derwent and surrounding country. Its chief advantage, however, as a
magnetic station, arises from its being placed
over a thick bed of sandstone, which having been
quarried to the depth of thirty or forty feet prevents all doubt as to the geological character of
the substratum, a circumstance of first importance
in all magnetic operations, and more especially so
in a country where are to be found such manifest
indications of its igneous origin.

The ships were warped further up the river, and
securely moored in a small cove off the government
grounds, in a situation convenient for ready communication with the Observatory, and out of the
bustle and confusion of the general commerce of
the colony. I strongly recommended this anchorage for the use of vessels of war visiting Hobart-
town, as being in every respect the most desirable;
and I am glad to find it has been very generally
resorted to by those of her Majesty's ships that
have touched there lately. During the stay of our
vessels at this place it was called, in almost ironical
compliment to them, Yacht Bay, but I perceive, in
the more recent plans that have been published, it
bears the name of Ross Cove.

The examination and refitting of the rigging,
and the necessary caulking, repairing, and painting
the ships, were proceeded with under the most

favourable circumstances, every facility and assistance being most cordially afforded to us by the gentlemen at the head of the various public offices; and I feel under especial obligations to the Assistant Commissary-general, George M'Lean, Esq., for his ready compliance with every demand made upon his department, the immediate removal of every difficulty, and the personal interest and trouble he took to obtain for us the unusually large supplies we required, and all of them of the very best kind, to our very great comfort, as well as real benefit to the service.

Under the daily personal superintendence of Sir John Franklin, the zealous co-operation of Major Kelsall, of the Royal Engineers, and the able and indefatigable exertions of Mr. Howe, the clerk of the works, the building of the Observatory proceeded most rapidly, and the whole was completed and roofed in, the stone pillars fixed upon the solid sandstone rock, the instruments placed on them, and all their delicate adjustments fulfilled, a few hours before the term-day observations of the 27th of August were to be commenced. Thus the erection of this Observatory was accomplished in the brief period of nine days,—an instance of what may be done where the hearts and energies of all are united to promote the common object of their endeavours. I should be doing injustice to my own feelings were I to neglect to express my admiration of the cheerful enthusiasm which the convicts employed in the building displayed throughout the work; as an instance of this, I may mention that after they had been labouring from six o'clock on Saturday morning until ten at night, seeing that a few more hours of work would complete the roofing in, they entreated permission to finish it before they left off; but as it would have broken in upon the Sabbath morning, their request was very properly refused: this is only one of several such instances of their disinterested zeal in the cause, for, from their unfortunate situation, they could not derive any benefit from their additional labour, and must have, on the occasion above mentioned, suffered much fatigue from their unusually prolonged exertions.

By these means we were enabled to begin the observations at this station some months earlier than we could have done under ordinary circumstances, and much sooner than I could have possibly anticipated. The ships' portable observatories had also been put up at convenient distances from the permanent observatory; and by the aid of some volunteer assistants we obtained a very complete and satisfactory series of observations throughout the 27th and 28th of August, with two sets of magnetometers, in which the three instruments of each were simultaneously recorded at every interval of two and a half minutes throughout the twenty-four hours.

The great advantage of obtaining the readings of *all three* instruments at each interval over the method proposed in the instructions with which I was furnished, and pursued by many of the foreign observatories, in which only one of the instruments was noted at each interval, was so manifest on looking over the series, that I resolved to continue this method throughout the remainder of our voyage; it was subsequently adopted at my earnest recommendation at the observatories of St. Helena, Cape of Good Hope, and Toronto, and by all those established by the liberality of the Russian government throughout its extensive dominions.

As soon as the August term-day observations were obtained, the instruments belonging to the permanent observatory were removed to allow the fitting up of the interior of the building, and to line it throughout, in order to prevent as much as possible great changes of temperature. The building, which is forty-eight long by sixteen broad, is entirely of wood, and care was taken that not the smallest particle of metal of any kind was used in its construction, the whole of the fastenings being of wooden pegs. The instruments are placed on pillars of sandstone, fixed in the solid rock, of the same formation, and defended from any influence the heat of the body of the observer might have upon them by the intervention a closely-fitted deal partition; the observer reading off the instrument by means of a telescope also fixed on a smaller pillar of the same kind, through a small aperture in the wooden partition several feet distant from the instrument.

In the astronomical observatory the transit instrument was properly adjusted, the clocks fixed
in their places, and observations with the invariable
pendulums for determining the figure of the earth
commenced by myself; Commander Crozier having
under his more immediate superintendence the
magnetometric observations, which were now continued uninterruptedly every hour throughout the
day and night, and afforded full occupation to all
the officers of the Expedition who had not other
duties to perform.

These several buildings were all included within
the boundary palings of the government grounds,
and formed a pretty-looking little village; and here,
without interruption or annoyance, the gratifying
and unceasing round of observations proceeded
most comfortably and satisfactorily.   The results
of these operations are already in part published
in "The Philosophical Transactions of the Royal
Society," and the remainder are in course of publication, at the expense of government, under the
superintendence of Lieutenant-Colonel Sabine, of
the Royal Artillery.

The most interesting news that awaited us on
our arrival at Van Diemen's Land related to the
discoveries made, during the last summer, in the
southern regions by the French expedition, consisting of the Astrolabe and Zelée, under the command
of Captain Dumont D'Urville, and by the United
States expedition, under Lieutenant Charles Wilkes,
in the frigate Vincennes.

I

The accounts published, by the authority of Captain D'Urville, in the local papers stated, that the French ships sailed from Hobart-town on the 1st of January, 1840, and discovered land on the evening of the 19th; on the 21st some of the officers landed upon a small islet lying some distance from the main land, and procured some specimens of its granitic rock. D'Urville traced the land in a continuous line one hundred and fifty miles, between the longitudes of 136° and 142° east, in about the latitude of the antarctic circle. It was entirely covered with snow, and there was not the least appearance of vegetation: its general height was estimated at about one thousand three hundred feet. M. D'Urville named it " Terre Adélie." Proceeding to the westward, they discovered and sailed about sixty miles along a solid wall of ice one hundred and fifty feet high, which he, believing to be a covering or crust of a more solid base, named " Côte Clairée." It must have been extremely painful to the enterprising spirit of D'Urville to be obliged to relinquish a more extended exploration of this newly-discovered land; but the weakly condition of his crews imperatively demanded of him to discontinue their laborious exertions, and return to a milder climate to restore the health of his enfeebled people, upon finding that the western part of the Côte Clairée turned away suddenly to the southward. He accordingly bore away on the 1st of February, and reached Hobart-town on the 17th of the same month, after an

absence of only seven weeks. Although the western
point of Côte Clairée had been seen by Balleny in
the preceding summer, it was mistaken by him
for an enormous iceberg, and the land he at first
imagined he saw behind it he afterwards thought
might only be clouds. These circumstances are
mentioned in the log-book of the Eliza Scott, but
are not inserted here with the least intention of
disputing the unquestionable right of the French
to the honour of this very important discovery.

The result of the American expedition was, in
compliance with the instructions of the government, kept profoundly secret on their return to
Sydney, and nothing appeared in the local papers
respecting their extensive operations but uncertain
conjectures and contradictory statements. I felt
therefore the more indebted to the kind and generous consideration of Lieutenant Wilkes, the distinguished commander of the expedition, for a long
letter on various subjects, which his experience had
suggested as likely to prove serviceable to me, under
the impression that I should still attempt to penetrate to the southward on some of the meridians he
had visited; a tracing of his original chart accompanied his letter, showing the great extent of
his discoveries, pointing out to me those parts of
the coast which he thought we should find most
easily accessible. These documents would, indeed,
have proved of infinite value to me, had I felt myself compelled to follow the strict letter of my instructions; and I do not the less appreciate the

motives which prompted the communication of those papers, because they did not eventually prove so useful to me as the American commander had hoped and expected: and I avail myself of this opportunity of publicly expressing the deep sense of thankfulness I feel to him for his friendly and highly honourable conduct.

The arduous and persevering exertions of this expedition, continued throughout a period of more than six weeks, under circumstances of great peril and hardship, cannot fail to reflect the highest credit on those engaged in the enterprise, and excite the admiration of all who are in the smallest degree acquainted with the laborious and difficult nature of an icy navigation: but I am grieved to be obliged to add, that at the present time they do not seem to have received either the approbation or reward their spirited exertions merit. The narrative of their comprehensive labours is now in the hands of the public: I need, therefore, make no further remark here on the subject; but as I shall have occasion hereafter to refer to the documents I received from Lieutenant Wilkes, they are printed in the Appendix.

That the commanders of each of these great national undertakings should have selected the very place for penetrating to the southward, for the exploration of which they were well aware, at the time, that the expedition under my command was expressly preparing, and thereby forestalling our purposes, did certainly greatly surprise me. I

should have expected their national pride would
have caused them rather to have chosen any other
path in the wide field before them, than one thus
pointed out, if no higher consideration had power to
prevent such an interference.

They had, however, the unquestionable right to
select any point they thought proper, at which to
direct their efforts, without considering the embarrassing situation in which their conduct might have
placed me. Fortunately, in my instructions, much
had been left to my judgment under unforeseen
circumstances; and impressed with the feeling that
England had ever *led* the way of discovery in the
southern as well as in the northern regions, I considered it would have been inconsistent with the
pre-eminence she has ever maintained, if we were to
follow in the footsteps of the expedition of any
other nation. I therefore resolved at once to avoid
all interference with their discoveries, and selected
a much more easterly meridian (170° E.), on which
to endeavour to penetrate to the southward, and if
possible reach the magnetic pole.

My chief reason for choosing this particular meridian in preference to any other was, its being that
upon which Balleny had in the summer of 1839,
attained to the latitude of sixty-nine degrees, and
there found an open sea; and not, as has been asserted, that I was deterred from any apprehension
of an equally unsuccessful issue to any attempt we
might make where the Americans and French had
so signally failed to get beyond even the sixty-

seventh degree of latitude. For I was well aware how ill-adapted their ships were for a service of that nature; from not being fortified to withstand the shocks and pressure they must have been necessarily exposed to had they ventured to penetrate any extensive body of ice, they would have equally failed had they tried it upon the meridian I had now chosen, for it will be seen we met with a broad belt of ice, upwards of two hundred miles across, which would have been immediate destruction to them to have encountered; but which, in our fortified vessels, we could confidently run into, and push our way through into the open sea beyond; without such means it would be utterly impossible for any one, under such circumstances, however bold or persevering, to attain a high southern latitude.

The colony of Van Diemen's Land was in a most flourishing condition at the time of our visit; although, in common with all the other Australasian settlements, it afterwards suffered severely from the ruinous system of over-trading, but not to any thing like the same extent. Under the wise and judicious government of Sir John Franklin the revenue of the colony had so greatly increased, that although involved deeply in debt when he arrived in the country, by prudent and well-arranged measures, the debt had been liquidated, and a superabundant income produced. A great amount of statistical information which I collected during our stay at Hobart-town, by the kind permission of Sir John Franklin, from Mr. Forster, acting as colonial secretary, during the temporary absence of Mr. Montague, and Mr. Henslowe, the governor's private secretary, being now but of little general interest, from much later information on the various subjects having already been published (showing a far less prosperous state of affairs, owing to the sad mismanagement of our colonial legislators in England); but more especially because of the admirable work lately published by Count Strzelecki, whose opportunities of traversing the country, and by whose fidelity and ability a far better account has been laid before the public than I could give, I consider it unnecessary for me to enter at all upon the subject of the present condition of the colony.

Constant occupation at the observatory prevented my seeing much of the interior of this most interesting and valuable country; two short excursions only, which I made with Sir John Franklin after the pendulum observations were completed, served to confirm all I had heard of its great resources; and to prove to me that, unlike the more northern colonies of these regions, its climate has not the effect of deteriorating the British character or constitution of the rising generation.

The society of Hobart-town is most perfectly English, and therefore most agreeable to visitors from the mother country. The houses even of the wealthier colonists are smaller and more unpretending in appearance than those of persons of more limited means in England; but there is no want of the characteristic substantial comforts of an English residence bordering often on elegance and luxury; whilst the true open-hearted hospitality we experienced during our prolonged residence amongst them was the best proof to us that this precious peculiarity of our country thrived as vigorously here as in any part of the British empire; and the pleasing remembrances of the many happy hours we passed amongst them will long be cherished by us with deep emotions of gratitude and warmest sentiments of regard. To Lieutenant-Colonel Elliott, and the officers of the 51st Regiment, we were all greatly indebted for their kind hospitality, and the friendship which grew up between the officers of the regiment and those of our ships will long continue amongst the more pleasurable recollections of our voyage. The constant, frank, and cordial intercourse between the barracks and the vessels proved a gratifying kind of united-service amalgamation, now so happily manifested, under all circumstances, between the army and navy.

There is one serious evil, however, which I cannot forbear adverting to, but too evident in every house you enter, and which will require prompt and immediate attention to prevent its baneful effects extending more widely and permanently, — I mean the want of sufficient means of education for the rising generation. It was quite distressing to witness the contrast between the English educated parents and their grown-up children, whose manners and ideas seemed barely equal to those of the lower uneducated order of society at home.

This evil the worthy governor had set his heart
upon remedying, and had made great exertions to
obtain from the home government a charter for a college to be formed on a liberal scale; the legislative
council of the colony also went so far as to vote a sum
of 2500l. for the purpose. At the recommendation
of the late Dr. Arnold, of Rugby, the Rev. J. P. Gell
was sent from England to organise such an institution as should meet the wants of the people. After
much deliberation, a site for the building was chosen
on part of the government land at New Norfolk;
and on the 7th November, 1840, the foundation-
stone was laid with great ceremony by Sir John
Franklin, in the presence of the members of the
executive and legislative councils, and a large assemblage of the inhabitants of the district; but
thus it remains, I believe, to this day, through the
opposition and intrigues of the defeated but influ-
ential parties, whose interests required that it should
be built in Hobart-town, whilst the claims of the
different religious denominations of all classes of
Christians to have a voice in its councils, occasioned
such violent disputes that the colonial office at
home abandoned the measure; and thus the benevo-
lent intentions of the governor have been, for the
present, frustrated.

But just at this time the Bishop of Tasmania has
resumed the endeavour with great earnestness, and is
making strenuous efforts to have formed a "collegiate
body possessing property (by royal charter, when it
can be obtained, till then a trust), to be the source

of education to the colonists, in the principles of the Church of Christ, and in all useful knowledge," by means of private subscription; and the Venerable Archdeacon Marriott, of Hobart-town, is in England for the purpose of carrying the views of the bishop into effect upon this as well as some other points connected with the welfare of the church in Tasmania.

It is calculated that 5000*l*., raised in England, may, together with landed and other endowments in the colony, produce such an annual income as will enable the bishop to proceed at once to organise the college: as the payments of the pupils will supply what may further be needed for obtaining the lease of suitable premises, for the general expenses of the institution, and for the accumulation of a fund for the erection of college buildings at a future time.

The bishop will, with the advice and assistance of proper persons in the colony, "hereafter to be named, invest the funds, and the property will be held in trust for the college, and made over to it in the event of its being incorporated; and from the yearly income provision will be made for the warden and fellows, and for scholarships, exhibitions, and other expenses."

We cannot doubt that a design so calculated to promote the well-being of the church in that colony, and to extend the blessings of a sound religious education to a population of sixty thousand souls, so greatly requiring it, will meet with ready sup-

port and assistance from the mother country. Sir
John Franklin, the late Lieutenant-Governor, has
manifested his undiminished interest in the welfare
of those over whom he for several years presided (and
during whose period of government so much moral
benefit was diffused through the society of the place
as to secure for him the lasting gratitude and attach-
ment of all right-minded people), by a donation of
five hundred pounds; and his amiable lady, on
leaving that country, made over four hundred acres
of land which she had purchased in the neighbourhood of Hobart-town, with an elegant museum
she had built upon it, to trustees for the benefit
of any collegiate institution which might be
founded with the approbation of the bishop of the
diocese. These acts of munificence we may hope
will be followed by the charitable and wealthy; and
by thus furnishing an adequate means of religious
instruction and general education, afford the most
efficient means of counteracting the existing evil,
which however can only be rendered effectual by
the persevering efforts of good and pious men, and
by the blessing of Almighty God on their labours.

The completion of Rossbank observatory proceeded satisfactorily, and long before the second
term-day arrived the magnetometers were replaced,
so that again on the 23d of September we had two
complete sets of instruments observed at the same
place, forming a most perfect comparison between
them.

To effect this desirable object we had again to avail ourselves of the aid of volunteers under Sir John Franklin, who, in his zeal for the advancement of science, took his share of the duties of that day, which, as on the previous occasion, amounted to twelve of the twenty-four hours' observations, at intervals of two and a half minutes. The observations in the ships' observatory were made by Captain Crozier, the officers of both ships, and myself: those in the permanent observatory by his Excellency, and the following gentlemen, who had devoted some time to acquire accuracy in reading off the instruments, — Rev. John Philip Gell, M. A., Trin. Coll., Cambridge; Rev. Dr. Turnbull, Mr. Henslowe, Lieut. Bagot, A. D. C. 51st; Mr. Cracroft, Mr. Nairne, Lieut. Kay, of the Terror, and two mates. I had thus the satisfaction of witnessing the effectual working of the observatory on those days on the enlarged plan of observation I contemplated, and which, by the unabated zeal of the volunteers, continued without interruption, on every succeeding term-day.

The regular hourly observations were next commenced by Lieutenant Kay, whom I had selected to conduct the magnetic and meteorological experiments at this important station, in co-operation with the numerous observatories established in different parts of the globe, and who had shown great diligence and application in making himself acquainted with the instruments to be employed in these investigations, and the various and delicate adjustments and corrections necessary to ensure

accuracy; the result has most fully justified my
confident expectations. Mr. Scott, mate of the
Terror, and Mr. Dayman, of the Erebus, were appointed as his assistants, and a marine from each ship
completed the establishment of the observatory.

In order that a more complete comparison might
be instituted between the observations at Hobart-
town and those to be made in more southern stations to be visited by the Expedition, the expanded
system of observation we had hitherto used was to
be continued by Lieutenant Kay; but as these
periods of exact comparison occurred so seldom,
and seemed to me scarcely sufficient to detect many
of the curious phenomena that might be expected
to present themselves on more frequent comparisons
of even shorter intervals, I considered it advisable
to arrange that one additional hour of continued observation should be made every night; and the time
selected for this purpose was that most favourable
for seeing the aurora, which has been known to exer-
cise so powerful an influence on the magnetometers,
and most suited for watching its several phases. I
especially directed the attention of Lieutenant Kay
and his assistants, during our absence, to notice the
frequency, direction, form, altitude, and all the
changes in the appearance of auroræ, as they would
also have formed, had we been so fortunate as to have
found a place in which to pass a winter in the Antarctic regions, circumstances of corresponding and continual observation, and perhaps serve to account for
many irregularities that might appear in the summer

observations in those latitudes, where the continual presence of the sun would prevent the detection of the aurora. Although, unfortunately, we had no opportunity of making any corresponding observations in high southern latitudes, those additional hours of labour to Lieutenant Kay's party have not been in vain, for by the ready zeal evinced by Mr. Caldcott, the superintendent of the magnetic observatory at Trevandrum, simultaneous observations were made at that place, and their comparison will, I have no doubt, afford very valuable results.

In addition to the magnetometric and meteorological instruments, some others were supplied to Lieut. Kay for astronomical purposes; and before we left Hobart-town arrangements were made for the erection of a more suitable and comfortable building for the party to reside in, and at a convenient distance from the observatory. The observatory was named Rossbank by His Excellency Sir John Franklin. It is in lat. 42° 52′ 27·4″, long. 147° 27′ 30″; and is situated one hundred and five feet above the level of the sea at mean tide. The mean magnetic dip, 70° 40′ S. and the variation (in May, 1841), 10° 24′ 24″ E.

As the proper season for our southern voyage drew near, the ships were made ready for sea. All defects had been repaired, and when we bent sails we had the great happiness to feel assured that our ships and crew were even more effective than the day we sailed from England. We had to lament the loss of one of our best men, Edward Bradley,

on the 24th of October, by an accident; and,
before our departure, were under the necessity of
invaliding Mr. Molloy, mate of the Terror, whose
constitution was considered unequal to the hard-
ships and severity of climate he would have been
exposed to, and whose present state of health rendered his return to England necessary. On the
5th of November the ships were dressed with
flags, and a salute fired on the occasion of His
Excellency Sir John Franklin laying the foundation-
stone of the new Government House, within sight
of the vessels.   The want of a building suitable to
the advanced importance of the colony, and the
comfort and dignity of the Governor, had long been
felt and acknowledged.

CHAPTER VI.

THE remaining few days were spent in completing
our preparations for sea; and adverse winds and
weather continued to detain us at our anchorage
until the morning of the twelfth, on which day we
weighed at daylight, and stood down the river
under favourable circumstances. Sir John Franklin
and some other friends came on board to accompany
us as far as the mouth of the river, and the government tender followed.

Soon after noon we passed the lighthouse on the
east point of the entrance of the river, and being
fairly out to sea by 1·30 P.M., our warm-hearted
friends took leave of us, giving us three cheers at
parting, which were most cordially returned from
our ships, as we stood out of Storm Bay. If the
deep-felt gratitude of thankful hearts be any gratification to our excellent friend Sir John Franklin,
who not only evinced the most anxious desire, but
sought every opportunity of promoting the objects
of our enterprise, and contributing to the comfort
and happiness of all embarked in it. I am sure
there is not an individual in either of our ships
who would not most heartily wish to express those
sentiments towards him, and also to every member
of his family, for their great kindness to us during
our prolonged stay at Hobart-town.

K

1840.

The evening was squally, with rain; but the wind still so favoured us, that we cleared the land before dark, and shaped our course for Auckland Island —distant between eight and nine hundred miles from Hobart Town.

Nov. 13.

The favouring breeze continued, and we carried all sail, the Terror keeping company with difficulty. Several beds of sea-weed were passed; and the albatross as well as several other kinds of petrel were seen in considerable numbers. The cloudy weather that prevailed during the nights, pointed out in my instructions for observing " falling stars," prevented our witnessing any of those remarkable exhibitions of almost regular periodical occurrence

14.

Being nearly calm at 9 A. M., we tried for soundings with six hundred fathoms of line, without success, and obtained the temperature at various depths: that of the surface being 51°; at 150 fathoms 49°·8; at 300 fathoms 48°; at 450 fathoms 46°·5, and at 600 fathoms 45°·6: the indices of the thermometer having been set to 51°, showed, on each occasion, they had passed through a stratum of water at the higher temperature of 52°·5, and certainly at a less depth than 100 fathoms; but a strong breeze arising from the eastward, prevented our ascertaining its depth and breadth with accuracy.

15.

At noon we were in latitude 45°·33' south, and longitude 152°·45' east, and found we had been set by a current thirty miles S. 60° E., in two days: the wind after noon veered to the southward, and

between 11 P. M. and midnight, we observed some
faint coruscations of Aurora Australis; but no " falling stars " were seen, although carefully looked for
throughout this remarkably clear night.

During this, as well as the following three days,   Nov. 16.
we observed much sea-weed, although four hundred
miles from any land; numerous luminous patches in
the water were also passed.   At eight o'clock in the
evening of the nineteenth, being within twenty miles   19.
of the land, and blowing a strong westerly gale, we
rounded to on the port tack to wait for daylight, and
tried for soundings occasionally throughout the
night with from 140 to 200 fathoms, but without
striking ground.

At 3·30 A. M. we bore away to the south-east, and   20.
soon afterwards North-west Cape was seen directly
a-head of us; a thick fog almost immediately
again concealed it from our view, so that had we
not fortunately got sight of it just at the time we did
we should have had no other opportunity of making
the land during the whole day.   The wind increased to a strong gale, attended with fog and
rain, and kept us in some anxiety, until the cape
again appeared through the haze at less than a
mile from us, and we were enabled to run along
the northern side of the island under its protection.   The north-west cape is a very remarkable
headland, with a rocky islet and a curious conical
rock off it; just to the eastward of it is a dark-
looking promontory, called Black Head, with a deep
cavernous indentation at its base: this we after-

wards found to be only a short distance from the westernmost part of Laurie Harbour; it was reached by Mr. M'Cormick and some other officers, by following the course of the stream that empties its waters into the head of the harbour, and whose source is in the hills above Black Head: these hills are from eight to nine hundred feet high.

Bristow Rock, which is reported to lie between eight and nine miles due north from Enderby Island, and level with the water's edge, we did not see, but is a danger to be carefully avoided by ships approaching the northern harbour. I may also mention that there is a narrow entrance to the harbour between the west end of Enderby Island and Rose's Island, which is only a channel fit for boats. The sea was breaking right across the opening when we passed it; but in calm weather it might be mistaken by strangers as a safe passage.

On rounding the N. E. cape of Enderby Island, we passed through some strong whirlpools, occasioned by the meeting of the tides off this point; and although we did not find soundings with our ordinary hand lines, it is by no means improbable that some shoals or rocky patches may have some influence in producing these strong and dangerous eddies.

As we opened the harbour, the squalls came down from the western hills with much violence, threatening to blow us out to sea again; and it required the utmost vigilance and activity of the officers and crew in beating up, at times, to maintain the ground we had gained. There is, however,

ample space, and no concealed dangers, the belts of
sea-weed, *Macrocystus* and *Laminaria*, which line
the shores and rocks, point out the shallow or dangerous parts. After five hours of hard contending
with the fierce westerly squalls, we anchored at
1 P. M. in a small cove on the western shore, in ten
fathoms.

Two painted boards, erected upon poles in a
conspicuous spot, attracted our attention, and an
officer was immediately sent to examine them.
They proved to be records of the visits of the
French expedition under D'Urville, and of one of
the vessels of the American exploring expedition.
The first, a white board with black letters, as follows :— " Les corvettes Françoises L'Astrolabe et
la Zélée, parties de Hobart Town le 25 Février,
1840, mouillées ici le 11 Mars, et réparties le 20
du dit pour la New Zéland. Du 19 Janvier au 1
Février, 1840, découverte de la Terre Adélie et
détermination du pôle magnétique Austral !"

The second, a black board with white letters,
stated, — " U. S. brig Porpoise, 73 days out from
Sydney, New Holland, on her return from an exploring cruize along the antarctic circle, all well;
arrived the 7th, and sailed again on the 10th
March, for the Bay of Islands, New Zealand."

A paper was also found inclosed in a bottle, which
had been so imperfectly corked that some water had
got into and so obliterated some parts of the writing, that we had difficulty in deciphering it. Its
purport was, that the Porpoise had touched here for

water, and that during their cruize they had coasted along the Icy Barrier, and had touched here for water. We were all much surprised that no mention was made of the " Antarctic Continent" discovered by Lieutenant Wilkes, but supposed that secrecy had been enforced upon him, as to any discoveries he might make, or that having parted from the Vincennes, his track had been more northerly, and therefore less fortunate than his commodore. I have reason now to believe the latter to be the more correct conjecture.

By the side of a small stream of water, and on the only cleared spot we could find, the ruins of a small hut was discovered, which I have since learnt formed for several years the wretched habitation of a deserter from an English whale ship and a New Zealand woman.

The ships being securely moored in a well-sheltered anchorage, on the west side of the harbour, the observatories were landed, and all hands employed clearing away the trees and digging for a foundation; the upper surface was a complete mass of peat bog, and the deeper we dug down the softer it became, so that we had great difficulty and labour in making a foundation sufficiently firm for our purpose: this was, however, accomplished by filling the deep holes with large blocks of stone, and after they had settled, placing casks filled with sand upon them; the instruments being then secured upon the casks. The term-day was so nigh at hand, we had not time to seek for a more suit·able place, and we now felt the great advantage of

being able to form three small houses of the materials of the second observatory; for there was not
sufficient level space to have put it up as one house.

By the twenty-fifth the instruments were all
fixed and adjusted, and we had the satisfaction of
finding, during three days' preliminary observations, that the foundation remained perfectly steady,
and the results were most satisfactory.

The term-day observations were made on the
twenty-eighth, and afforded, as we afterwards found,
a most interesting comparison with those made at
the Rossbank observatory, Van Diemen's Land,
showing the same instantaneous movements of the
instruments as occur in the northern regions; and
thus our principal purpose of coming here was fulfilled to our wishes.

Hourly and additional observations agreed upon
before we sailed from Hobart Town were continued
until we had obtained seven days of uninterrupted
results, when we considered the magnetometric
operations complete : the absolute determinations
were next to be attended to; but in these we found
very considerable difficulty. The place proved to
be a most remarkable corroboration of what I have
already said respecting the uncertainty and inac-
curacy of magnetic observations made on land. In
our course from Van Diemen's Land we found a
gradual increase of dip, in exact proportion to the
distance we sailed during each day towards these
islands, from which we could determine with very
great accuracy the amount of dip due to their geo-

graphical position; but the first observations we obtained here gave us too small a dip by more than two degrees. The cause I of course immediately attributed to local attraction, and directed observations to be made at several different stations. At a position only thirty yards distant from the first station the dip, with the same instrument, was found to be nine degrees less, and therefore eleven degrees in error. The rocks at this point had a peculiar ferruginous appearance, and on presenting some of them to a delicate compass they turned it round and round as swiftly as the hand could move; and moreover were found to possess a powerful degree of polarity, the north and south pole of the fragments depending entirely upon the direction in which they were found lying with reference to the magnetic meridian. They were not however loose stones, as those of a beach, but taken from the laminated rocks of which the land consists, so that we may esteem the whole mass to be one great magnet. Mr. Smith, whom I entrusted with this service, made many observations on various parts of the harbour, all of which are recorded, and will prove an useful lesson to magnetic observers. At the point where we had placed the magnetometers we found the dip accordant with our computations; but this was purely accidental. The dip obtained from observations on board the Erebus, sufficiently removed from the pernicious influence of the land, was that upon which we were obliged to depend, and was pro-

bably very near the truth; and the variation at
these two places also accorded very nearly. The
observations on board the Terror were vitiated by
her proximity to Shoe Island, so much so as to
mask the local attraction of the iron of the ship, and
to render useless their observations to determine
its amount, when they swung the vessel for that
purpose. Numerous specimens of the rocks from
other parts of the island were brought to me by
Mr. M'Cormick, proving how extensively this magnetic power was distributed over it. It is not at all
improbable that considerable effects might be produced upon this magnetic island by the action of the
sun upon a surface so constituted, and therefore even
differential observations cannot be depended fully
upon under a frequent change of clear or cloudy
weather, or great differences of temperature of the
land, whether occasioned by the absorption or radiation of heat.

Auckland Islands were discovered by Abraham
Bristow, commander of the ship Ocean, a southern
whaler belonging to Messrs. Enderby, on the 18th
of August, 1806, during a third voyage round the
world, and is recorded in the log-book, from which,
by the kindness of C. Enderby, Esq., of Greenwich,
I am permitted to make the following extract: —
" Moderate and clear: at daylight saw land, bearing west by compass, extending round to the north
as far as N.E. by N., distant from the nearest
part about nine leagues. This island or islands,
as being the first discoverer, I shall call Lord

Auckland's (my friend through my father), and is situated according to my observation at noon in lat. 50° 48′ S., and long. 166° 42′ E., by a distance of the sun and moon, I had at half-past 10 A.M. The land is of a moderate height, and from its appearance I have no doubt but it will afford a good harbour in the north end, and I should suppose lies in about the latitude of 50° 21′ S., and its greatest extent is in a N.W. and S.E. direction. This place I should suppose abounds with seals, and sorry I am that the time and the lumbered state of my ship do not allow me to examine."

Captain Bristow again visited these islands in 1807, in the ship Sarah, also belonging to Messrs. Enderby: he then took formal possession of them and landed some pigs, which have increased in numbers in a surprising manner.

I have not been able to refer to the log-book of the Sarah: but the names on the annexed survey are taken from a plan of the Island published by the Admiralty in 1823, from information derived from Captain Bristow.

The group consists of one large and several smaller islands, separated by narrow channels. The largest island is about thirty miles long, and its extreme breadth is about fifteen miles. It contains two principal harbours, whose entrances are both from the eastward, and whose heads or terminations reach within two or three miles of the western coast, and only five or six miles from each other. Rendez-vous Harbour, which is at the north extreme of the island, contains several secure an-

chorages. The outermost of these, though convenient for stopping at a short time only, is a small
sandy bay on the south side of Enderby Island,
and about a mile and a half from its N.E. cape.
It is well protected from all winds except those
from the south-eastward, and the holding ground
a good tenacious clay. It is probable that there
may be found good anchorage also to the west of
Enderby Island. After passing Ocean and Rose's
Islands, a ship may anchor in perfect safety in any
part, but the most convenient will be found to be
between those islands and Erebus Cove, where
abundance of wood and water may be obtained, as
also at Terror Cove. The upper end of the inlet,
called Laurie Harbour, is the most suitable for
ships wanting to heave down or to undergo any extensive repair. It is perfectly land-locked, and the
steep beach on the southern shore affords the greatest facility for clearing and re-loading the vessel.

I was so struck with the many advantages this
place possesses for a penal settlement, over every
other I had heard named, to which to remove convicts
from the now free colonies of New South Wales,
New Zealand, and Van Diemen's Land, that I addressed a letter on the subject to Sir John Franklin
on my return to Hobart Town, recommending its
adoption. This letter was forwarded to the Secretary of State for the Colonies; but I believe
Chatham Island, as being seated in a milder climate,
has been preferred, although I am not aware of any
other advantages it possesses; whilst the want of

good harbours will be found a great drawback, and the two tribes of New Zealanders from Port Nicholson, who took possession of it in 1835, after eating the half of the aborigines they found there, and making slaves of the other half, will prove a difficult people to dispossess of the land they have gained by conquest.

The southern harbour of Auckland Island is said to be capacious, but the water too deep over the greater part of it for anchoring: there are several coves on either side of it, where good anchorage may be found, and well protected; but as we did not visit that inlet, I cannot answer for the accuracy of these statements, which I received from masters of whalers. Laurie Harbour is well calculated for the location of an establishment for the prosecution of the whale fishery: many black and several sperm whales came into the harbour whilst we were there; and from such a situation the fishery might be pursued with very great advantage. I am rejoiced to hear that the enterprising merchant, Charles Enderby, Esq., is making application to the government for a grant of the Islands for that purpose, and from the circumstance of their having been discovered by the commander of one of his ships, he may with some justice claim to be entitled to greater privileges than others.

We arrived there in the spring of the year, November being equivalent to April of the northern latitudes; and although less than eight degrees to the southward of the latitude of Hobart Town, we

ABSTRACT OF THE METEOROLOGICAL JOURNAL OF HER MAJESTY'S
SHIP EREBUS.—NOVEMBER, 1840.

Day	Mean Temperature of the			Mean (corrected) barometer.	Winds.		Weather.	Remarks.
	Air in shade.	Sea at surface.	Dew point.		Direction.	Force.		
1	57·0	54·5	47	Inches. 30·139	N.W.	2	5 b. c.†	Auckland off Hobart Town. W. L. Lat. 42° 52' S.
2	59·0	55·0	50	072	W.N.W.	1	4 b. c.	
3	57·1	56·0	51	005	{A.M. N.W. / P.M. East}	2	{A.M. 4 b.c. / P.M. 2 b.c.d.}	
4	54·8	55·9	45	103	S.E.	1	7 b.c.v.	
5	54·0	55·4	45	019	Westerly	2	5 b.c.v.	
6	55·6	57·3	45	102	Easterly	1	7 b.c.v.	
7	51·3	53·6	42	29·985	{A.M. N.W. / P.M. S.E.}	1	7 b.c.v.	
8	57·4	57·7	52	728	S.E.	1	4 b.c.	
9	53·1	58·0	53	699	S.E.	1	{A.M. 3 b.c.p.r. / P.M. 0 g.p.r.}	
10	48·8	56·0	*49	582	Southerly	1	0 g.r.	
11	45·6	53·8	*43	630	S.W.	2	{A.M. 0 q.r. / P.M. 3 b.c.}	
12	49·3	54·3	*50	879	S.W.	{A.M. 1 / P.M. 4}	2 b.c.g.p.r.	
13	52·7	52·8	*53	755	Westerly	5	{A.M. g.r. / P.M. 3 b.c.}	
14	46·8	49·7	*47	608	Easterly	{A.M. 1 / P.M. 4}	0 d.r.	At sea.
15	49·4	48·9	47	705	Southerly	2	3 b.c.g.d.	
16	50·6	49·2	48	941	Westerly	3	{A.M. 6 b.c.v. / P.M. 2 b.c.g.p.r.}	
17	51·2	47·4	50	462	N.W.	4	0 m.f.	
18	46·0	44·4	48	233	S.W.	5	{A.M. 1 b.c.g.p.r. / P.M. 3 b.c.q.}	
19	46·4	44·2	46	329	W.N.W.	5	2 b.c.g.q.p.r.	
20	44·6	42·7	43	332	W. by S.	5	3 b.c.p.q.r.	
21	47·0	45·5	*47	468	W.N.W.	4	0 q.r.	
22	47·1	45·0	44	305	West	6	{A.M. 0 g.q.r. / P.M. 4 b.c.q.}	Auckland Island. Lat. 50° 32' S.
23	46·2	44·2	48	553	W.N.W.	3	3 b.c.m.q.	
24	42·4	42·7	45	232	Westerly	3	3 b.c.q.r.s.	
25	40·0	40·1	*40	051	N.S.W.	3	3 b.c.q.r.s.	
26	40·1	39·4	36	284	S.S.W.	2	3 b.c.q.r.s.	
27	42·4	42·4	*40	562	Westerly	1	0 g.r.d.	
28	46·8	44·5	*48	481	W. by S.	2	0 g.r.m.	
29	47·8	45·6	40	535	Westerly	2	{A.M. 1 b.c.m. / P.M. 2 b.c.g.d.}	
30	46·4	45·2	45	639	N.S.W.	2	4 b.c.p.b.	*
	49·23	49·38	46·2	29·6472		2·57		

* Rain falling.   † For the key to these symbols, see Appendix.

ABSTRACT OF THE METEOROLOGICAL JOURNAL OF HER MAJESTY'S
SHIP EREBUS.—DECEMBER, 1840.

Day	Mean Temperature of the			Mean (corrected) barometer.	Winds.		Weather.	Remarks.
	Air in shade.	Sea at surface.	Dew point.		Direction.	Force.		
	°	°	°	Inches.				
1	43·2	42·0	38	29·899	S.W.	2	2 b.c.g.†	
2	45·4	43·7	37	865	Westerly	1	A.M. 3 b.c. / P.M. 0 g.p.r.	
3	44·9	44·3	39	757	S. Westerly	3	A.M. 2 b.c.g. / P.M. 0 g.q.p.r.	
4	45·1	43·9	46	698	S. Westerly	5	4 b.c.q.g.	
5	47·1	45·2	45	941	W.S.W.	3	4 b.c.g.	Auckland Islands.—Lat. 50° 32′. S.
6	47·2	46·1	39	955	S.W.	3	5 b.c.q.d.	
7	47·9	46·0	40	738	W. by S.	3	A.M. 3 b.c.o.g. / P.M. 0 q.r.	
8	47·9	46·2	45	628	S. Westerly	2	0 m.p.r.	
9	50·1	48·4	*51	453	W.N.W.	3	0 g.m.r.	
10	47·5	47·1	*50	240	S. Easterly	1	A.M. 0 g.m.r. / P.M. 0 g.	
11	46·7	45·7	48	542	W.S.W.	A.M. 2 / P.M. 4	2 b.c.q.r.	
12	48·8	46·6	49	829	N. Westerly	4	A.M. 3 b.c.g. / P.M. 1 b.c.f.r.	
13	48·8	46·4	47	830	W.N.W.	2	A.M. 5 b.c.q. / P.M. 2 b.c.f.d.	Campbell's Is. Lat. 52° 33′. S.
14	48·5	47·0	*49	653	W.N.W.	2	A.M. 0 q.f.r. / P.M. 0 f.	
15	46·7	45·2	42	649	S.W. by W.	2	4 b.c.g.	
16	44·3	42·6	38	962	W.S.W.	2	4 b.c.	
17	46·7	45·2	*48	838	Westerly	A.M. 3 / P.M. 6	0 q.d.r.	52·44
18	42·4	40·6	40	756	S.W.	5	3 b.c.g.	54·21
19	41·4	39·7	42	417	Westerly	A.M. 5 / P.M. 3	0 g.q. / 0 m.r.	55·56
20	39·0	37·3	38	179	S.W. by W.	A.M. 8 / P.M. 6	2 b.c.q.p.r.	56·44
21	39·0	36·4	36	300	W.S.W.	4	2 b.c.p.d.	57·47
22	37·4	34·3	30	133	A.M. S.W. / P.M. Nthly.	3 / 2	0 g.f.p.d.	59·0
23	36·1	34·9	*35	28·996	S. Easterly	A.M. 2 / P.M. 4	1 b.c.p.s. / 3 b.c.g.p.s.	59·41
24	35·7	33·4	32	29·435	S.W.	3	A.M. 3 b.c.p.s. / P.M. 5 b.c.v.	60·32
25	36·2	33·4	*35	029	N.N.W.	A.M. 5 / P.M. 6	0 g.r.s. / 0 m.r.	62·10
26	36·8	34·3	38	667	W. by N.	5	0 m.	62·3
27	31·9	29·5	28	784	S.W.	A.M. 5 / P.M. 8	1 b.c.q.p.s. / 3 b.c.q.	62·43
28	31·3	29·5	29	28·934	Easterly	3	A.M. 1 b.c.o.p.s. / P.M. 0 p.s.	62·40
29	30·2	29·1	24	29·119	S. Easterly	A.M. 4 / P.M. 2	0 g.	64·6
30	32·2	30·8	32	28·991	A.M. N. / P.M. Wstly.	2	1 b.c.o.p.s.	64·32
31	30	29·8	29	826	E.S.E.	A.M. 4 / P.M. 2	2 b.c.p.s. / 5 b.c.p.	66·0
	41·83	40·15	39·3	29·5175		3·29		

* Rain falling.   † For the key to these symbols, see Appendix.

found a very great difference in the temperature, amounting to about ten degrees of the thermometer, but still greater to our feelings, owing to the increased humidity of the atmosphere, the temperature of the dew point being nearly the same in both places notwithstanding so great a difference of temperature. Abstracts of the Meteorological Journal of the Erebus for November and December are annexed, to show the differences of climate of Auckland and Campbell Islands, from that of Van Diemen's Land. The temperature cannot be considered severe, when we remember that in England, which is very nearly in the same latitude, the mean temperature for April, the corresponding month, is 46°.* Our stay was too short to justify any further remarks on the climate of these islands; but a series of well conducted observations, continued for two or three years, could not fail to prove highly interesting and important to the advancement of meteorological science.

Mr. M'Cormick, who remarks that the formation of these, as well as Campbell Islands, is volcanic, and constituted chiefly of basalt and green-stone, especially calls attention to "Deas' Head," a promontory of Auckland Island, as being of great geological interest, exhibiting fine columns, three hundred feet high, which are highly magnetic. The loftiest hill, Mount Eden, to the S.W. of our anchorage, attains an elevation of thirteen hundred feet, is rounded at the top, and clothed with grass

* Greenwich Observations, 1841, p. 37., and 1842, p. 34.

to its summit.   Another hill in the west rises to
nearly one thousand feet.

The following observations on the vegetable productions are by Dr. Hooker :—

"Perhaps no place in the course of our projected
voyage in the southern ocean promised more
novelty to the botanist than Auckland Islands.
Situated in the midst of a boisterous ocean, in a
very high latitude for that hemisphere, and far
removed from any tract of land but the islands of
New Zealand, it proved, as was expected, to contain, amongst many new species, some of peculiar
interest, as being antarctic forms of genera otherwise confined to the last-mentioned group.

"Possessing no mountains rising to the limits
of perpetual snow, and few rocks or precipices, the
whole land seemed covered with vegetation.   A
low forest skirts all the shores, succeeded by a
broad belt of brushwood, above which, to the
summits of the hills, extend grassy slopes.   On
a closer inspection of the forest, it is found to be
composed of a dense thicket of stag-headed trees,
so gnarled and stunted by the violence of the gales,
as to afford an excellent shelter for a luxuriant
under-growth of bright green feathery ferns, and
several gay-flowered herbs.   With much to delight
the eye, and an extraordinary amount of new
species to occupy the mind, there is here a want of
any of those trees or shrubs to which the voyager
has been accustomed in the north ; and one cannot
help feeling, how much a greater pleasure it would

be to find new kinds of the pine, the birch, willow, or the oak, than those remarkable trees which have no allies in the northern hemisphere, and the mention of which, suggesting no familiar form to compare them with at home, can interest few but the professed botanist.

"The woods consist entirely of four or five species of trees, or large shrubs, which are here enumerated in the order of their relative abundance. 1. A short and thick-trunked tree (*Metrosideros lucida*), which branches at top into a broad crown; this is more nearly allied to the classical myrtle than to any other European plant. 2. *Dracophyllum longifolium*, (Fl. Antarct. * TAB. xxxi. and xxxii.), a black-barked tree, with slender erect branches, bearing grassy leaves at the ends of the twigs. 3. *Panax simplex*, a tree allied to the ivy. 4. *Veronica elliptica*, this is the *V. decussata* of our gardens, a Tierra del Fuego plant, but which was originally detected in New Zealand, during Cook's second voyage. 5. A species of *Coprosma* (*C. fœtidissima*, TAB. xiii.), whose leaves emit when bruised, and especially in drying, an intolerably fœtid odour. Under the shade of these, near the sea beach, about fifteen different *Ferns* grow in great abundance, the most remarkable of which is a species of *Aspidium* (*A. venustum*, of the French South Polar Voyage), with short trunks

* The Plates quoted all refer to those published in the *Botany of the Antarctic Expedition.*

2-3 feet high, crowned with a tuft of spreading feathery fronds, each 3-5 feet long : this is one of the most graceful and ornamental productions of the group. The *Aralia polaris*, Homb. and Jacq.*, and the *Pleurophyllum criniferum* (TAB. xxiv. and xxv.), are two highly remarkable plants, very common near the sea; the former is allied to the ivy, but has clusters of green waxy flowers as large as a child's head; and its round and wrinkled leaves, of the deepest green, measure a foot and a half across. They form the favourite food of the hogs which run wild on these islands.

" It is upon the hills, however, that the more beautiful plants abound; amongst which the most striking is a liliaceous one, allied to *Anthericum* (*Chrysobactron Rossii*, TAB. xliv. and xlv.), whose conspicuous racemes of golden flowers are often a span long, and many specimens have three or four such spikes. The *Pleurophyllum speciosum* (TAB. xxii. and xxiii.), resembles a large *Aster*, bearing numerous purple flowers, the size of a large marigold. The *Celmisia vernicosa* (TAB. xxxi. and xxxii.), has linear glossy leaves, spread out on the ground like the spokes of a wheel, and pure white flowers, with a purple eye, as large as those of the last-named plant. Finally, the *Veronica Benthamii* (TAB. xxxix. and xl.), may be mentioned; it is of shrubby growth, with spikes of flowers of a deep ultramarine blue. Amongst those of humbler stature,

---

* Figured in the Botany of the French South Polar Expedition.

several European genera occur, as species of *Cardamine, Ranunculus, Plantain, Geranium,* and *Epilobium,* two beautiful white and red-flowered *Gentians* (TAB. xxxv. and xxxvi.), and a *Forget-me-not* (TAB. xxxvii.), with flowers much larger than those of any English species.

" The vegetation is characterised by a luxuriance of these fine species, and the absence of such weeds as grasses and sedges, &c. Eighty flowering plants were found, a small number, but consisting of species more remarkable for their beauty and novelty than the flora of any other country can show, no less than fifty-six being hitherto undescribed, and one half of the whole peculiar to this group, or Campbell Island, as far as is at present known.

" The ships of Captain Vancouver's expedition touched at the southern extremity of New Zealand, from whence the naturalist attached to that voyage, the late venerable Mr. Menzies, brought a richer store of cryptogamic plants than had ever before reached Europe. Nor did Lord Auckland's group prove less productive, having afforded no less than upwards of two hundred species of *mosses, lichens, Hepaticæ,* and *sea-weeds,* &c.; of which a very large proportion are new to science.

" A few botanical remarks on the flora of this group are best incorporated with those on the vegetation of the island next visited. It may here be remarked, however, that probably nearly all of the native plants were collected ; that the vegetation is characteristic of New Zealand, but contains many new forms typical of the antarctic regions. The proportion which the smaller division of flowering plants (*Monocotyledones*) bears to the greater (*Dicotyledones*), is very large, being as 1 to 2·2 ; in either hemisphere this division increases on attaining a high latitude; but that of Melville Island must be reached in the north, to meet with a similar ratio. It is worthy of notice that this large pro portion does not depend on an increased number of *grasses*, which form a smaller item in this flora than they do in that of the Falklands or of Melville Island ; but is due to the number of *Cyperaceæ* and *Orchideæ*, both of which equal the *grasses* ; and probably also to the small amount of *Compositæ* amongst the *Dicotyledones*."

Respecting the zoology of these islands, Mr. M'Cormick observes : — " There is no species of land animal, with the exception of the domestic pig, introduced several years ago, and now in a wild state. The birds are all New Zealand species, from which country these islands have unquestionably been colonised by the feathered tribe. Of land birds there are not more than seven or eight species, and of these the beautiful " Tooe " bird of New Zealand, and a small olive-green species allied to *Meliphagidæ*, are the chief choristers of the woods, which are in many places almost impenetrable, the trees and underwood forming dense thickets. The water birds consist of a New Zealand species of duck (*teal*), a mergus (*Merganser*), a species of phalarocrocorax,

(*cormorant*), a snipe, a penguin, and two kinds of
gull, the black-backed, and small ash-backed, fre-
quenting the bays in great abundance. The albatross (*Diomedea exulans*) was breeding in considerable numbers on the tops of the cliffs to the north-
westward of the harbour. Their nest is formed,
upon a small mound of earth, of withered grass and
leaves matted together, above six feet in circumference at the base, and about eighteen inches in
height; it is the joint labour of the male and
female birds. Like most of the petrel tribe, the
albatross lays only one egg, of a pure white,
varying in weight from fifteen to twenty-one
ounces. In one instance only, out of above one
hundred nests that were examined, were two eggs
found in the same nest.

"Its greatest enemy is a fierce raptorial gull,
very strongly resembling the Skua gull, both in its
predatory habits and general aspect, and is probably an undescribed species.

"Several kinds of petrel were breeding in holes
underground, and on the sides of the cliffs bounding the bays; a solitary ring-plover was seen, but
no specimen was obtained."

Of insects we observed a great variety, and a
large collection was made. The sand-flies were
very troublesome during the heat of the day, and
their stings painful.

The party employed cutting fire-wood found a
cat's nest with two kittens in it, still blind: they
were of course destroyed, but the old cat escaped.

The pigs that were left on the island by Captain
Bristow have become very numerous.   Their food
consists of the Arabia polaris, "one of the most
beautiful and singular of the vegetable productions
of the island it inhabits, growing in large orbicular
masses on rocks and banks near the sea, or amongst
the dense and gloomy vegetation of the woods; its
copious bright green foliage, and large umbels of
waxy flowers, have a most striking appearance.*
The whole plant has a heavy and rather disagreeable rank smell, common to many of its natural
order.   But it is, nevertheless, greedily eaten by
goats, pigs, and rabbits."   And more especially the
Pleurophyllum criniferum †, a very common and
striking plant, often covering a great extent of
ground, and according to Dr. Hooker, forming the
larger proportion of the food of the hogs which now
run wild upon the main island of this group.   It is
indeed so abundant in the marshy spots, that these
animals frequently live entirely amongst it, particularly where it grows near the margins of the
woods, where they form broad tracks through the
patches, grubbing up the roots to a great extent, and by trampling down the soft stems and
leaves, make soft and warm places for them, to
litter in.

One of these animals was shot by Mr. Hallett,
the purser, and although in poor condition its flesh

* Flora Antarctica, p. 20.
† Ibid. p. 32. Plates 24, 25.

was considered well-flavoured, though by no means equal to that of our own well-fed pigs.

In order to increase the stock of useful animals, I directed a ram and two ewes, which we had brought from Hobart Town in the Erebus for the purpose, to be landed on the western side of the harbour; and a ram and two ewes brought by the Terror were taken several miles inland to the southward. Besides these were landed from our private stores some pigs, poultry, and rabbits. These last, together with a quantity of cabbage, turnip, mustard and cress, radish, and other seeds, were sent to me by Mr. Anstey, of Hobart Town, as well as a pair of goats, but one of them unfortunately died the day before we arrived at the Aucklands. Some seeds of each kind were sown in the small place we had cleared; and a great many gooseberry and currant bushes, and raspberry and strawberry plants, with which Sir John Franklin had directed us to be supplied from the Government garden, were distributed over various parts of the island by Dr. Hooker, and I have no doubt will for the most part thrive, and may hereafter prove a benefit to vessels calling there. The hens had formed nests in well-concealed situations, and had laid several eggs before we left the place. We found some small roots of potatoes and some plants of Siberian kale that had been left by some of our predecessors, and we planted some more of the former.

Whilst the magnetic observations were being

made on shore, the other officers and crew of the ships were engaged procuring firewood, completing the water, and making the necessary preparations in the vessels for our voyage to the southward.

Mr. Tucker and Mr. Davis were employed under my directions surveying and sounding the harbour. Mr. Oakley was sent to examine Enderby Island, where also he landed some rabbits, and brought back with him the nests and young birds of several small kinds of petrel he found there. The medical officers having fortunately no sick to attend to, zealously devoted themselves to increase our collections of natural history in all its branches. Dr. Hooker brought on board a tree fern between three and four feet high, with fronds between four and five feet long: this and Campbell Island are the highest south latitudes they have yet been found in; and many curious and beautiful sea-weeds were gathered along the shores of the inlet. The seine was hauled, but with very indifferent success. A seal was seen with a good-sized fish in its mouth, proving their presence; but only two or three were taken, — a small flat-fish, near the head of Laurie Harbour, and the others about nine inches long, are described by Dr. Richardson under the name of *Notothenia**, of which genus he remarks the designation has reference to its high southern habitat, where it is probably represented by one or more species in almost every degree of longitude.

* Zoology, by Dr. Richardson, p. 5. Plate 3.

Some of our officers finding it very laborious
walking through the dense brushwood in their way
to the western hills, opened a road by setting fire
to the dried grass and sticks, which being fanned
by a strong breeze, spread with great rapidity in
all directions, burning a great part of the wood
near which our Observatory was fixed; but fortunately did not approach to within half a mile of
it. The whole country appeared in a blaze of
fire at night. The scene as viewed from our ships
was described as one of great magnificence and
beauty. It was nevertheless a thoughtless prank,
and might have been productive of great mischief,
besides destroying so much valuable wood.

The result of our observations gave for the latitude of the spot, marked + on the plan, where the
Observatory stood, 50° 32′ 30″ S., the longitude,
166° 12′ 34″ E. The magnetic dip 73° 12′, and the
variation 17° 40′ E. High water at the full and
change of the moon took place at twelve o'clock,
and the highest spring tides scarcely exceeded three
feet. A remarkable oscillation of the tide when near
the time of high water was observed; after rising to
nearly its highest, the tide would fall two or three
inches, and then rise again between three and four
inches, so as to exceed its former height rather
more than an inch. This irregular movement
generally occupied rather more than an hour, of
which the fall continued about twenty minutes,
and the rise again upwards of fifty minutes of the
interval. The time here given as that of H. W. at

1840.

full and change, is that of the last or greatest height of tide recorded.

Dec. 12.

Our observations being completed, we re-embarked the instruments and observatories, and having repeated our experiments for determining the amount of deviation produced on the compass and dipping needle by the iron of the ships, we weighed on the morning of the 12th, and stood out to sea. As we passed Shoe Island at a distance of about fifty feet, the compasses were deviated nearly two points from their proper direction; showing in a striking manner the very extraordinary magnetic power of its component rocks. Three or four miles to the eastward of Ewing Island we found a very strong tide ripple; when, being well clear of the land, we shaped our course for Campbell Island, distant about one hundred and sixty-three miles. The weather throughout the day continued moderate and favourable, but a dense haze over the Auckland Islands soon concealed them from our view.

13th.

Campbell Island was seen at 7h. 50m. A.M., four or five leagues distant. I had been recommended before we left Van Diemen's Land to take the ships into the harbour near the north-east point of the island, but from the entrance it appeared so exposed to winds from that quarter, we bore away for the southern harbour. At 10h. 30m. A.M., when we entered the heads, we were compelled to reduce our sail to double-reefed topsails and courses by the strong gusts of wind which came down from

the high lands to the westward, with astonishing
force; the more dangerous from succeeding the
light and baffling winds that occupy the intervals
between the squalls.   This occurrence of sudden
and violent rushes of wind is a remarkable characteristic phenomenon of all the islands in about this
latitude.   We observed it at Kerguelen Island, at
Auckland Island, and at Campbell Island; and the
trees of the latter island especially indicate, by
their prostrate position, the prevailing power of
the westerly storms.   The harbour is about four
miles in depth, running for more than two miles
in a W.N.W. direction, and thence after passing
a shoal point, with a warning bed of sea-weed
off it, about W.S.W. to its head.   In the outer
part of the harbour the water is too deep for convenient anchorage, but in the upper part, which is
completely land-locked, there is abundance of room
for a hundred ships to lie in the most perfect security, and where wood and excellent water can be
had in any quantity.   After four hours of hard
work, beating through the outer arm of the harbour,
we stood up to the head of it, and were just about
to let go our anchor, when we perceived the ship
stirring up the mud, and she soon after stuck fast.
Some hawsers were run out to the trees on the
shore; the ship warped off, and anchored in five
and a half fathoms.   At this time we observed the
Terror aground on the shoal point above-mentioned, and immediately sent our boats to her assistance; but the tide was falling so fast that all

their efforts to get her off were ineffectual; she had struck upon the shoal at the top of high water. On going on board of her I found Captain Crozier had made every preparation for heaving her off when the tide again flowed, having lightened the vessel as much as possible by starting the water, and landing the stores. As soon as the tide began to rise I returned to the Erebus with our boat's crews, and warped her near to the Terror, the more readily to afford her assistance, should it be required: but she floated off before high water without having sustained any damage, and anchored to the eastward of the point in six fathoms. Our boats were now employed refilling her water-tanks, whilst her own crew were re-embarking and stowing away the stores and provisions that had been landed to lighten her. Assisted by Mr. Tucker and Mr. Davis, I obtained the annexed survey of the harbour, and it employed those officers two entire days to complete the soundings. Our observations were made on a small beach near the shoal point, and is marked + on the plan of the harbour. It is in latitude 52° 33′ 26″ S., longitude 169° 8′ 41″ E., the magnetic dip 73° 53′, and the variation 17° 54′ E. The few days' observation of the tides, reduced to the times of full and change of the moon, gave high water at twelve o'clock; presenting also the same irregularities as were observed at Rendezvous harbour, Auckland Island. The amount of rise and fall at dead neap tides was forty-three inches.

The dip and variation above recorded are those

made on board the ships, for here also we found a
great amount of local attraction; the same instrument in different places giving widely different results, and proving how very liable to error all surveys
made by compass must be, and especially so upon
lands of volcanic formation; for, although so very
remarkable in these islands, it may here be observed
that there is scarcely any position on shore entirely
free from this source of confusion; and even in
our own country serious errors have been detected
in surveys where the compass alone had been used.

Campbell Island was discovered in 1810, by Fre-
derick Hazelburgh, in command of the brig Perseverance.   He states that "the island is thirty miles
in circumference, the country is mountainous, and
there are several good harbours, of which two on
the east side are to be preferred."   The southern
harbour of these two, in which we anchored, he
named after his brig, "Perseverance Harbour."

The highest hill seen from the harbour is on its
north side, and has an elevation of fifteen hundred
feet.   The shores on either side are steep, and rise
abruptly to between eight and nine hundred feet.
They are skirted by a belt of sea-weed, and the harbour is quite free from any danger except the shoal
point on which the Terror grounded; so that a ship
may run in or beat up with perfect confidence and
safety.   The hills from being less wooded have a
more desolate appearance than those of the Auckland Islands, and although there is abundance of
wood in the sheltered places, the trees nowhere

attain so great a height as at the Auckland Islands. The seine was hauled on two promising-looking places near the head of the harbour, but without success. A rich collection of marine insects and shell-fish were obtained, and had our time permitted I think we should have found fish in a lake that some of the officers discovered by tracing a small stream to the southward, which emptied its superabundant waters into the upper corner of the inlet.

Those officers whose duties did not confine them to the vicinity of the ships made several excursions across the island, in various parts, especially Dr. Hooker, pursuing his botanical researches, and whose remarks on that department of natural science are here entered.

" Although Campbell's Island is situated 120 miles to the southward of Lord Auckland's group, and is of much smaller extent, it probably contains fully as many native plants. This arises from its more varied outline, and from its steep precipices and contracted ravines, affording situations more congenial to the growth of grasses, mosses, and lichens. Its iron-bound coast and rocky mountains, whose summits appear to the eye bare of vegetation, give it the aspect of a very desolate and unproductive rock, and it is not until the quiet harbours are opened, that any green hue save a few grassy spots is seen. In these narrow bays the scene suddenly changes ; a belt of brushwood, composed of some of the trees mentioned as inhabitants of the

last-visited island, but in a very stunted state, form
a verdant line close to the beach. This is succeeded by bright green slopes, so studded with the
Chrysobactron as to give them a yellow tinge, visible
a full mile from the shore. Most of the beautiful
plants of Lord Auckland's group, including the
elegant caulescent ferns, are equally abundant here,
and from many of them growing in this higher
latitude at a proportionally lower elevation, their
beauty strikes every one on first landing.

   "The stay of the expedition here was necessarily
very short, and though two days sufficed to collect
between 200 and 300 species, the island cannot be
considered as sufficiently explored to justify any
rigid numerical comparison between its Flora and
that of the Aucklands; still some few relative observations may be offered. Sixty-six flowering
plants were detected, of which fourteen were not
seen in the neighbouring group. Thus, in two
degrees of latitude, thirty-four species had disappeared from the Flora of this longitude, and been
replaced by at least twenty other plants, producing as great a concomitant change in the proportions of the two groups of flowering plants as
was to be expected from the higher latitude. The
new species are almost all typical of an antarctic
climate, and consist both of species confined to
the island, and of others hitherto considered peculiar to Antarctic America. The proportion of
monocotyledonous plants is increased from being
$1 : 2.2$, to $1 : 1.4$. The grasses, instead of bearing

the small ratio of 1 : 14, which they do in Lord Auckland's group, here appear as 1 : 4·5. *Cyperaceæ* and *Orchideæ* have proportionally decreased, and the *Compositæ*, which were to all *Dicotyledones* as 1 : 10·4, are here as 1 : 5·6. These are not the signs of the vegetation of a more rigorous latitude alone, but of one differing more widely from that of New Zealand than Lord Auckland's group did, where only one-seventh of the plants were common to other antarctic regions, whilst in Campbell's Island fully one-fourth are natives of other longitudes in the Southern Ocean.

"Considering the aggregate of the plants in the islands to the southward of New Zealand as composing one Flora, a comparison of it with those of other countries is not out of place here. The flowering plants amount to one hundred species, or about the same number as have been collected in the whole group of arctic islands to the northward of the American coast. Of these one-fourth have been found in New Zealand, whilst many of the others belong to genera whose abundance is characteristic of that country. Only one-thirteenth of the whole are known to be Tasmanian, and one-sixth are common to Tierra del Fuego. Since there is no other country with which these islands possess any marked botanical features in common, their Flora may be considered a continuation of that of New Zealand, differing only in that it is more typical of the antarctic regions.

"The remarkable points of resemblance to

the last-named group with which we have compared this Flora, are the preponderance of *Ru-
biaceæ*, *Araliaceæ*, *Epacrideæ*, *Orchideæ*, and *Myr-
sineæ*; the small amount of surface occupied by
Compositæ, *Caryophylleæ*, *Cruciferæ*, and *Ericeæ*;
and the entire want of *Saxifrageæ*, *Leguminosæ*,
Labiatæ, and *Amentaceæ*, all scantily represented
in New Zealand. The more striking points of
difference are the increased proportion of *Monocotyledones*, which are there* as 1 : 3·2, and in
these two islands as 1 : 1·8; of grasses, which bear a
proportion there to other flowering plants of 1 : 13,
and here of 1 : 6·8 ; and of *Compositæ*, which there
appear as 1 : 8, and as 1 : 4·4 here. This Flora
further departs from that of New Zealand in possessing none of its numerous species of pine or beech,
of which latter genus five are now known to grow
there, and this is the more remarkable because all the
beeches and several of the pines are alpine, both in
New Zealand and in Van Diemen's Land, only
reaching the level of the sea in the southern parts of
those islands. The pines of the southern hemisphere
are, however, exceedingly local, nor are they so antarctic as some of those in the northern hemisphere
are arctic.   Of the ten New Zealand species it is not
certain that more than two or three are natives of
the middle island, or that any of them are peculiar

---

* The calculations relating to the New Zealand Flora are
founded on the Prodromus of Mr. Cunningham, and the results
must be considered as probable approximations only.

M

to a latitude south of 40°. Not only do Lord Auckland's group and Campbell's Island exhibit no inconsiderable number of Fuegian plants, considering the immense intervening tract of ocean (upwards of 4,000 miles), but in all the particulars in which their Flora differs from that of New Zealand, it more closely approximates to that of Antarctic America. Strong though the resemblance is in the numerical proportions of the orders, and in the similarity of many of the smaller plants, the trees and shrubs of the one differ in every respect from those of the other locality; for beeches extend from a latitude in the American continent which corresponds to their principal parallel in New Zealand beyond the latitude of Lord Auckland's group, as far south as Cape Horn itself, in the 57th degree.

" The relation between the Flora now under consideration and that of the northern regions is but slight; and the same may be said, though not to an equal extent, of any two countries in the higher latitudes of the opposite hemispheres. This group lies in the latitude of England, yet we recognise in it only three indigenous plants of our own island,—the *Cardamine hirsuta*, *Montia*, and *Callitriche*. Of the sixty genera twenty-two are English, and twenty-eight natives of a more northern latitude than England. Hardly any of these belong to the divisions *Calyciflora*, *Compositæ*, or to the higher orders of the *Monocotyledones;* while, on the other hand, they include the whole of the *Thalamiflora*,

Monochlamydeæ and grasses, and most of the
Cyperaceæ. Such genera as *Sieversia, Trisetum,*
and *Hierochlœ* have their analogues chiefly in the
arctic regions; whilst *Myosotis, Ranunculus, Cardamine, Stellaria, Veronica, Luzula, Juncus,* and all
the grasses, are predominant in the arctic Flora.
There are, however, slight points of resemblance,
rendering the want of a larger amount of their
congeners more remarkable, and also of others
which in the north generally accompany them, as
saxifrages, heaths, and *Vaccinia, Leguminosæ,* pines,
beech, and especially oak, birch, and willow; for
most of which no representative has hitherto been
found in the high southern latitudes."

The geology of this island is very similar to that
of the Aucklands, except in the total absence of
land-birds, of which the Aucklands possess seven
or eight species. The albatross had formed their
nests on the tops of the north-western cliffs of
the island, and a great many of their eggs were
obtained, but none of the young had yet appeared.

The remains of some huts were found on each
side of a cove to the north of the Erebus anchorage,
as also the graves of several seamen who had evidently been employed on the seal-fishing, and
amongst them that of a French woman who had
been accidentally drowned by the upsetting of a
boat in the harbour. There had also been an
establishment by the side of a stream in the north-
west corner of the harbour, but its situation was
not so good for the purpose as that of the cove.

1840.   During the 15th and 16th we were busily engaged completing wood and water, and making all
necessary preparations for our southern voyage,
which may be considered to have commenced on
leaving this harbour. I now communicated to
Commander Crozier my intention of proceeding
direct to the southward upon the meridian of this
island rather than upon that of Hobart Town, and
was gratified to find he entirely concurred with my
views upon this subject. He received his final
orders, and a complete list of rendezvous, containing instructions how to act in case of the ships
unavoidably parting company, so as to ensure our
meeting again without loss of time. And by
the evening of the 16th, the day having been unusually favourable, we had fully accomplished all
the purposes of our visit to this place, and the
ships were ready for sea.

CHAPTER VII.

WITH a moderate breeze from the westward, we weighed at 9 A. M., and stood out of the harbour. As soon as we had cleared the land we shaped our course directly south; and the wind soon freshening to a strong gale, with thick weather and rain, we lost sight of Campbell Island about noon.

The fifteen months which had elapsed since we took our departure from England had in no degree diminished our eagerness for the southern voyage; and now that we had at length the prospect before us of entering upon those labours from which we all hoped the most remarkable and important results of our voyage might be fairly anticipated, joy and satisfaction beamed in every face; and although I could not but look forward with much anxiety of mind to the issue of our exertions, yet this was greatly diminished by the assurance that we were in possession of the best of human means to accomplish our purposes. Our ships were in every respect most suitable for the service, with three years' provisions, and stores of the best kind, and supported by officers and crews in whom I had reason to entertain the utmost confidence that they would endure every trial and hardship with credit to themselves and the country. I felt that we had nothing to desire but the guidance and blessing of Almighty God throughout the arduous duties we were about to commence, and without which all human skill and courage must prove utterly unavailing.

It blew a strong gale from the south-west, so that we could not maintain a direct course. At noon we were in lat. 54° 22′ S., long. 169° 12′ E., having completed a distance of one hundred miles to the southward. At midnight a bright appearance was observed in the clouds, between south-east and south, resembling the diffused light of aurora australis, at an altitude of 12°.

Stormy weather continued throughout the 19th and 20th, during which time we had no opportu-
nity of sounding; and on the 21st were so unfortunate as to lose two of our self-registering thermometers by the line breaking. By Commander Crozier's experiment the temperature at two hundred and thirty fathoms below the surface was 39°·5, that of the surface being 42°. We were at that time in lat. 57° 52′. S., long. 170° 30′ E.

Although Midsummer-day of the southern regions, and in so low a latitude, the temperature of the air was at no time during the day above 40°, having very gradually declined as we advanced to the southward. The smaller kind of petrel became much more numerous; several patches of seaweed were seen during the day; and we were kept in expectation of meeting with some new land, of which these, and the numbers of penguins of two or three kinds we saw, were considered to be indications.

The next day it was nearly calm in the afternoon, and some interesting experiments on the
temperature of the sea were made: at the surface
it was 37°, at one hundred and fifty fathoms 38°·5,
at three hundred fathoms 39°·5, at four hundred
and fifty fathoms 39°·7, at six hundred fathoms,
39°·7; showing that since yesterday we had crossed
the point of uniform temperature of the ocean
throughout its whole depth; and that the effect
of the radiation of its heat from the surface extended to below three hundred fathoms. Our lat.
59° S., long. 171° E.

Snow and sleet accompanied a moderate south-
easterly breeze, and reduced the temperature of
the surface of the sea to 32°. The elegant little
blue petrel passed us in large flocks, going to the
southward. The albatross and smaller petrels hovered about in considerable numbers; and a few
bottle-nosed whales were seen.

During the last three days we had felt the influence of a current, drifting us to the north, between ten and eleven miles each day.

Christmas-day was passed by us in a strong
gale, but it did not prevent our enjoying the usual
festivities of the joyous season. Constant snow
and rain, which as usual attended the northerly
gale, and the expectation of meeting with ice, as
well as the possibility of passing new land, deterred
me from running during the continuance of such
unfavourable weather; we therefore hove-to under

the close-reefed topsails. At noon we were in lat. 62° 10′ S., and long. 170° 24′. E.

The wind veered to the westward, but the weather was still so thick that we continued hove-to until 2 P. M., when we wore round, and stood to the southward.

On the 27th we had a strong south-westerly gale, with clear weather, violent squalls, and frequent snow-showers. The temperature of the sea fell to 29° at 5 A. M., at which it remained all day, and led us to expect soon to meet with ice.

The gale moderated early the next morning, and was succeeded by a calm between 5 and 9 A. M., when an easterly breeze sprang up, and enabled us to resume our southerly course, having been driven back to the northward very considerably by the late storm.

A great many whales were seen during the afternoon; and at 4 P. M., when in lat. 63° S. and long. 174° 30′ E., we tried for soundings, with six hundred fathoms, without striking the ground. The temperature at the surface was 30°, at one hundred and fifty fathoms 35°·5, at three hundred fathoms 38°·2, and at six hundred fathoms 39°·7, at which depth the mean temperature of the ocean was reached by the thermometers.

At 7 20 P. M. the first iceberg was seen, in latitude 63° 20′ S.; several others came in sight shortly afterwards, and before eight o'clock fifteen were counted from the deck. Unlike the icebergs of the arctic seas, they presented very little variety of

form, but were generally of large size and of very
solid appearance, bounded by perpendicular cliffs
on all sides, their tabular summits, varied from
one hundred and twenty to one hundred and eighty
feet in height, and several of them more than two
miles in circumference. As we passed through this
chain of bergs we observed large masses continually falling from them, giving proof of their rapid
destruction, even in this high latitude, and forming
long streams of heavy loose fragments to leeward
of them.

1840.

We continued our course to the southward,
amongst numerous icebergs and much drift ice. A
great many whales were seen, chiefly of the common black kind, greatly resembling, but said to be
distinct from, the Greenland whale: sperm, as well
as hunchbacked whales, were also observed; of the
common black species we might have killed any
number we pleased: they appeared chiefly to be
of unusually large size, and would doubtless yield
a great quantity of oil, and were so tame that our
ships sailing close past did not seem to disturb
them. During a short period of calm in the
afternoon many marine invertebrata were taken,
amongst them the Clio borealis and beautiful little
Argonauta arctica, upon which, doubtless, the
whales were feeding, as it is well known that these
creatures constitute the whale's food in the northern
seas.

Dec. 29.

A light southerly breeze brought with it almost
constant snow-showers and thick weather, so that

we were compelled to shorten sail and keep close to the wind during the night, being amongst a great many bergs, which we could not see until almost touching them, and expecting also that the main pack was not far distant: there was also a heavy swell amongst the bergs, which rendered our situation one of no small anxiety. The roar of the waves against their precipitous faces was generally the first knowledge we had of our proximity to them.

30. The next morning, at 7 A. M., we bore away to the southward, the wind having changed to the westward, with more favourable weather. The bergs and loose pieces of ice became gradually less numerous, so that throughout the day we seldom had more than ten or twelve of the former in sight at a time, and generally not so many.

Soon after noon we crossed the track of the Russian navigator, Bellinghausen, in lat. 64° 38′ S. and long. 173° 10′ E.; and, being becalmed at 2 P. M., we had a good opportunity of trying for deep soundings. Five thousand fathoms of line had been prepared for the purpose, but only one thousand five hundred and sixty fathoms had run off the reel when the weight struck the bottom. The temperature at the surface was 31°·, at one hundred and fifty fathoms 35°·2, at three hundred fathoms 37°·2, at four hundred fathoms 38°·8, and at six hundred fathoms 39°·8. I regretted that the thermometers constructed to sustain the pressure at a great depth, which I had written to England for, had not arrived at Hobart

Town before our departure. The specific gravity
of the water at the surface and that taken up from
six hundred fathoms was exactly the same, being
1·0272, in both cases at a temperature of 32°.

The current was found to be setting to the
E.S.E., at the rate of eight miles per diem.

At 6 P. M. a fine breeze sprang up from the eastward, and we carried a press of sail all night,
passing a great many bergs, and much loose ice in
long narrow streams, as we advanced to the southward. A beautiful white petrel was seen in the
evening, giving notice of our approach to a large
body of ice, although we were not at the time
aware that these birds never wander far from the
main pack.

At noon the next day we were in lat. 66° 0′ S.
and long. 171° 50′ E. At this time the weather
was beautifully clear, and a strong ice-blink in the
sky, from S. W. to S. E., pointed out the situation
of the pack. The streams of ice became more numerous, but fewer bergs were seen during the day.
At 9 P. M. a line of ice was seen from the masthead,
from E. by S. to S. by E., which proved to be the
pack edge; but falling perfectly calm soon afterwards, we were not able to approach it until 8 A. M.
the next morning, when a light northerly wind
sprang up, bringing thick weather and snow-
showers. We steered to the southward, passing
great quantities of drift ice; at ten o'clock we
crossed the antarctic circle, and came to the edge
of the main pack, of which, however, we could only

1841.

see a very small extent, owing to the thick weather; we were therefore obliged, after running a short distance along the edge of it, to haul off to the northward, to prevent getting entangled amongst the loose ice, with a considerable swell, and too little wind to make any way through it. At noon we were in lat. 66° 32' S. and long. 169° 45' E. The magnetic dip 82·35, and the variation 28·21.

Jan. 1.

Being New-Year's-day, an additional allowance of provisions was served to the ships' crews, as was the practice on all the arctic voyages; and a complete suit of warm clothing was issued gratis to each individual; this had been provided by the liberality of the government, and on our entering the icy regions, could not but prove to be as useful and acceptable a new-year's gift as they could have received. Mutual congratulations passed between the officers and crews of the ships, and the day was kept, as in old England, in conviviality and re-joicing. Being amongst numerous icebergs and having a great deal of loose ice about us, added greatly to the interest of the day to those who had never been amongst it before; and those who had could not but share in some degree the excitement and delight of their companions. We had, indeed, met with the pack in a much lower latitude than we had anticipated; but from the little we had seen of it we were by no means dispirited by the early appearance of so serious an obstruction to our progress, for it presented none of those evidences of impenetrability we had been led to expect.

Several whales were seen, and the white petrel
(Procellaria nivea) was flying about in great numbers.   In the evening a boat was lowered down,
and several good specimens of this beautiful bird
were added to our collection : a seal was also seen.
During a partial clearing of the weather we had a
good view of the pack, which extended as far as
the eye could discern to the southward.   Some
large holes of water were seen beyond the edge,
which, as usual, consisted of the heaviest pieces
closely set together, but afforded us a confident
hope of being able to make our way through it
whenever circumstances should admit of the attempt: at that time it was perfectly calm, with
a considerable swell from the northward, so that
our ships were for several hours nearly unmanageable.

At 5 A. M. a berg was observed at a short distance, with a large piece of rock upon it, and nearly
covered with mud and stones.   It had much the appearance of a small island; and Mr. Smith was sent
to examine and bring specimens of the rock.   It
proved to be of volcanic origin, and must have
been of many tons weight.   At 8 A. M. a fresh breeze
sprang up from the eastward, with thick snow-
showers ; the barometer also falling fast, led me to
expect bad weather: we therefore stood off to the
northward, to get into more clear water, and to
wait a favourable opportunity of entering the pack.
Thick weather prevailed throughout the day, and
accompanied by a strong breeze and high sea, ren-

dered our situation critical and anxious. As we stood away from the pack the temperature of the sea rose from 28° to 30° at the distance of seven or eight miles; when, having got into a much clearer space, we kept the ship under easy sail all the next Jan. 3. day, waiting for more favourable weather. Several whales, a few seals, and many white petrel, were seen during the day, also three penguins.

Towards midnight the barometer began to rise, and other indications of the weather improving, we wore round and stood to the southward; we carried all sail, passing through several narrow streams of heavy ice, formed of the fragments of broken-up bergs, which rendered the greatest vigi- Jan. 4. lance necessary during the thick snow-showers that passed over us in quick succession, and were some- times of long continuance; nor was it until the after- noon that the clear blue sky was again seen and the sun shone forth in all its splendour,—the numerous bergs, of strange and curious forms, reflecting its brilliant rays in every beautiful variety of colour, and forming, as our ships pursued their devious way amongst them, a scene of much interest and grandeur.

At noon we were in lat. 65° 22′ S., long. 172° 42′ E.; the magnetic dip 81° 40′, variation 25° 1′. By a remarkable, and of course in some degree accidental coincidence, exactly the same dip and variation were signalled from both ships.

The power of the sun's radiation was measured at 9 P. M., by means of a thermometer whose bulb was blackened with Indian ink: it rose from 33° to 40°·2, the sun's altitude being at the time only four degrees. Heavy clouds were soon afterwards observed rising both at east and north-west: those in the latter direction were of a peculiarly threatening appearance, with hard rugged outlines, like the cumulus clouds of the equatorial regions, with bright reflections of light from their more prominent points, affording a strong contrast to the extreme darkness of the frowning mass. The setting sun was also a very remarkable object, being streaked across by five dark horizontal bands, of nearly equal breadth, and flattened into a most irregular form by the greater refraction of its lower limb as it touched the horizon, at $11^h 56^m 51^s$; skimming along to the eastward, it almost imperceptibly descended until its upper limb disappeared exactly seventeen minutes and thirty seconds afterwards. The difference of the atmospheric refraction at the upper and lower limb of the sun was carefully determined by several measurements of the horizontal and vertical diameter, and found to amount to 5′ 21″, the horizontal diameter being 32′ 31″, and the vertical diameter only 27′ 10″, that given in the Nautical Almanac being 32′ 34″; thus showing also that the flattened appearance of the sun was not produced in the least degree by the elongation of the horizontal diameter, as some have supposed. We also remarked the peculiar purple colour that the vapour of very low altitudes exactly opposite to the setting sun reflects so constantly in the arctic regions, and sometimes even in our own country. It did not exceed two degrees of altitude when the sun's centre was on the horizon.

In approaching the pack we had passed a great many bergs, but after midnight comparatively few were seen. The wind freshened to a strong breeze from the north-westward, and carried us rapidly to the southward. At 8 A. M. we again came in sight of the main pack, and ran several miles along the edge of it to examine it. From the mast-head it seemed sufficiently open to admit of our penetrating as far as we could see to the southward; and although other circumstances were not so favourable for taking the pack as I could have wished, owing to the unsettled state of the weather and the wind blowing so directly upon the ice as to preclude our regaining the open water if thought desirable, I nevertheless determined to make the attempt, and push the ships as far into it as we could get them. The signal was made to the Terror, and we bore away before the wind, selecting the most favourable point to break through the outer edge of the pack, which, as usual, was formed of much heavier ice than the rest, and which we accomplished without sustaining any serious injury, although necessarily receiving some very heavy blows.

After about an hour's hard thumping, we forced our way into some small holes of water, connected by narrow lanes, for which we had purposely steered; and, closely followed by the Terror, we found the ice much lighter and more scattered than it appeared to be when viewed from the distance. It consisted chiefly of small floes of ice, of last winter's formation, with a quantity of hummocky ice of much older date, formed by great pressure into very heavy masses; but it was by no means of so formidable a character as we had been led to expect from the accounts we had received of the southern barrier in those parts where the American and French expeditions had encountered it.

At noon we were in latitude 66° 55′ S., and longitude 174° 34′ E. The clear sea was no longer discernible from the masthead; with nothing but ice around, and fortunately a clear sky above us, we pursued our way through the pack, choosing the clearest "leads," and forcing the interposing barriers as they occurred; the way continued, if not to open before us, still sufficiently so to enable us to navigate freely amongst the ice, without danger or difficulty as we proceeded, at times sustaining violent shocks, which nothing but ships so strengthened could have withstood.

A remarkable appearance of land was reported in the evening, and, continuing for many hours without any alteration of figure, several of the officers imagined it was really land they saw, assuming the appearance of many pointed hills perfectly covered with snow, and so calculated to deceive the inexperienced eye, that had we been prevented proceeding further, they would doubtless have asserted on our return to England that we had discovered land in this position. This appearance of land was, however, nothing more than the upper part of a cloud, marking, by a well-defined but irregular line, the limit to which vapour can ascend in these latitudes; below is vapour in every degree of condensation, above, the clear cold space which vapour can never attain. It is always near the margin of the ice that these appearances of land are most remarkable and most deceptive. It proved a useful lesson to some of our new hands, who could not be persuaded it was not land until we had actually passed over the place of their baseless mountains.

We saw many seals, as we sailed along, basking on the ice, and several penguins; these curious birds actually followed our ships, answering the call of the sailors, who imitated their cry; and although they could not scramble over the ice so fast as our ships sailed past it, they made up for it when they got into the water, and we soon had quite a flock of them in our wake, playing about our vessel like so many porpoises.

The elegant white petrel was also very numerous, and a single stormy petrel, of a different and larger species than our European procellaria pelagica, was seen.

The wind gradually moderated as we got farther into the pack, and had declined to quite a gentle air at midnight, by which time we were between sixty and seventy miles from the pack edge; there was, however, still so much motion amongst the ice, that I have no doubt it was blow-

ing a strong gale in the open sea to the northward;
the clouds drifted swiftly over our heads, and thick
showers of snow fell, but we had, at intervals, an
extensive view from the crow's nest, which enabled us to pursue our southerly course with confidence, though under diminished sail, throughout the
night.

Early the next morning the ice became much
closer, compelling a more varying course, and
greatly retarding our progress; a strongly marked
" water-sky," which was seen to the south-eastward, raised our hopes of being able to reach an
open sea at no great distance, and all our means
were employed to force the ships onward through
the ice in that direction; but early in the afternoon
we found it so close as to baffle all our exertions,
and we were obliged to heave to in a small hole of
water, out of which we could find no way to the
southward, and wait until the ice opened.

We saw great numbers of penguins of a different
species from those we had met with at Kerguelen
and Auckland Islands, and a boat being sent in
pursuit of them, several were procured and added
to our collection.

Commander Crozier came on board in the evening,
and we had the satisfaction to hear that all on
board the Terror were in the same good health and
spirits as we were, not an individual being on the
sick list of either ship. One of his boat's crew fell
overboard, and although quite unable to swim, he
floated on the surface without an effort until picked

up by one of our boats, no worse for his cold immersion.

Some whales were seen, but not in such numbers as near the pack edge. At noon we were in lat. 68° 17′ S., long. 175° 21′ E., and found we had been driven by a current twenty-six miles to the S. E. during the last two days; another proof to us that there Jan. 7. must be open space in that direction. But the ice remained so close until the afternoon of the following day, that we could not make any way through it; and whilst thus detained we tried for soundings, but without reaching the ground with 600 fathoms. The temperature at that depth, 39°·8; at 450 fathoms, 39°·2; at 300 fathoms, 38°·2; at 150 fathoms, 37°·5; at the surface, 28°.

Late in the evening the ice slackened a little, and we bored through it seven or eight miles to the south-east, towards the encouraging dark water-sky, that we had never lost sight of, and which we appeared to have approached very considerably, since it was first observed.

At 11 P. M. a thick fog came on, and the ice being much too compact for us, we were obliged to heave to for several hours.

Jan. 8. At 4 A. M. we recommenced our labour, aided by a light south-westerly wind, and succeeded in forcing the ships several miles through the pack by noon, when it fell perfectly calm. Our observations to-day showed that the whole body of ice had during the last two days been carried fourteen miles to the northward by the late southerly winds.

I availed myself of the opportunity the calm
afforded me of making some magnetic observations
upon a large piece of ice near the ship, well suited
to the purpose. The dip and intensity observations agreed exactly with those we had previously
obtained on board our vessels, satisfactorily proving
that the corrections we employed for the effect of
the ship's iron on the instruments continued to
give accurate results. We were then in lat. 68° 28'
S., and long. 176° 31' E. Dip 83° 36' S., and
variation 34° 39' E.

A new species of seal was killed by some of the
crew of the Terror, differing from all others hitherto
known, in the total absence of ears; not the smallest
orifice could be detected where they usually are
placed in these animals; and this remarkable peculiarity was afterwards confirmed on its being dis-
sected by Dr. Robertson.

A great change in the ice was produced by the
calm opening it out in all directions, as we always
found to be the case in the Arctic Seas; and a
breeze springing up from the northward at 8 P. M.
we made some way through the pack, pressing forward under all sail towards the south-east water.
We sustained many severe shocks in breaking
through the interposing barriers of closer ice.
Thick weather and snow prevented our seeing to
any distance before us or selecting our way, whilst
the increasing breeze impelled us rapidly onward.
So that at 5 A.M. the next day we had accomplished   Jan. 9.
the object of our exertions, and found ourselves

again in a clear sea. The northerly breeze soon after increased to so strong a gale as to reduce us to close reefed topsails, which, with the continuous snow and thick weather, compelled us at noon to haul to the wind after having run about thirty miles to the southward since leaving the pack.

At noon we were in lat 69° 15′ S., and long. 176° 15′ E.

The wind veered round gradually to the eastward, so that we continued to make some progress to the southward notwithstanding the fog and snow being so thick that we could seldom see more than half a mile before us, and sometimes not so far; but as we met with no icebergs, and only a few straggling pieces of ice and a heavy sea having arisen, we felt assured that we had gained an open space of great extent.

The storm blew with great violence from the eastward until 2 A. M. the next day, when it began to abate, and by nine o'clock had moderated so much as to admit of our setting reefed courses. The fog also began to disperse about that time, and at noon we had a most cheering and extensive view; not a particle of ice could be seen in any direction from the mast-head. Our observations gave us a lat. 70° 23′ S., long. 174° 50 E. and the magnetic dip had increased to 85°.

We now shaped our course directly for the Magnetic Pole, steering as nearly south by compass as the wind, which soon afterwards veered to the south-east, admitted. Our hopes and expectations

of attaining that interesting point were now raised
to the highest pitch, too soon, however, to suffer as
severe a disappointment. A strong "land-blink"
made its appearance in the horizon as the ships
advanced, and had attained an elevation of several
degrees by midnight. All of us were disposed to
doubt that which we so much apprehended, owing
to its much paler colour than the land-blinks we
had seen in the northern regions, but soon after
2 A. M. the officer of the watch, Lieutenant Wood,
reported that the land itself was distinctly seen
directly ahead of the ship.

It rose in lofty peaks, entirely covered with perennial snow; it could be distinctly traced from
S.S.W. to S.E. by S. (by compass), and must have
been more than one hundred miles distant when
first seen.

The highest mountain of this range I named
after Lieutenant-Colonel Sabine, of the Royal Artillery, Foreign Secretary of the Royal Society,
one of the best and earliest friends of my youth,
and to whom this compliment was more especially
due, as having been the first proposer and one of
the most active and zealous promoters of the expedition.

At noon we were in the highest latitude
(71° 15') attained by our great navigator in 1774,
during his several attempts to penetrate to the
south. We had by this time run fifteen leagues
directly towards Mount Sabine, and still it appeared
to be very distant: more land came in view as we

N 4

advanced, mountainous ranges extending to the right and left of that we first discovered.

At 6 P. M., when we had closed the land seventy miles, we were about two leagues from the shore, which was lined with heavy pack-ice. We steered close along the edge of it towards a small bay, where we hoped to effect a landing, but the wind being on the shore, and a high sea beating heavily along the pack edge, we found it quite impracticable. We therefore stood to the S. E. for the purpose of rounding the eastern extreme of a close body of ice, and of getting to leeward of a projecting point of the coast, off which we observed several small islands, that we expected would afford such protection as to admit of our landing with less difficulty.

The cape which formed the southern promontory of the bay was, at the request of Commander Crozier, named Cape Downshire, after his kind and lamented friend, the late estimable marquis. Its northern point was called Cape Adare, after my friend Viscount Adare, M. P. for Glamorganshire, who always evinced a warm interest in our undertaking. It is a remarkable projection of high, dark, probably volcanic, cliffs, and forms a strong contrast to the rest of the snow-covered coast. Some rocks, that were observed to lie several miles to the north and west of Cape Adare, showing their black summits conspicuously amongst the white foam of the breakers, were named Dunraven rocks. We obtained soundings in one hundred and sixty-five fathoms, and several small black stones, which came up with the lead, tended to confirm my conjectures of the volcanic origin of the newly-discovered land. Cape Adare at the time bore N. 52 W., distant about five or six miles.

It was a beautifully clear evening, and we had a most enchanting view of the two magnificent ranges of mountains, whose lofty peaks, perfectly covered with eternal snow, rose to elevations varying from seven to ten thousand feet above the level of the ocean. The glaciers that filled their intervening valleys, and which descended from near the mountain summits, projected in many places several miles into the sea, and terminated in lofty perpendicular cliffs. In a few places the rocks broke through their icy covering, by which alone we could be assured that land formed the nucleus of this, to appearance, enormous iceberg.

The range of mountains extending to the N. W. was called Admiralty Range, of which the higher and more conspicuous were distinguished by the names of the Lords Commissioners of the Admiralty under whose orders I was serving. Mount Minto, Mount Adam, and Mount Parker were named after the Right Honourable Earl Minto, the first Lord; Vice-Admiral Sir Charles Adam, K.C.B., now Commander-in-Chief in the West Indies; and Vice-Admiral Sir William Parker, Bart., G.C.B., and Commander-in-Chief in the Mediterranean, the two senior naval lords; and I cannot forbear here expressing the deep gratitude I must ever feel

to them for the efficient manner in which our ships
were fitted out under their auspices; for the ample
means we were provided with by their liberality;
and for the encouragement we received previous
to our departure, by witnessing the warm, personal
interest they took in perfecting the equipment of
the expedition; as well as for the many instances
of friendship with which they honoured me; the
remembrance of which often, during the voyage,
proved a powerful stimulus to renewed exertion.
Mount Troubridge, Mount Pechell, and Mount
Dalmeny were named after Rear-Admiral Sir
Edward Thomas Troubridge, Bart., C.B.; Captain
Sir Samuel J. Brooke Pechell, Bart., C.B., K.C.H.;
and the Right Honourable Lord Dalmeny; the
three junior lords. The positions of these mountains are given in the Geographical Table in the
Appendix to this volume. Mount Dalmeny formed
the western extreme of the Admiralty Range, as
also the westernmost land in sight, and was distant
from us between seventy and eighty miles. The
height of Mount Sabine was found, by means of
several measurements, to be rather less than ten
thousand feet, and about thirty miles from the
coast. The elevations of the other mountains were
not determined with accuracy, but we judged them
to vary from seven to nine thousand feet; and altogether they presented as grand and magnificent a
view as can well be imagined. A cape to the westward of Cape Adare, having a deep bay between
them, was named after Charles Wood, Esq.,

First Secretary to the Admiralty; and another
cape, still further to the westward, surmounted
by a remarkable conical hill, was distinguished by
the name of Sir John Barrow, Bart., the father of
modern arctic discovery, by whose energy, zeal,
and talent our geographical knowledge of those
regions has been so greatly increased; and we
may hope, by God's guidance and blessing attend-
ing the exertions of the expedition that has so
recently left our shores, he may live to see the
great object of his heart, the discovery of a N. W.
passage through Barrow Straits to the Pacific
Ocean, accomplished.

The dip had increased to eighty-six degrees, and
the variation amounted to forty-four degrees.
These observations place the magnetic pole in lat.
76° S., long. 145° 20′ E., therefore in the S. W.
(true) from us, and distant above five hundred miles.
But the land interposed an insuperable obstacle
to our direct approach to it, and we had to choose
whether we should trace the coast to the north-west,
with the hope of turning the western extreme of
the land, and thence proceed to the south; or follow
the southerly coast line round Cape Downshire,
and thence take a more westerly course.   The latter
was preferred, as being more likely to extend our
researches into higher latitudes, and as affording a
better chance of afterwards attaining one of the
principal objects of our voyage: and although we
could not but feel disappointed in our expectation
of shortly reaching the magnetic pole, yet these

mountains being in our way restored to England the honour of the discovery of the southernmost known land, which had been nobly won by the intrepid Bellinghausen, and for more than twenty years retained by Russia.

Favoured by very fine weather during the night, we succeeded in approaching within two or three miles of the small islands lying a short distance from the main land by nine o'clock the next morning, at which time, accompanied by several of my officers, I left the ship in charge of Lieutenant Bird, and pulled towards the shore, followed by Commander Crozier and some of the Terror's officers.

We found the shores of the mainland completely covered with ice projecting into the sea, and the heavy surf along its edge forbade any attempt to land upon it; a strong tide carried us rapidly along between this ice-bound coast and the islands amongst heavy masses of ice, so that our situation was for some time most critical; for all the exertions our people could use were insufficient to stem the tide. But taking advantage of a narrow opening that appeared in the ice, the boats were pushed through it, and we got into an eddy under the lee of the largest of the islands, and landed on a beach of large loose stones and stranded masses of ice. The weather by this time had put on a most threatening appearance, the breeze was freshening fast, and the anxious circumstances under which we were placed, together with the recal-flag flying at the ship's mast-

head, which I had ordered Lieutenant Bird to hoist
if necessary, compelled us to hasten our operations.

The ceremony of taking possession of these
newly-discovered lands, in the name of our Most
Gracious Sovereign, Queen Victoria, was immediately proceeded with; and on planting the flag of
our country amidst the hearty cheers of our party,
we drank to the health, long life, and happiness of
Her Majesty and His Royal Highness Prince
Albert. The island was named Possession Island.
It is situated in lat. 71° 56′, and long. 171° 7′ E.,
composed entirely of igneous rocks, and only accessible on its western side. We saw not the smallest
appearance of vegetation, but inconceivable myriads
of penguins completely and densely covered the
whole surface of the island, along the ledges of the
precipices, and even to the summits of the hills,
attacking us vigorously as we waded through their
ranks, and pecking at us with their sharp beaks, disputing possession; which, together with their loud
coarse notes, and the insupportable stench from the
deep bed of guano, which had been forming for ages,
and which may at some period be valuable to the
agriculturists of our Australasian colonies, made us
glad to get away again, after having loaded our
boats with geological specimens and penguins.
Owing to the heavy surf on the beach, we could
not tell whether the water was ebbing or flowing;
but there was a strong tide running to the south,
between Possession Island and the main land, and
the Terror had some difficulty to avoid being car-

ried by it against the land ice. Future navigators should therefore be on their guard in approaching the coast at this place.

After a long and heavy pull we regained our ships only a short time before so thick a fog came on, with a strong northerly breeze, that to have been a few minutes later, would have rendered our return to the ships impossible, and compelled us to have borne away for the shore again, to take up our quarters with the penguins, until the ships could have again approached it with safety. The weather obliged us now to stand out to sea. At night we had high winds with constant snow, and not meeting with any icebergs or loose ice, we kept the ships under easy sail, waiting a change of weather.

Some few whales and large flocks of Cape pigeons were seen; but the elegant white petrel, which seldom goes to any distance from the main pack, had, to our great satisfaction, quite deserted us.

The next morning a southerly gale came on, which reduced us to close-reefed topsails, and storm staysails; the weather also being very thick, we stood to the eastward, uncertain what we might meet with and were kept throughout the day and night in a state of great anxiety and watchfulness: but we were not sorry to find the ship labouring in a heavy sea, a sure indication of a great space of open water to windward, in the direction we were now most anxious to get.

At noon we were in lat. 72° 3′ S., and long. 172° 9′ E. Although blowing a hard gale with a

high sea, we were enabled, by means of Mr. Fox's
instrument, to obtain observations for the dip,
86° 25′ in both ships.

The land was seen several times during the day;
the same we had before discovered, and we carried
all sail to prevent being driven back to the northward. In the evening we wore and stood towards
the land, hoping for fairer weather by the time we
closed it; but the storm continued with unabated
violence, so that when we were by our reckoning
within ten or twelve miles of the shore, and unable
to see to any distance on account of the almost
uninterrupted snow-showers and thick foggy weather, we were obliged again to stand off to sea, still
struggling under all sail to maintain our ground.

At noon we were in lat 71° 50′, and long.
172° 20′, which, under the circumstances, we considered more favourable than we expected, having
lost only eighteen miles during this violent gale.

In the course of the day a great number of
whales were observed; thirty were counted at one
time in various directions, and during the whole day,
wherever you turned your eyes, their blasts were to
be seen. They were chiefly of large size, and the
hunch-back kind: only a few sperm whales were distinguished amongst them, by their peculiar manner
of " blowing," or " spouting," as some of our men
who had been engaged in their capture called it.
Hitherto, beyond the reach of their persecutors,
they have here enjoyed a life of tranquillity and
security; but will now, no doubt, be made to con-

tribute to the wealth of our country, in exact proportion to the energy and perseverance of our
merchants; and these, we well know, are by no
means inconsiderable. A fresh source of national
and individual wealth is thus opened to commercial
enterprise, and if pursued with boldness and perseverance, it cannot fail to be abundantly productive.
We observed great quantities of molluscous and
other minute marine animals, on which, no doubt,
the whales were feeding; and large flocks of the
young of the Cape pigeon were playing about, and
feeding with them.   In the evening the wind rather
moderated, and the weather becoming more clear
we were induced again to try and approach the
land.   The barometer also had risen to nearly
twenty-nine inches, which we had now learnt to
consider to indicate fine weather in these latitudes,
although in England such a depression would be
regarded very differently.

Jan. 15.   Early this morning we had a fine view of the
magnificent chain of mountains that we had seen
stretching away to the southward some days before,
but then more imperfectly.   With a moderate
southerly wind we had beautifully clear weather,
and we now saw them to great advantage; and as
we stood towards them, we gazed with feelings of
indescribable delight upon a scene of grandeur and
magnificence far beyond anything we had before
seen or could have conceived.   These mountains
also were completely covered to their sharply-
pointed summits with snow, and the elevation

that were measured roughly, varied from twelve to upwards of fourteen thousand feet. These were named after the eminent philosophers of the Royal Society and British Association, at whose recommendation the government was induced to send forth this expedition. I had great satisfaction in having it in my power thus to record the names of those distinguished gentlemen from whose exertions in the cause of science these discoveries resulted. Herschel, an imperishable name, rendered still more illustrious by the scientific labours and achievements of the greatest philosopher of our own time, was given to the most conspicuous of the mountains, after Sir John F. W. Herschel, Bart., President of the British Association; by whom, in the double capacity of Chairman of the Committee of Physics of the British Association, as well as of the Royal Society, the recommendations of those scientific bodies were communicated to Her Majesty's government. Mount Northampton was named after the Most Noble the Marquis of Northampton, President of the Royal Society, who took a personal and active interest in promoting the great system of magnetic co-operation throughout the civilised world, and in recommending a voyage of magnetic research to the antarctic seas. Cape Roget and Cape Christie, which are formed by the terminations of Mount Herschel and Mount Lloyd, to seaward, were named after Dr. Peter Mark Roget, Secretary of the Royal Society, and his colleague, Professor Samuel Hunter Christie, of the Royal Military Academy, Woolwich.

Cape Wheatstone was named after Professor Wheatstone, the inventor of the electric telegraph; and Cape Daniell after my much-lamented friend the late Professor of Chemistry of King's College, and Foreign Secretary of the Royal Society.

Mount Peacock, Mount Whewell, Mount Lloyd, and Mount Robinson were named in compliment to the Very Reverend Dr. George Peacock, Dean of Ely; the Reverend Dr. William Whewell, Master of Trinity College, Cambridge; the Reverend Dr. Humphry Lloyd, of Trinity College, Dublin; and the Reverend Dr. Robinson, of Armagh; the more zealous and active promoters of magnetic research in the antarctic regions, and who, together with Sir John Herschel and Colonel Sabine, constitute a Committee of the British Association for the purpose of conducting the magnetical and meteorological co-operation, and for the reduction of meteorological observations.

Contending with a strong southerly breeze, we beat to windward close along the chain of islets which extends about ten miles to the southward of Possession Island. It consists of eight dark-coloured rocks of small size and curious shapes: an arched perforation was observed in one of them, through which the coast of the main land was seen; another was considered to resemble a ship's capstan.

At noon we were in lat. 71° 56′ S., Possession
Island bearing (true) west of us, distant seven or
eight miles.   Whenever we approached the land
we found ourselves attended by shoals of penguins,
which kept playing about our ships and alongside
of them, much as porpoises do in our own seas,
probably attracted by the shining copper.   Whales
also were seen in considerable numbers during the
day; and they who may hereafter seek them in
these latitudes will do well to keep near and under
the lee of extensive banks of ice to protect themselves from the heavy sea they will have to encounter,
and from which we experienced much inconvenience whenever we tacked off to the eastward, the
ship pitching her bowsprit under very frequently,
nothing but the great care of the officers of the
watches prevented our losing some of the spars.
We nevertheless made progress to the southward,
assisted by a strong tide, or more properly a current, since it had been setting us to windward for
more than twelve hours.   We sounded always as
we approached the land, and found from sixty to
ninety-two fathoms, when at two and a half to four
miles' distance.

Whilst measuring some angles for the survey,
an island I had not before noticed appeared,
which I was quite sure was not to be seen two or
three hours previously.   It was above one hundred
feet high, and nearly the whole of the summit and
eastern side perfectly free from snow.   I was much
surprised at the circumstance, and on calling the

attention of some of the officers to it, one of them
remarked that a large berg which had been an object
of observation before, had disappeared, or rather
had turned over unperceived by us, and presented
a new surface, covered with earth and stones, so
exactly like an island that nothing but landing on
it could have convinced us to the contrary had not
its appearance been so satisfactorily explained; and
moreover, on more careful observation a slight rolling motion was still perceptible.

I was very desirous to find a harbour in which
to secure the ships and obtain magnetometric observations on the 20th of this month, being one of
the term days agreed upon for simultaneous observations; well knowing the great interest and importance that would attach to a complete series of such
experiments, within 500 miles of the south magnetic pole; and for this purpose I had closely examined every indentation of the coast that presented
itself. These were, however, all filled with drifted
snow from the mountains, and formed a mass of
ice several hundred feet thick; and thus we found
it impossible to enter any of the valleys or breaks
in the coasts where harbours in other lands usually
occur. Still we hoped to meet with lower land, or
amongst some of the islands to find a place of shelter
for our ships and suitable for our purpose; therefore
we kept as close to the shore as circumstances would
admit throughout the day, and in the evening stood
out to sea, as we then found the tide near the land
had turned, and was carrying us fast to leeward.

At 10 p. m., when distant between twenty and
thirty miles from the land, it presented a remarkable
appearance; a bank of dense clouds concealed the
lower parts of the mountains, and their snowy
pointed summits alone appeared above the cloud,
contrasting strongly with the beautifully clear blue
sky, and conveying to the mind the idea of an im-
mensity of elevation beyond their measured height.

Our operations were retarded by a strong south-
west gale, against which we struggled in vain, the
whole of the next day, under our storm-sails. Such
a continuance of stormy weather in the middle of
summer we were not at all prepared to expect, and
we could not but feel anxious as day after day of
the brief season of navigation passed away without
any material advance in the desired direction. At
noon we were in lat. 72° 12′ S., but were driven
back to the northward by the violence of the storm,
which continued until noon of the following day,
about twenty-five miles.

As the wind moderated the reefs were shook out
of the topsails and courses, and we increased the
sail with good effect, the wind having veered to the
westward, so as to admit of our steering a more
southerly course. New portions of land opened to
our view as we proceeded to the southward. The sun
shone forth with great brilliancy, the more acceptable to our feelings, perhaps, from having been so
long concealed by unceasing showers of rain; and
its beams were reflected from the now distant
mountains in every variety of tone and modification

of light which the different forms of their icy coverings exhibited; and which, whilst attracting the admiration, and delighting the eye, could not fail also to improve the mind; for how was it possible thus to admire the stupendous and magnificent fabric, without our thoughts rising in adoration of the Author, and Maker, and Preserver of all?

The fine afternoon proved a source of real enjoyment after so much bad weather, and a proof of the extraordinary clearness of the atmosphere occurred worthy of notice. We had been sailing directly off to the eastward during the whole of the late gale, and on the fog and snow clearing away, both the angles and observations concurred in placing us at a distance of ninety miles from the mountains, which we still saw so clearly that many, unaccustomed to the deceptive appearances and uncertainty in estimating distances from land, would have supposed we were not more than thirty or forty miles from them. Mount Herschel subtended an angle with the horizon of thirty-six minutes, and might have been seen under equally favourable circumstances at thirty or forty miles further off. A heavy stream of ice, about a mile broad, lying in the direction of the wind, and extending to the north and south beyond the reach of vision from the mast-head, was passed through without difficulty, and with only a few severe blows as we forced our way amongst it. The temperature of the sea had fallen to 28°, and we naturally expected soon to meet with the main pack, of which a strong

ice-blink to the eastward appeared to give us warning; but in this we were mistaken, it proved to be
only a fog-bank.

During the afternoon an unusual degree of refraction was remarked to the south-westward, which
had the effect of bringing, at times, clearly into
view land we had not before seen, and then again
removing it from our sight.   This land having
been thus discovered at a distance of more than
one hundred miles on the birth-day of a lady to
whom I was then attached, and whom I have now
the happiness of calling my wife, I gave her name
to the extreme southern point—Cape Anne; and
the land afterwards proving to be an island, was
named Coulman Island, after her father, Thomas
Coulman, Esq., of Whitgift Hall, Goole.   The
northern point of the island was named Cape
Wadworth, in compliment to her uncle, Robert
John Coulman, Esq., of Wadworth Hall, Don-
caster; a spot of many happy associations.

Moderate breeze from the S. W. and fine weather:
we stood away to the S.S. E. on the starboard tack
until we lost sight of the land, at a great distance
from us; but we were sailing in an unexplored
space, perfectly free from either bergs or loose ice.
A few whales, penguins, cape-pigeons, and stormy
petrel were our only companions.   We were also
increasing our southing, and at noon were in 72° 57'
S. long., 176° 6' E.   At 1 P.M., having run three
miles S.S. E., we hove to, and obtained soundings
in two hundred and thirty fathoms.   Small stones

1841.

Jan. 18.

and shells, with some pieces of coral and a crustaceous animal (*nymphon gracile*), common in the Arctic Seas, came up with the lead. The temperature at that depth was 34°·6; at one hundred and fifty fathoms, 33°·8; that of the surface being 30°, and of the air 31°; the specific gravity of water brought up from various intermediate depths was the same as at the surface, 1·0277, at a temperature of 35°. This experiment was repeated with exactly the same result, in consequence of the Terror, which was less than a mile distant from us, having found only one hundred and seventy-four fathoms on a sandy bottom, showing a very remarkable irregularity in the bed of the ocean at this part. At 5 P. M., when in lat. 73° 3′ S., we tacked and stood towards the land; at 8 we sounded in one hundred and ninety, and at midnight in one hundred and eighty fathoms, on a bottom of sand and broken shells, having at that time run twenty-four miles true W. by N. The land was again seen soon after 9 P.M. W.N.W. true, at one hundred and twenty miles' distance, the sky of course being beautifully clear in that direction: we considered

Jan. 19.

it a curious circumstance finding the water so shallow at so great a distance from such high land. Numbers of the young pintado were flying about, and one shot by Mr. M'Cormick fell on board; it was the first specimen of the kind we obtained.

At four o'clock in the morning, we had one hundred and seventy fathoms, at eight o'clock two hundred and ten fathoms, and at noon had increased the depth of water to two hundred and seventy fathoms, although we had closed the land more than forty miles since midnight. Coulman Island, which we had only before seen by refraction, now formed the southern extreme point in view, and a new range of mountains was observed stretching away to the south-west from Mount Northampton, forming a kind of crescent-shaped ridge. A remarkable conical mountain to the north of Mount Northampton was named in compliment to the Rev. W. Vernon Harcount; one to the southward of it, after Sir David Brewster, the joint-founders of the British Association, which has so eminently contributed to the advancement of science in Great Britain. Mount Lubbock, to the southward of Mount Brewster, was named after Sir John Lubbock, Bart., treasurer of the Royal Society; and two other mountains, still further to the southward, were named after Sir Roderick Impey Murchison, the general secretary, and Professor Phillips, the assistant secretary, of the British Association.

Becalmed for two or three hours after noon, the dredge was put over in two hundred and seventy fathoms water, and after trailing along the ground for some time was hauled in. It was found to contain a block of grey granite, composed of large crystals of quartz, mica, and felspar, with apparently a clean and recent fracture, as if lately broken off from the main rock, and had probably been deposited by the agency of an iceberg. Besides this there were a great many stones of vari-

ous kinds of granitic and volcanic structure; but
the most remarkable circumstance was drawing
up from so great a depth beautiful specimens of
living coral, which naturalists and geologists have
hitherto concurred in believing unable to work
beyond the pressure of a few fathoms below the surface.   Corallines, Flustræ, and a variety of marine
invertebrate animals, also came up in the net, showing an abundance and great variety of animal life.
Amongst them I detected two species of Pycno-
gonum; Idotea Baffini, hitherto considered peculiar
to the Arctic Seas; a chiton, seven or eight bivalves
and univalves, an unknown species of *Gammarus*,
and two kinds of Serpula, adhering to the pebbles
and shells. I am indebted to the kindness of Charles
Stokes, Esq , for some remarks on the very interesting species of corals obtained by us on this
occasion, which will be found in the Appendix to
this Volume, and the beautiful drawings he has
made will appear in the zoology of the voyage now
publishing.

It was interesting amongst these creatures to
recognise several that I had been in the habit of
taking in equally high northern latitudes; and although contrary to the general belief of naturalists,
I have no doubt that from however great a depth
we may be enabled to bring up the mud and stones
of the bed of the ocean we shall find them teeming
with animal life; the extreme pressure at the greatest
depth does not appear to affect these creatures;
hitherto we have not been able to determine this

point beyond a thousand fathoms, but from that
depth several shellfish have been brought up with
the mud.

At 3 P. M. a favourable breeze sprang up, and
we made all sail to the south, steering direct for
Coulman Island, which still formed the eastern
extreme of land in sight, having a broad passage between it and the main land. A deep bight
was observed to the southward of a remarkable
cape, high, black, and cloven at the top; further to
the north, Cape Wheatstone, the right-hand point
of an apparent inlet, had the whole of its precipitous
face quite clear of snow, though it thickly covered
its rounded summit. The evening continued beautifully fine; but we well knew that a northerly wind
would most assuredly bring over us fog and snow,
its never-failing accompaniments; and the barometer
falling fast warned us to make the best of the brief
period of fine weather. All sail was crowded on both
our ships, and once again we had all the studding
sails on both sides set, and were running directly
before a fine breeze. The scene was most animating
and cheering; the harassing, tedious, and laborious
work of contending against adverse winds and
weather were forgotten in the full expectation we
now enjoyed of soon passing into a higher latitude
than had ever before been attained; and few on
board either of the ships closed their eyes that
night, so great were their anxiety and excitement. Soon after three o'clock the next morning
thick fog and snow limited our view at times to

less than a quarter of a mile, and we could seldom see beyond a mile; we, however, continued our course under all sail until six o'clock, when, during a partial clearing, we saw a great body of ice extending across our bows, fortunately in time to enable us to haul off to the eastward, and clear the point of it, passing through only a small quantity of scattered pieces at its outer edge. Soon afterwards we perceived that the ice extended from the north cape of Coulman Island (Cape Wadworth) several miles to the northward, and the whole space between it and Cape Jones, named after my friend Captain William Jones, R. N., was filled with a solid field of ice that appeared as if it had not yet broken up this season. We resumed our course to the southward, after clearing some loose streams off the main body of the ice, and at noon were in latitude, by dead reckoning, 73° 47′ S., long. 171° 40′ E., the sun not affording us an observation for latitude, for which we now most anxiously wished.

Penguins, white and stormy petrel, were seen in abundance, as also were several seals. Falling calm at 1·30 P. M. we sounded in 320 fathoms, the deep-sea clamms coming up full of a stiff green mud, sand, and small stones, some fragments of starfish, and pieces of coral. A strong ripple indicated a tide or current; and we found the ship was drifting to the south by the lead and bearings of the land, at the rate of three quarters of a mile per hour. At this time, Cape Anne, the high, perpendicular, extreme point of Coulman Island, bore

W. N. W. twenty-five miles.   Light baffling winds
prevailed for several hours, but eventually settled
in a stiff breeze from the southward.   We stood to
the S. W. to close the mainland, which we observed
had taken a considerable turn to the westward, but
without being able to get sight of it, owing to the
thickness of the weather, until 4 A. M. : when being
close in with the main pack edge we could observe
the land ice stretching round to the southward, a
firm unbroken mass, with a considerable quantity
of loose ice off its edge, which seemed to have been
recently broken away from the main body.

We tacked and stood off to the eastward to wait
for clear weather, and on standing in again the
land was distinctly seen : a high-peaked mountain,
bearing true west, was named Monteagle, after
the Chancellor of the Exchequer; and one of very
great elevation, the highest by estimation that we
had yet seen, but which we had not the opportunity of measuring accurately, was named Mount
Melbourne, after the Right Honourable Lord Viscount Melbourne, Prime Minister of England when
our expedition was proposed to her Majesty's government, and upon whom and his colleagues the
representations of the great philosophers of the day
had their due influence.   The form of Mount Melbourne had so general and striking a resemblance
to Mount Ætna, that for distinction's sake it went
by that name for several days amongst the officers
of both ships; but its elevation must be very much
greater than that of the Sicilian mountain.

The land ice, although not more than five or six feet above the surface, and therefore probably not more than forty feet in thickness, blends so imperceptibly with the snow which descends from the mountains at this part and extends far into the sea, that it was almost impossible to form any idea of the exact position of the coast line; thus from the edge of the land ice, it seemed at no great distance from its margin gradually to ascend until it reached the summits of the highest mountains.   To the N.W. the space between Coulman Island and the main land was occupied by a similar kind of land ice that appeared not to have been broken away for many years: in this particular more like the barrier described by Lieut. Wilkes, as extending from the shores of the lands discovered by him near the Antarctic Circle.   It was sufficiently evident that it was impossible to penetrate this mass of ice to the westward, as there was not even a crack or hole of water to be seen in any part of it. I therefore made up my mind to proceed along its edge to the southward, hoping to be able afterwards to pursue a westerly course to the Magnetic Pole, which we still continued to approach very considerably, the dip now amounting to 87° 39′.

At noon we were in lat. 74° 15′ S. by our reckoning, but the observation gave only 74°, showing that we had been driven to the northward by a current, which was the more mortifying as we had already begun to congratulate ourselves in the belief that we had reached as high a south latitude as had ever before been attained, and with every prospect of being permitted to extend our researches very much further.   In spite of all our exertions we found the ships unable to contend against the combined influence of the southerly wind and northerly current, which still carried us back to the northward, and when it fell calm in the afternoon, we could do nothing but watch the gradually retrograde motion of the ships.

It was the most beautiful night we had seen in these latitudes, the sky perfectly clear and serene. At midnight, when the sun was skimming along the southern horizon at an altitude of about two degrees, the sky over head was remarked to be of a most intense indigo blue, becoming paler in proportion to the distance from the zenith.

We got soundings in three hundred fathoms, and the dredge being again put over, and allowed to trail along the bottom for two or three hours, brought up many animals, some corallines, and a quantity of sand, mud, and small stones.   Amongst them we found several entirely new forms of creatures, of which accurate drawings were taken by Dr. Hooker, which, together with their descriptions, are now in course of publication, and constitute one of the more interesting features of our researches.   It is well known that marine invertebrate animals are more susceptible of change of temperature than land animals; indeed they may be isothermally arranged with great accuracy.   It will, however, be difficult to get naturalists and philosophers to believe that these fragile creatures could possibly exist at the depth of nearly two thousand fathoms below the surface: yet as we know they can bear the pressure of one thousand fathoms, why may they not of two? We also know that several of the same species of creatures inhabit the Arctic, that we have fished up from great depths in the Antarctic, Seas. The only way they could have got from the one pole to the other must have been through the tropics; but the temperature of the sea in those regions is such that they could not exist in it, unless at a depth of nearly two thousand fathoms. At that depth they might pass from the Arctic to the Antarctic Ocean without a variation of five degrees of temperature; whilst any land animal, at the most favourable season, must experience a difference of fifty degrees, and, if in the winter, no less than one hundred and fifty degrees, of Fahrenheit's thermometer — a sufficient reason why there are neither quadrupeds, nor birds, nor land-insects common to both regions.

success. Observations at noon placed us in lat. 74° 44′, long. 169 °30′, dip 87° 54′ S., var. 67° 13′, from which we deduced the place of the magnetic pole to be distant two hundred and forty-nine miles. We had penetrated the pack as far as the ice admitted to the westward by half-past eight in the evening, when we tacked and obtained observations by which we found we had approached so much nearer the Pole that the dip had increased to 88° 10′. We tried for soundings with three hundred fathoms line, but it did not reach the bottom. Mount Melbourne and Mount Monteagle were here seen to great advantage ; the immense crater of the former, and the more pointed summit of the latter, rose high above the contiguous mountains ; and they form two of the more remarkable objects of this most wonderful and magnificent mass of volcanic land.

Whilst struggling to get through the pack, we found it drifting, under the influence of the wind and current, rapidly to the northward, which seemed to encourage a hope, that, if defeated in our attempt to pass round its southern extremity, we might be able, at a later period of the season when more of the land-ice should have drifted away, to penetrate to the shore, and find some place wherein to secure the ships for the winter. For several days past we had seen very few whales, which was the more remarkable on account of the very great numbers we met with not more than sixty or seventy miles to the northward. There must be doubtless some cause for their absence from this spot, which

The gale, which rather freshened during the night, gradually veered more to the eastward; we therefore wore round and stood towards the land on the port tack; but, owing to the continuance of thick and snowy weather during the whole of Sunday, we did not get sight of it until 7 P. M., when it was indistinctly seen ahead of the ship. At midnight we were in lat. 74° 29′ by observation. We carried all sail, and both wind and sea abating, we approached the land rapidly; the barometer which had been rising throughout the gale, reached the unusual height of 29·33 at 4 A. M. the next morning; the line of coast was at this time distinctly seen, but at a great distance: a heavy pack extended at least forty or fifty miles from the shore, into which we stood amongst the loose ice as far as we could without getting beset; this I did not think proper to hazard, as it would assuredly have occasioned considerable loss of time without any equivalent advantage, and every hour at this period of the season was of much importance to us. I have no doubt that, had it been our object, we might have penetrated it several miles further, for although heavy-looking ice, it was not very densely packed, nor any thing like the solid land-ice we had seen further to the northward, and we should certainly have made the attempt, had not the land imposed an insuperable barrier to our reaching the Pole, which we still hoped to accomplish by a more circuitous route; and we were not then in a condition to be content with any thing short of complete

success. Observations at noon placed us in lat.
74° 44', long. 169 °30', dip 87° 54' S., var. 67° 13',
from which we deduced the place of the magnetic
pole to be distant two hundred and forty-nine miles.
We had penetrated the pack as far as the ice admitted to the westward by half-past eight in the
evening, when we tacked and obtained observations
by which we found we had approached so much
nearer the Pole that the dip had increased to 88° 10'.
We tried for soundings with three hundred fathoms
line, but it did not reach the bottom.   Mount Melbourne and Mount Monteagle were here seen to
great advantage; the immense crater of the former,
and the more pointed summit of the latter, rose high
above the contiguous mountains ; and they form two
of the more remarkable objects of this most wonderful and magnificent mass of volcanic land.

Whilst struggling to get through the pack, we
found it drifting, under the influence of the wind
and current, rapidly to the northward, which seemed
to encourage a hope, that, if defeated in our attempt
to pass round its southern extremity, we might be
able, at a later period of the season when more of
the land-ice should have drifted away, to penetrate
to the shore, and find some place wherein to secure
the ships for the winter.   For several days past we
had seen very few whales, which was the more remarkable on account of the very great numbers we
met with not more than sixty or seventy miles to
the northward.   There must be doubtless some
cause for their absence from this spot, which

perhaps future observation may supply; for it is desirable to know where they are not to be found as well as where they are, that valuable time may not be thrown away by those who go in pursuit of them.

On reaching the clear water, we found a short irregular sea, in which the ships pitched heavily under the easiest sail we could prevail on ourselves to carry, which seemed to indicate a change of tide to windward. As we pursued our way along the pack edge to the southward, we saw a great many of the beautiful snowy petrel, and some penguins. The temperature of the air varied only one degree during the twenty-four hours, from 25° to 26°, which was sufficiently low to freeze into ice the sprays that fell on board. the ship, and soon accumulated such a load about our bows as to keep the watch continually at work clearing it away, and beating it off the running ropes. At noon we had increased the dip to 88° 33′, so that the magnetic pole was now only one hundred and seventy-four miles from us in a W. by S. (true) bearing. Mount Melbourne bore W. by N. eighty miles.

In the afternoon, as we got further from the pack, the uneasy irregular sea subsided, and the wind becoming more westerly enabled us to stand direct for the east extreme of the " land blink," which bore S.W. by S. (true) from us; and at this time some strong indications of land appeared, which we all hoped would prove a "Cape Flyaway," as many others had done before. As we increased our distance from the pack, the temperature of the sea at its surface gradually rose from 28° to 31°, at about twelve miles off, although the air was at the time at 25°·5.

Light baffling winds, which prevailed for two or three hours, were succeeded by a moderate breeze from the eastward; all sail that the ships could spread was immediately set; and although the fog and rain came on so thick as to prevent our seeing more than half a mile before us, we continued to run with studding-sails on both sides set to the south-westward until nearly eight o'clock, when we were suddenly taken aback by the wind shifting to that quarter, and on the fog clearing away, we found that we had been steering into a deep bight of the main ice, which we now saw stretching across from the extreme point of the main land to an island bearing (true) south of us, and thus preventing our proceeding any further to the westward in this part; after closely examining the pack, in which no opening was to be seen, we stood away to the southward to endeavour to land on the island.

At noon we were in lat. 75° 48′, S. long. 168° 33′ E., dip 88° 24′, variation 80° 50′ E. At 3 P. M. we sounded in 200 fathoms, on fine black sand and small black stones, about twelve miles north of the island. At five o'clock when we were within two or three miles of it, I left the ship, accompanied by several officers, and soon after-wards followed by Commander Crozier, and a party from the Terror, we pulled towards the shore. A high southerly swell broke so heavily against the

cliffs, and on the only piece of beach we could see as
we rowed from one end of the island to the other, as
almost to forbid our landing ; a mortification not to
be endured if possible to be avoided : the Terror's
whale boat being more fit for encountering such a
surf than the heavy cutter of the Erebus, I got into
her, and by the great skill and management of the
officers and crew I succeeded, by watching the opportunity when the boat ·was on the crest of the
breakers, in jumping on to the rocks.   By means
of a rope, some of the officers landed with more
facility, but not without getting thoroughly wetted ;
and one having nearly lost his life in this difficult
affair, I was obliged to forbid any more attempting
to land, to their very great disappointment.   The
thermometer being at 22°, every part of the rocks
which were washed by the waves was covered with
a coating of ice, so that in jumping from the boat,
he slipped from them into the water, between her
stern and the almost perpendicular rock on which
we had landed, and but for the promptitude of
those in the boat, in instantly pulling off, he must
have been crushed between it and the rocks.   It
was most mercifully ordered otherwise, and he was
taken into the boat without having suffered any
other injury than being benumbed with the cold.
We proceeded at once therefore to take possession
of the island in due form ; and to the great satisfaction of every individual in the expedition, I
named it " Franklin Island ;" in compliment to His
Excellency Captain Sir John Franklin of the

Royal Navy, to whom, and his amiable lady, I have already had occasion to express the gratitude we all felt for the great kindness we received at their hands, and the deep interest they manifested in all the objects of the expedition. Having procured numerous specimens of the rocks of the island, we hastened our departure, in consequence of the perishing condition of our unlucky companion, and succeeded in embarking without any further accident; we gained the ships before nine o'clock, all of us thoroughly drenched to the skin, and painfully cold.

Franklin Island is situate in lat. 76° 8′ S., long. 168° 12′ E. It is about twelve miles long and six broad, and is composed wholly of igneous rocks; the northern side presents a line of dark precipitous cliffs, between five and six hundred feet high, exposing several longitudinal broad white, probably aluminous, bands of several feet thickness; two or three of them were of a red ochre colour, and gave a most strange appearance to the cliffs. We could not perceive the smallest trace of vegetation, not even a lichen or piece of sea-weed growing on the rocks; and I have no doubt from the total absence of it at both the places we have landed, that the vegetable kingdom has no representative in antarctic lands. We observed that the white petrel had its nests on the ledges of the cliffs, as had also the rapacious skua gull; several seals were seen, and it is by no means improbable that the beach on which we in vain attempted to land may, at the proper season, be one of their places of resort, or "*rookeries*" as they are termed by the seal fishers.

At between two and three miles distance from the land, the soundings were regular, in thirty-eight to forty-one fathoms, on a bed of fine sand and black stones, and probably good anchorage might be found near the shore with southerly winds. A high cliff of ice projects into the sea from the south and south-west sides, rendering it there quite inacessible, and a dangerous reef of rocks extends from its southern cape at least four or five miles, with apparently a deep water passage between them and the cape; several icebergs of moderate size were aground on the banks to the northward and westward of the island. At midnight the bearings of eight separate islands are given in the log of the Erebus; but as these afterwards proved to be the summits of mountains, at a great distance, belonging to the mainland, they do not appear upon the chart as islands. With a favourable breeze, and very clear weather, we stood to the southward, close to some land which had been in sight since the preceding noon, and which we then called the "High Island;" it proved to be a mountain twelve thousand four hundred feet of elevation above the level of the sea, emitting flame and smoke in great profusion; at first the smoke appeared like snow drift, but as we drew nearer, its true character became manifest.

The discovery of an active volcano in so high a
southern latitude cannot but be esteemed a circumstance of high geological importance and interest,
and contribute to throw some further light on the
physical construction of our globe. I named it
"Mount Erebus," and an extinct volcano to the eastward, little inferior in height, being by measurement ten thousand nine hundred feet high, was
called "Mount Terror."

A small high round island, which had been in
sight all the morning, was named "Beaufort Island,"
in compliment to Captain Francis Beaufort, of the
Royal Navy, Hydrographer to the Admiralty, who
was not only mainly instrumental in promoting the
sending forth our expedition, but afforded me much
assistance, during its equipment, by his opinion
and advice: and it is very gratifying to me to pay
this tribute of respect and gratitude to him for
the many acts of kindness and personal friendship
I have received at his hands. At 4 P.M. we were
in lat. 76° 6' S., long. 168° 11' E.   The magnetic
dip 88° 27' S., and the variation 95° 31 'E.: we
were therefore considerably to the southward of
the magnetic pole, without any appearance of being
able to approach it on account of the land-ice, at a
short distance to the westward, uniting with the
western point of the "High Island," which, however, afterwards proved to be part of the main
land, and of which Mount Erebus forms the most
conspicuous object.   As we approached the land
under all studding-sails, we perceived a low white

line extending from its eastern extreme point as
far as the eye could discern to the eastward. It
presented an extraordinary appearance, gradually
increasing in height, as we got nearer to it, and
proving at length to be a perpendicular cliff of ice,
between one hundred and fifty and two hundred
feet above the level of the sea, perfectly flat and
level at the top, and without any fissures or pro-
montories on its even seaward face. What was
beyond it we could not imagine; for being much
higher than our mast-head, we could not see any
thing except the summit of a lofty range of mountains extending to the southward as far as the
seventy-ninth degree of latitude. These mountains, being the southernmost land hitherto discovered, I felt great satisfaction in naming after
Captain Sir William Edward Parry, R. N., in grateful remembrance of the honour he conferred on
me, by calling the northernmost known land on the
globe by my name*; and more especially for the
encouragement, assistance, and friendship which he
bestowed on me during the many years I had the
honour and happiness to serve under his distinguished command, on four successive voyages to
the arctic seas; and to which I mainly attribute the
opportunity now afforded me of thus expressing
how deeply I feel myself indebted to his assistance
and example. Whether "Parry Mountains" again
take an easterly trending, and form the base to

* Parry's Polar Voyage, p. 121.

which this extraordinary mass of ice is attached, must
be left for future navigators to determine. If there
be land to the southward, it must be very remote, or
of much less elevation than any other part of the
coast we have seen, or it would have appeared
above the barrier. Meeting with such an obstruction was a great disappointment to us all, for we
had already, in expectation, passed far beyond the
eightieth degree, and had even appointed a rendezvous there, in case of the ships accidentally separating. It was, however, an obstruction of such a
character as to leave no doubt upon my mind as to
our future proceedings, for we might with equal
chance of success try to sail through the Cliffs of
Dover, as penetrate such a mass. When within
three or four miles of this most remarkable object,
we altered our course to the eastward, for the purpose of determining its extent, and not without the
hope that it might still lead us much further to the
southward. The whole coast here from the western
extreme point, now presented a similar vertical cliff
of ice, about two or three hundred feet high. The
eastern cape at the foot of Mount Terror was named
after my friend and colleague Commander Francis
Rawdon Moira Crozier, of the Terror, to whose zeal
and cordial co-operation is mainly to be ascribed,
under God's blessing, the happiness as well as success of the expedition: under the circumstances we
were placed in, it is impossible for others fully to
understand the value of having so tried a friend,
of now more than twenty years' standing, as com-

mander of the second ship, upon whom the harmony and right feeling between the two vessels so greatly depends. I considered myself equally fortunate in having for the senior lieutenant of the Erebus, one whose worth was so well known to me, and who, as well as Commander Crozier, had ever shown so much firmness and prudence during the arduous voyages to the arctic regions, in which we sailed together as messmates, under the most successful arctic navigator; in compliment to him, I named the western promontory at the foot of Mount Erebus, " Cape Bird." These two points form the only conspicuous headlands of the coast, the bay between them being of inconsiderable depth. At 4 P.M. Mount Erebus was observed to emit smoke and flame in unusual quantities, producing a most grand spectacle. A volume of dense smoke was projected at each successive jet with great force, in a vertical column, to the height of between fifteen hundred and two thousand feet above the mouth of the crater, when condensing first at its upper part, it descended in mist or snow, and gradually dispersed, to be succeeded by another splendid exhibition of the same kind in about half an hour afterwards, although the intervals between the eruptions were by no means regular. The diameter of the columns of smoke was between two and three hundred feet, as near as we could measure it; whenever the smoke cleared away, the bright red flame that filled the mouth of the crater was clearly perceptible; and some of the officers believed they

could see streams of lava pouring down its sides
until lost beneath the snow which descended from
a few hundred feet below the crater, and projected
its perpendicular icy cliff several miles into the
ocean. Mount Terror was much more free from
snow, especially on its eastern side, where were
numerous little conical crater-like hillocks, each of
which had probably been, at some period, an active
volcano; two very conspicuous hills of this kind
were observed close to Cape Crozier. The land
upon which Mount Erebus and Terror stand com-
prised between Cape Crozier and Cape Bird, had the
appearance of an island from our present position;
but the fixed ice, not admitting of our getting to
the westward of Cape Bird, prevented our ascertaining whether it was so or not at this time.

The day was remarkably fine; and favoured by a
fresh north-westerly breeze, we made good progress
to the E. S. E., close along the lofty perpendicular
cliffs of the icy barrier. It is impossible to conceive a more solid-looking mass of ice; not the
smallest appearance of any rent or fissure could we
discover throughout its whole extent, and the intensely bright sky beyond it but too plainly indicated the great distance to which it reached to the
southward. Many small fragments lay at the foot
of the cliffs, broken away by the force of the waves,
which dashed their spray high up the face of them.

Having sailed along this curious wall of ice in
perfectly clear water a distance of upwards of one
hundred miles, by noon we found it still stretching

1841.

Jan. 29.

to an indefinite extent in an E. S. E. direction. We were at this time in lat. 77° 47' S., long. 176° 43' E. The magnetic dip had diminished to 87° 22' S., and the variation amounted to 104° 25' E. The wind fell light shortly before noon, but we fortunately had time to increase our distance from the barrier before it fell calm; for the northerly swell, though by no means of any great height, drifted us gradually towards it without our being able to make any effort to avoid the serious consequences that must have resulted had we been carried against it. We had gained a distance of twelve or fourteen miles from it, and as the Terror was getting short of water, I made the signal to Commander Crozier to collect some of the numerous fragments of the barrier that were about us; whilst in the Erebus we were engaged making observations on the depth and temperature of the sea. We sounded in four hundred and ten fathoms, the leads having sunk fully two feet into a soft green mud, of which a considerable quantity still adhered to them. The temperature of three hundred fathoms was 34° 2', and at one hundred and fifty fathoms, 33°; that of the surface being 31°, and the air 28°.* So great a depth of water seemed to remove the supposition that had been suggested, of this great mass of ice being formed upon a ledge of rock, and to show that its outer edge at any rate could not be resting on the ground.

* Current S. by E. twelve miles per diem.

We had closed it several miles during the calm, but all our anxiety on that account was removed on a breeze springing up from the south-east. I went on board the Terror for a short time, this afternoon, to consult with Commander Crozier, and compare our chronometers and barometers *, and on my return at half-past four, we made all sail on the starboard tack to the eastward; but not being able to fetch along the barrier, and the weather becoming thick with snow, we lost sight of it before nine o'clock in the evening. Several gigantic petrel were seen, and one that was badly wounded by Mr. Abernethy falling at too great a distance for us to send a boat after it, was immediately attacked by two others of the same kind, and torn to pieces. Many white petrel, stormy petrel, small penguins, and some of the Skua gull were also seen. The breeze freshened very much, and drew more round to the eastward. The barrier was occasionally seen between the frequent snow-showers; and as we made but slow progress along it, we could quite clearly determine its continuity. At midnight we had gained the lat. of 78° S., in 180° of E. long. At this time the wind was blowing fresh from E. S. E., bringing a considerable swell along the face of the barrier, to which

---

* After an absence now of nearly three months from Van Diemen's Land, the chronometers of the two ships were found to differ only 4″ of time, equal to a mile of longitude, or in this latitude less than a quarter of a mile of distance; a sufficient proof of the excellence of the instruments with which we were furnished : — the agreement of the barometers was perfect.

our ships pitched heavily, and greatly retarded our progress ; but it was a gratifying evidence to us that there was still much clear water in that direction.

The wind and sea had increased so much that our dull-sailing ships could no longer gain any ground by beating to windward ; making two points of leeway, they could only sail again and again over the same space upon each successive tack. I thought it therefore advisable to make a long board under all sail to the north-east, so as to pass over as great an extent of unknown space as possible during the continuance of the adverse wind, and resume the examination of the barrier from the point we had last seen whenever the circumstances of wind and weather became favourable for doing so. The whole aspect of the sky indicated a very unsettled state of the atmosphere, whilst heavy clouds of snow drifting frequently over us obscured every thing from our sight, I therefore considered it desirable at any rate to get a greater distance from the barrier, in case of a change of wind making it a lee shore to us of the most dangerous character. The intervals of clear weather between the showers afforded us opportunities of seeing sufficiently far ahead to prevent our running into any very serious difficulty, so that we could venture to proceed with confidence. Several heavy pieces of ice were passed, evidently the fragments of the barrier or broken-up bergs, of which it was very remarkable we had not seen one during a run of one hundred and sixty miles along the barrier ; from which, no doubt, some must occasionally break away. But a little reflection soon furnished an explanation: in summer the temperature of the atmosphere and of the ocean seldom differ more than three or four degrees, the air being generally the colder, but never more than eight or ten degrees: it is therefore probably of rare occurrence that any great disruption should occur at that season of the year, the whole mass being then of so uniform a temperature. But in the winter, when the air is probably forty or fifty degrees below zero, and the sea from twenty-eight to thirty degrees above, the unequal expansion of those parts of the mass exposed to so great a difference of temperature could not fail to produce the separation of large portions. These, impelled by the prevailing southerly winds, drift to the north as soon as the winter breaks up, and are met with abundantly in the lower latitudes, where they rapidly melt away and break in pieces. We have often in the arctic regions witnessed the astonishing effects of a sudden change of temperature during the winter season, causing great rents and fissures of many miles extent; especially on the fresh-water lakes of those regions, where the ice being perfectly transparent, affords better means of observing the effects produced: a fall of thirty or forty degrees of the thermometer immediately occasions large cracks, traversing the whole extent of the lake in every variety of direction, and attended with frequent, loud explosions; some of the cracks opening in places several inches by the contraction of the upper surface in

ABSTRACT OF THE METEOROLOGICAL JOURNAL KEPT ON BOARD
HER MAJESTY'S SHIP EREBUS.—JANUARY, 1841.

Day.	Position at Noon.		Temperature of the Air in Shade.			Mean Temperature of Sea at Surface.	Temp. at 9 A.M.	
	Lat. S.	Long. E.	Max.	Min.	Mean.		Air.	Dew point.
1	66·32	169·45	31	27	28·9	28·8	28	*
2	66·28	170·14	32	26	29·7	29·1	31	31
3	65·39	170·48	30·5	29·5	30·0	30·0	31	31
4	65·22	172·40	32	30	31·2	30·6	32	32
5	66·55	174·31	32	29	30·3	29·3	31	28
6	68·17	175·21	30·5	24·5	28·2	28·7	32	24
7	68·31	175·37	32	24·5	27·8	27·4	28	24
8	68·28	176·31	41·5	29·5	34·2	29·8	36	33
9	69·15	176·14	30·5	28·5	29·6	28·8	30	*
10	70·23	174·48	31	28	29·5	28·8	30	30
11	71·15	171·15	40·5	29·5	32·4	30·5	31	29
12	71·49	170·52	31·5	29	30·2	30·0	32	30
13	72·07	172·19	30·5	29	29·2	29·6	30	29
14	71·51	172·40	30·5	28·2	29·6	29·6	30	30
15	71·56	171·51	31	28·5	29·6	29·5	32	29
16	72·12	172·13	29·5	27	27·5	27·9	28	27
17	72·09	173·35	31·5	26·5	28·9	28·3	29	29
18	72·56	176·06	31	28·5	29·7	28·6	30	25
19	72·31	173·39	39·5	28·5	31·8	29·3	30	23
20	73·47	171·50	31·5	27·5	28·8	29·4	31	29
21	74·00	170·43	34·2	28	29·9	27·7	29	28
22	73·55	172·20	35	28·5	31·4	29·9	32	23
23	74·23	175·35	31	27·5	29·8	29·7	31	31
24	74·35	173·01	29·5	26·5	27·6	27·9	28	*
25	74·44	169·43	29	25·5	27·6	27·3	29	22
26	75·03	169·04	26·5	25	25·7	29·3	27	23
27	75·47	168·59	30	24	26·2	29·9	26	23
28	76·57	169·25	33	23	27·9	29·9	30	18
29	77·47	176·43	31	22·5	26·4	29·4	30	22
30	77·35	181·20	29	26	27·5	30·4	29	*
31	77·06	189·06	26	19·5	22·7	29·3	25	24
			41·5	19·5	29·02	29·18		

* Snow falling.

ABSTRACT OF THE METEOROLOGICAL JOURNAL KEPT ON BOARD
HER MAJESTY'S SHIP EREBUS.—JANUARY, 1841.

Day.	Barometer.			Winds.		Weather.
	Max.	Min.	Mean.	Direction.	Force	
1	29·079	28·886	29·017	W.N.W.	2	0 p.s.*
2	·057	·453	28·747	N. Easterly	3	A.M. 5 b.c. / P.M. 0 m.s.
3	28·551	·422	·468	West	4	0 m.s.
4	29·181	·563	·886	Southerly	3	A.M. 0 p.s. / P.M. 5 b.c.
5	·180	·814	·999	W.S.W.	4	4 b.c.
6	28·922	·789	·869	W.S.W.	3	5 b.c.v.
7	29·073	·905	·958	Southerly	2	0 g.
8	·179	29·075	29·134	S.S.W.	1	0 g.
9	·045	28·446	28·664	E.N.E.	5	0 q.s.
10	·349	·553	·982	Easterly	A.M. 6 / P.M. 3	0 q.s. / 0 g.
11	·386	29·183	29·286	W.S.W.	3	7 b.c.v.
12	·372	·138	·273	W.N.W.	2	0 g.m.
13	·110	28·688	28·890	S.E.	6	0 g.q.p.s.
14	28·990	·699	·850	S.E.	6	A.M.0 g.q.s. / P.M. 1 b.c.g.p.s.
15	29·148	29·003	29·094	S. Easterly	4	5 b.c.
16	·126	·010	·065	S.E.	6	A.M. 0 q. / P.M. 2 b.c.q.p.s.
17	·167	·030	·103	South	A.M. 6 / P.M. 3	0 q.s. / 5 b.c.
18	·259	·157	·188	South	3	4 b.c.
19	·310	·154	·255	A.M. S.S.E. / P.M. N.N.W.	2	5 b.c.
20	·132	28·937	·005	A.M. N.N.E. / P.M. S.E.	3	0 g.m.
21	·098	·959	·036	E.S.E.	2	1 b.c.o.g.
22	·085	29·041	·062	S.E.	3	6 b.c.v.
23	·043	28·935	28·987	S.S.E.	5	0 g.q.s.
24	·339	29·022	29·154	E. by S.	5	0 q. s.
25	·352	·165	·201	S.S.E.	3	5 b.c.
26	·146	·015	·086	Southerly	3	2 b.c.
27	·020	28·902	28·950	S.S.W.	2	A.M. 2 b.c.p.s. / P.M. 4 b.c.
28	28·959	·841	·873	S.W. by W.	4	5 b.c.v.
29	29·093	·951	29·049	Easterly	3	A.M. 3 b.c.g. / P.M. 0 g.p.s.
30	·004	·950	28·966	N.E.	4	0 q.g.s.
31	·006	·911	·943	E. by S.	3	3 b.c.g.
	29·386	28·422	29·061		3·48	

* For the explanation of these symbols, see Appendix.

1841.

contact with the extreme cold of the atmosphere. In those regions we have also witnessed the almost magical power of the sea in breaking up land-ice or extensive floes of from twenty to thirty feet thick, which have in a few minutes after the swell reached them, been broken up into small fragments by the power of the waves.

But this extraordinary barrier of ice, of probably more than a thousand feet in thickness, crushes the undulations of the waves, and disregards their violence: it is a mighty and wonderful object, far beyond any thing we could have thought or conceived.

Thick squally weather, with constant snow prevailing, we stood away to the E.N.E. all day, without meeting either land or ice until 8 P.M., when, the snow clearing off, we could discover the strong iceblink of the barrier to the southward, and soon afterwards several icebergs were seen ahead of us: they were chiefly of the tabular form, perfectly flat on the top, precipitous in every part, and from 150 to 200 feet high: they had evidently at one time formed a part of the barrier, and I felt convinced, from finding them at this season so near the point of their formation, that they were resting on the ground. The lines were immedi-

Jan. 31. ately prepared, and when we got amongst them at 3 A. M. the next morning we hove to, and obtained soundings in two hundred and sixty fathoms, on a bottom of stiff green mud, leaving no doubt on our minds that all the bergs about us,

after having broken away from the barrier, had
grounded on this curious bank, which being two
hundred miles from Cape Crozier, the nearest
known land, and about sixty from the edge of the
barrier, was of itself a discovery of considerable
interest.

We continued our course to the eastward,
sailing amongst many large bergs and much loose
ice. Whales were again seen during the day,
but in no great numbers; white petrels were very
numerous, and a king penguin of unusual size was
seen on a piece of ice. At noon we were in lat.
77° 6', long. 189° 6'. The dip had diminished to
86° 23'; and although the compasses again began
to act with more precision, we here observed an
unaccountable decrease of variation from 96 E. to
77 E., and then again an increase of sixteen degrees. The observations were numerous and very
satisfactory, so that I have no doubt we had passed
one of those extraordinary magnetic points first
observed during Sir Edward Parry's second voyage* to the Arctic Seas, near the eastern entrance
of the Hecla and Fury Straits, but either of much
less power or at a greater distance. These observations should not be employed in determining the
position of the magnetic pole, as they would tend
to throw it very considerably to the southward of
the truth. At 1 P.M. we sounded in three hundred
fathoms; but here there were no bergs in sight

* See p. 297.

q 3

1841. even from the mast-head. A strong ice-blink to the eastward led us to expect to find the barrier in that direction, but it proved to be occasioned by a heavy loose pack, which we entered at half-past four o'clock, and penetrated about twelve or thirteen miles, when it became too close for us to venture further. We were at this time in 192° east longitude, when we tacked to get back into the open water; this, however, we found more difficult, for the ice had closed so much since we entered the pack that it was not without receiving many severe blows, and losing some of our copper, as we bored through the heavier streams, that we regained a more open space. A boat was sent after a small seal that was seen asleep on the ice, and brought it on board; it was of the common kind, and very prettily marked with dark spots: its stomach was full of small red shrimps. Several whales were also seen at the edge of the pack: young ice was observed to be forming in every sheltered situation under the lee of the larger pieces of ice, the temperature of the air being 19°. The wind continued too strong from the southward for us to make any way by beating to windward: we therefore stood back to the westward during the night upon nearly the same line as we had sailed during the day, but in the opposite direction.

Feb. 1. A calm of three hours' duration was followed at 9 A.M. by a gentle breeze from the north-westward, which again enabled us to stand towards the barrier. At noon, in lat. 77° 5′ S., long. 188° 27′ E.,

we obtained soundings in two hundred and fifty
fathoms, on soft green mud and small stones. We
also found the temperature of the sea at that depth
33° 2', and at one hundred and fifty fathoms 33°,
the surface being 32°; the current was setting to
the northward at the rate of three quarters of a
mile per hour, its strength being greater no doubt
over the shallow bank than in the deeper water.
In the evening, whilst running with all studding
sails set, the wind suddenly shifted to the south-
eastward, and the Terror being between two and
three miles astern, we shortened sail to wait for her.

During a snow shower of four or five hours' continuance, and variable winds and squalls, we kept
company by firing muskets every quarter of an
hour, the ships not being more than an eighth of
a mile from each other, but perfectly concealed
by fog and snow.   These cleared off at 5 A. M.,
but the whole morning was lost to us by alternate
calms and light baffling winds.   At noon, in lat.
77° 46′ S., long. 187° E., we got soundings with two
hundred and eighty fathoms, greenish mud and
clay.   The top of the barrier at the time was distinctly visible from the deck, just rising above the
horizon.   We now made all sail to a light breeze
from the north-east directly towards it; the loose
ice became closer as we proceeded to the southward, and at a quarter past nine stopped our
further progress.   We were about ten or twelve
miles from the barrier, but the whole of the
intervening space was filled with packed heavy

ice; we therefore wore round, hove to, and sounded in two hundred and sixty fathoms. I made the signal for Captain Crozier to come on board, who concurring in opinion with me of the utter impracticability of penetrating the dense pack between us and the barrier, I determined to devote a few more days to tracing its extent to the eastward; for although we could not hope to be able to get much further to the southward so late in the season, yet we knew the land-ice must still be clearing away from the shores at the most probable place of our being able to approach most nearly to the magnetic pole. Our dead reckoning since noon placed us in latitude 78° 3', the Terror's 78° 5'; we therefore assumed 78° 4' as the true latitude, which proved to be the highest attained this season; the face of the barrier at this part was therefore in 78¼° S.; it was about one hundred and sixty feet high, and extended as far to the east and west as the eye could discern, continuing in one unbroken line from Cape Crozier, a distance of two hundred and fifty miles.

At 10 P. M. we made sail to the northwest, to get clear of the pack, and by midnight were again in open water. I obtained an observation of the sun at 28 minutes after midnight, which gave the latitude 77° 56' S., agreeing with the reckoning of the preceding and subsequent noon in placing our point of furthest south in latitude 78° 4'; at the same time an observation was made in the Terror, which, also, when reduced back to our position at 9·15 P. M., agreed exactly with the former determination.

With a moderate breeze from the north-eastward, we stood to the N. N.W. to gain an offing, as we were prevented by the pack making any way to the eastward, and the barometer falling gradually seemed to indicate the approach of unfavourable weather. But the wind veering to the south-east in the afternoon, and late in the evening to south, the weather, contrary to our expectations, continued clear, and the breeze freshening we made way to the eastward, having got to the northward of the pack, and having the barrier still in sight to the southward. We passed through several streams of loose ice, and saw a great many whales of small size; several of them marked with large white patches. In the evening a cask was put overboard in lat. 77° S. and long. 187° 24′ E., containing a brief account of our proceedings, and with a request that whoever might find it would forward the paper to the Secretary of the Admiralty. It was my practice to throw a bottle over almost every day containing a paper with our latitude and longitude marked on it, for the purpose of gaining information respecting the joint effects of the prevailing winds and currents in these parts; but amongst ice, and in so turbulent an ocean, I fear but few of them will ever be found to subserve the intended purpose.

The next day we had a strong breeze from the southward, and pushed our way through loose ice and amongst numerous bergs to the eastward; at noon we were in lat. 77° S., and long. 192° 15′ E., when the ice appearing more open, with smooth water, we began to beat up to the southward to endeavour to close the barrier: many seals and penguins were seen on the ice. At 8 P. M. we had reached lat. 77° 18′ and long. 193°, where we found the ice so close in every direction that we were unable to proceed any further, and were obliged to dodge about in a hole of water two or three miles in diameter to wait for a favourable change. We obtained soundings in two hundred and seventy fathoms, muddy bottom, at four o'clock the next

Feb. 5.
morning. The ice was so closely packed to the eastward and southward that we could make no way in either direction, so we continued beating about in the small hole of water in which we were shut up by the closing of the ice. We saw several of the large penguins, and three were brought on board: they were very powerful birds, and we had some difficulty in killing them: each of the two larger weighed sixty-six pounds, and the smallest fifty-seven pounds: their flesh is very dark, and of a rank fishy flavour. In the evening we made fast with warps to a heavy floe piece, and employed all hands in collecting ice to replenish our water, which was now getting rather short. Two seals were also captured to furnish us with oil for the winter. We cast off again at 10 P. M., having taken on board a sufficient quantity of ice, and stood out through a narrow opening we had watched forming

to the westward. We passed through much closely
packed ice to gain the clear water, which was seen
from the mast-head early in the morning, and which
we succeeded in accomplishing by noon, in lat.
77° 1′ S., long. 188° 26′ E.; the remainder of the
day was spent in beating to the south-west to get
away from the pack edge, on which the wind was
blowing, and threatening to drive us down upon
it.

It moderated during the next morning, and
the wind getting to the westward enabled us to
steer a more southerly course amongst loose ice,
passing only a few bergs, and occasionally through
a sheet of newly-formed ice: it fell calm at midnight, and continued so for several hours.

At 1 A. M. sounded in two hundred and eighty-
eight fathoms, muddy bottom. We passed a berg
which had a large rock upon it. At 8 A. M. a
steady breeze sprung up from the northward,
when we made all sail before it, running along
the pack edge in clear water: at noon we were
in lat. 77° 39′, and long. 187° 5′ E. After passing through several streams of young ice the
barrier was seen right ahead of us at 5 P. M. The
main pack now trending more to the south-eastward,
we hauled up along its edge, to run between it
and the barrier, the whole of the surface of the sea
being covered with "pancake" ice. At midnight,
when about seven miles from the barrier, we obtained soundings in two hundred and seventy-five
fathoms.

The low temperature of the air and the smoothness of the water combined to favour the rapid formation of young ice, which greatly retarded us, and rendered the attainment of our purpose of more than ordinary difficulty; although the heavy pack to the north of us was fast closing the barrier, it was still fourteen or fifteen miles distant, and favoured with a commanding breeze, we stood on between the pack and barrier towards a remarkable looking bay, the only indentation we had perceived throughout its whole extent; and as clear water was observed even to the foot of the barrier, I could not permit myself to relinquish so favourable an opportunity of getting quite close to it, although I must confess the hazard was greater than a due degree of prudence would have ventured to encounter. At 5 40 A. M., being within a quarter of a mile of its Icy Cliffs, we tacked and sounded in three hundred and thirty fathoms, green muddy bottom. We had now a better opportunity of measuring the elevation of this perpendicular barrier, which, far overtopping our mast-heads, of course limited our view to the cliffs themselves, and these we considered to be much lower than at other points of it which we had previously approached: our angles gave them an elevation of one hundred and fifty feet. The bay we had entered was formed by a projecting peninsula of ice, terminated by a cape one hundred and seventy feet high; but at the narrow isthmus which connected it to the great barrier it was not more than fifty feet high, affording us the only opportunity we had of seeing its upper surface from our mast-heads: it appeared to be quite smooth, and conveyed to the mind the idea of an immense plain of frosted silver. Gigantic icicles depended from every projecting point of its perpendicular cliffs, proving that it sometimes thaws, which otherwise we could not have believed; for at a season of the year equivalent to August in England we had the thermometer at 12°, and at noon not rising above 14°; this severity of temperature is remarkable also when compared with our former experience in the northern seas, where from every iceberg you meet with, streams of water are constantly pouring off during the summer.

Young ice formed so quickly in this sheltered position, and the whole space between the barrier and the main pack which was driving down upon us being occupied by pancake ice, we found ourselves in a situation of much difficulty, the ice becoming so thick from being pressed fold over fold, as to render it for some hours a question of doubt whether we should be able to force our way through it to the open water which we could not at this time see from the mast-head; but fortunately for us the breeze maintained sufficient strength to enable us, with the assistance of great exertions of the crews in breaking up the ice before the ships, to regain a clearer space; and then, when we required its aid no longer, the wind came directly against us from the westward, so that had we lingered longer near the barrier, or had the wind shifted half an hour sooner, we should certainly have been frozen up in a most dangerous situation between the barrier and the pack; and had we eventually escaped without more serious consequences, we should at any rate have lost some of the few remaining days of the navigable season. A thick fog which prevailed for several hours added to the embarrassment of our situation, and rendered it the more difficult to keep the ships together, by obliging us to carry more moderate sail whilst amongst so much heavy ice and so many bergs.

At noon we were in lat. 77° 56′ S., long. 190° 15′ E. At 4 p. m. the fog cleared away, and we were again enabled to press all sail on the ships, running to the westward close along the edge of the main pack; the wind freshening from the northward drove it quickly down upon the barrier; and soon the channel by which we had escaped was filled by heavy ice closely pressed together, so that not the smallest hole of water could be seen amongst it. I was most anxious to examine as great an extent of the barrier to the eastward as possible, in order to leave less to be accomplished the following year; but the season was now fast drawing to a close, and the present state of the pack rendered any attempt to penetrate it quite hopeless. I determined, however, to devote two or three days to seeking a passage through it further to the northward, and accordingly the whole of the tenth and eleventh was passed examining the pack edge, but without our being

able to get so far to the eastward as we had
been on the fourth and fifth by seventy or eighty
miles.

At noon we were in lat. 76° 11′ S., long. 187° 53′ E.,
and were very much hampered by the newly
formed ice, which was so thick, and extended so
far from the main pack, as to render our efforts to
examine it quite fruitless, and the fatigue and
labour excessive. We continued, however, to coast
along its western edge seeking for an opening;
but the severe cold of the last few days had completely cemented it together, and the thick covering of snow that had fallen had united it, to
appearance, into a solid unbroken mass: although
we knew quite well that it consisted entirely of
loose pieces, through which only a few days before
we had sailed upwards of fifty miles, yet we
could find no part of it now in which we could
have forced the ships their own length.

We had further evidence of the approach of
winter in the very great thickness of young ice
we had to pass through as we ran along the
pack edge, in many places between three and four
inches thick, and entirely covering the surface of
the sea for many miles around us: had we not
been favoured with a strong breeze of very precarious duration, which enabled us to force our
ships through it, we should certainly have been
frozen in; and I could not but feel that the object we were pursuing was by no means of sufficient importance to justify the hazard of thus

sacrificing the accomplishment of far more important purposes.

In the afternoon, whilst running before this favouring breeze, the main pack was reported in every direction of us except directly to windward; and we soon found that during the thick weather we had run down into a deep bight of it. The ships were instantly hauled to the wind, and it was with the greatest difficulty they were extricated from their dangerous situation before the wind increased to a violent gale that reduced us before midnight to a close-reefed main-topsail and storm stay-sails, under which we barely weathered a great number of very large bergs clustered together under our lee, and most probably aground; but we could not venture to try for soundings, being uncertain whether we might not be driven down amongst them: it was no doubt this chain of bergs that had arrested the main pack in its northerly course and spread it out so far to the westward. One of the bergs was nearly four miles long, though not more than one hundred and fifty feet high. For some hours we were in a state of considerable anxiety, not knowing how far to the westward the chain of bergs might extend, the thick falling snow preventing our seeing to any distance before us; the waves, as they broke over the ships, froze as they fell on the decks and rigging, and covered our clothes with a thick coating of ice, so that our people suffered severely during the continuance of the gale. We passed many bergs and loose pieces of ice during the early part of the next day, and were frequently obliged to bear away to clear them. In the afternoon the storm began to abate, and on the weather clearing up for a short time, we found ourselves in a more open space.

I now became convinced of the necessity of at once relinquishing any attempt to penetrate to the eastward, and of deferring the further examination of the barrier to the following season; and the wind having shifted to the eastward, we bore away before it for the purpose of making another attempt to reach the magnetic pole, and of seeking a harbour in its vicinity in which we might pass the winter.

Thick fog and constant snow, which prevailed during the remainder of this and greater part of the following day, obliged us to run under moderate sail, to prevent the ships separating, and to be in readiness to avoid any danger that might suddenly arise; we, however, were in a perfectly clear sea, not a single piece of ice to be seen during the whole time, and the temperature of the air had risen to the freezing point.

At noon we were in lat. 76° 22' S., long. 178° 16' E.; the dip had again increased to 87° as we approached the pole, now distant from us about three hundred and sixty miles, and the variation being 91°, showed us we were very nearly in its latitude: we continued, therefore, to steer direct south by compass. The mildness of the day, notwithstanding the constant snow, was much enjoyed by us, as it allowed us to open the hatches, which had been closely battened down during the late gale of three days' continuance. The condensation of vapour between decks had been so great as to run down the ship's sides in small streams. I therefore directed the warm-air stove to be put into operation, which speedily and effectually removed every appearance of damp, driving the vapours up the hatchways, and circulating in its place a dry, pure air. The admirable performance of this most invaluable invention of Mr. Sylvester cannot be mentioned in adequate terms of praise.

Towards evening the swell had greatly subsided, but there was still a strong wind blowing, and the snow falling so thick, that we could seldom see a mile before us : running down upon a lee shore under such circumstances was a measure of some anxiety, but the barometer was rising fast from its very low state, and promised an improvement of the weather.

We were still a hundred miles from Franklin Island, for which we were steering, and I was unwilling to lose the advantage of the favourable breeze, even at some degree of hazard; for I felt we had but a few days to do much that we still hoped to accomplish.

On the 27th of January we had not been able to approach the pole nearer than about eighty leagues, but during the time we had spent in examining the barrier, a period of nearly three weeks, we could not but hope that so much more of the land ice would have broken away as to admit of our getting very close to, perhaps even complete the attainment of the pole.

The wind veered to the southward, and the snow ceased; several pieces of ice with rock on them were passed, and at 11 A. M. Franklin Island was seen at a distance of seven leagues ahead of us. We ran to leeward of it at 3 P. M., and when five miles N. N. W. from it we sounded in fifty fathoms, rocky bottom. Some streams of ice appearing soon afterwards, we hauled more to the southward to avoid them; and as we closed the main land we got in amongst a great quantity of brash ice of a brownish yellow colour; some of it was collected and placed under a powerful microscope, but we were unable to ascertain the true nature of the colouring matter*; by most of us it was believed to be the fine ashes from Mount Erebus, not more than eighty miles south of us.

At 11 P. M., being nearly calm, we sounded in three hundred and eighty fathoms, greenish-coloured mud and clay: Beaufort Island at the time bearing true south.

The wind was so light and variable, and the sludge and pancake ice so thick, we could scarcely get the ships through it. Mount Erebus was seen at 2 30 A. M., and the weather becoming very clear, we had a splendid view of the whole line of coast, to all appearance connecting it with the main land, which we had not before suspected to be the case.

* See M. Ehrenberg's account of the minute forms of organic life of which this substance is composed, in the Appendix.

1841.   A very deep bight was observed to extend far to the south-west from Cape Bird, in which a line of low land might be seen; but its determination was too uncertain to be left unexplored; and as the wind, blowing feebly from the west, prevented our making any way in that direction through the young ice that now covered the surface of the ocean in every part, as far as we could see from the mast-head, I determined to steer towards the bight, to give it a closer examination, and to learn with more certainty its continuity or otherwise. At noon we were in lat. 76° 32′ S., long. 166° 12′ E., dip 88° 24′, and variation 107° 18′ E.

During the afternoon we were nearly becalmed, and witnessed some magnificent eruptions of Mount Erebus, the flame and smoke being projected to a great height; but we could not, as on a former occasion, discover any lava issuing from the crater; although the exhibitions of to-day were upon a much grander scale.

A great number of whales of two different kinds were seen, the larger kind having an extremely long, erect back-fin, whilst that of the smaller species was scarcely discernible. The Skua gull, white petrel, penguins, and seals were also about us in considerable numbers.

Feb. 17.   At 10 P. M. we sounded in three hundred and sixty fathoms, green mud. Soon after midnight a breeze sprang up from the eastward, and we made all sail to the southward until 4 A. M., although we had an hour before distinctly traced the land entirely round the bay connecting Mount Erebus with the main land. I named it M'Murdo Bay, after the senior Lieutenant of the Terror, a compliment that his zeal and skill well merited. The wind having shifted to the southward enabled us to resume our endeavours to approach the magnetic pole, and we accordingly stood away to the northwest, sailing through quantities of tough newly formed ice perfectly covered with the colouring matter I have before noticed. When the melted ice was filtered through bibulous paper, it left a very thin sediment, which on being dried became an impalpable powder, seeming to confirm our belief of its volcanic origin.

At 2 P.M. we had penetrated the pack so far as to have got within ten or twelve miles of the low coast line, when our further progress was stopped by heavy closely packed ice. To the north-westward we observed a low point of land with a small islet off it, which we hoped might afford us a place of refuge during the winter, and accordingly endeavoured to struggle through the ice towards it, until 4 P.M., when the utter hopelessness of being able to approach it was manifest to all; the space of fifteen or sixteen miles between it and the ships being now filled by a solid mass of land ice. We therefore wore round and hove to for Commander Crozier to come on board; and as he quite concurred with me in thinking it impossible to get any nearer to the pole, I determined at once to relinquish the attempt, as we could not hope at so late a period of the season that any more of the land ice would break

1841. away. The cape with the islet off it was named
after Professor Gauss, the great mathematician of
Göttingen, who has done more than any other philosopher of the present day to advance the science
of terrestrial magnetism.

We were at this time in latitude 76° 12′ S., longitude 164° E.; the magnetic dip 88° 40′, and the
variation 109° 24′ E.   We were therefore only one
hundred and sixty miles from the pole.*

Had it been possible to have found a place of
security upon any part of this coast where we
might have wintered, in sight of the brilliant burning mountain, and at so short a distance from the
magnetic pole, both of those interesting spots might
easily have been reached by travelling parties in
the following spring; but all our efforts to effect
that object proved quite unsuccessful; and although our hopes of complete attainment were not
realised, yet it was some satisfaction to know that
we had approached the pole some hundreds of miles
nearer than any of our predecessors; and from the
multitude of observations that were made in so
many different directions from it, its position may
be determined with nearly as much accuracy as if
we had actually reached the spot itself.

It was nevertheless painfully vexatious to behold

* Professor Barlow's formula, $\tan \delta = 2 \tan \lambda$, has been employed in this deduction; but as all the magnetic observations
made on board both our ships are published in the second part
of the Philosophical Transactions of the Royal Society for 1843,
those who desire to use any other mode of computing the place
of the pole will there find ample materials.

at an easily accessible distance under other circumstances the range of mountains in which the pole
is placed, and to feel how nearly that chief object
of our undertaking had been accomplished: and
but few can understand the deep feelings of regret
with which I felt myself compelled to abandon
the perhaps too ambitious hope I had so long
cherished of being permitted to plant the flag
of my country on both the magnetic poles* of our
globe; but the obstacles which presented themselves
being of so insurmountable a character was some
degree of consolation, as it left us no grounds for
self-reproach, and as we bowed in humble acqui-
escence to the will of Him who had so defined the
boundary of our researches, with grateful hearts we
offered up our thanksgivings for the large measure
of success which he had permitted to reward our
exertions.   Some amongst us even still indulged
a feeble hope, that to the westward of the Admiralty
Mountains, which we knew trended so suddenly to
the westward, we might find the coast there turn
to the southward, and by following it we might
yet approach the pole more nearly; but we could
not conceal from ourselves that from the late period
of the season and the early setting in of the winter,
we were in this case hoping against hope.

The range of mountains in the extreme west,
which, if they be of an equal elevation with Mount
Erebus, were not less than fifty leagues distant,

* For some remarks relating to the discovery of the north
magnetic pole, see the Appendix to the second volume.

and therefore undoubtedly the seat of the southern magnetic pole, was distinguished by the name of His Royal Highness Prince Albert, who had been graciously pleased to express a warm interest in the success of our expedition.

The whole of the great southern land we had discovered, and whose continuity we had traced from the seventieth to the seventy-ninth degree of latitude, received the name of our Most Gracious Sovereign Queen Victoria, as being the earliest and most remote southern discovery since Her Majesty's accession to the throne.

As soon as we had completed all the necessary observations at this interesting spot, we commenced the laborious work of retracing our way through the pack to the eastward; but the young ice had so greatly increased in thickness, that this was a measure of great difficulty, and for a long time we had great doubts whether it would not prove too strong for us, and that in spite of our utmost exertions we might be frozen fast; for when we got clear of the heavy pack, the whole surface of the sea presented to our view one continuous sheet of ice, through which, when the breeze freshened up, we made some way, but were sometimes more than an hour getting a few yards; the boats were lowered down, and hauled out upon each bow, and breaking up the young ice by rolling them, we found the most effectual means; for although it was sufficiently strong to prevent our ships sailing through it, yet it was not strong enough to bear the weight of a party of men to cut a passage with saws. The whole night was passed in this fatiguing work, and it was not until ten o'clock the next morning that we regained the clear water, and were enabled to bear away to the northward.

Notwithstanding my anxious wish to keep close along the shore, that we might complete the examination of that portion of the land which we had but imperfectly seen on our way to the southward, yet we were obliged to stand off so far to the eastward to prevent getting entangled in the ice, and the weather not proving favourable for our purpose, we found it impossible to distinguish the coast line between Cape Gauss and a fine headland to the south of Mount Melbourne, which I called Cape Washington after my friend and brother officer of that name, for several years the able Secretary of the Royal Geographical Society, and a zealous promoter of geographical research. The continuity of the land and its leading features were however clearly ascertained: it is of less elevation than any other part of Victoria Land, and the mountainous ridges appeared to recede much farther from the coast. An island or a large berg with much earth and rocks upon it, which was passed in the afternoon, is marked on the chart " Doubtful Island," as it was quite impossible to know which it really was. Several stars were observed about midnight, the first we had seen since entering the pack, and warning us of the approach of the winter.

Mount Erebus was in sight until 3 30 A.M. at a distance of fifty leagues, and would probably have been seen at a greater distance had not some clouds passed over it at that time.

At noon we were in lat. 75° 3′ S. long., 168° 40′ E., Cape Washington and Mount Melbourne bearing (true) N.W. by W. In the afternoon we got much closer to the shore, and observed a deep bay formed between Cape Washington and another fine bold cape, which I named Cape Johnson, after Captain Edward John Johnson of the Royal Navy. The bay between Cape Johnson and Cape Washington was called Wood's Bay, after the third lieutenant of the Erebus, whilst the north extreme cape received that of the second lieutenant, now Commander John Sibbald. Late in the evening we observed the land ice extending from Cape Sibbald to the north extreme of Coulman Island, which obliged us to stand out to the north-east to clear it; at the same time some islets were seen that had not before been noticed, to which I applied the name of Lieutenant Kay, director of the Rossbank observatory at Van Diemen's Land, and third lieutenant of the Terror.

Soon after midnight the breeze freshened to a gale. As we stood out of the bight to the eastward, we passed through a great quantity of newly formed ice, and amongst heavy pieces of pack ice; and it was not until 9 A.M. we got clear of it, when having rounded Cape Anne, at a few miles' distance, we again bore away before the gale under

close-reefed topsails and reefed foresail. At noon
we were in lat. 73° 10′ S., and long. 171° 26′ E.,
and nearly abreast of a high cape, the projecting
base of Mount Lubbock, which I named Cape Jones,
after my friend Captain William Jones of the
Royal Navy.   Cape Phillips, at the foot of Mount
Brewster, was named after Lieutenant Charles Ger-
rans Phillips ; and I had much satisfaction in now
bestowing the names of the other officers of the
expedition, by whose exertions these discoveries
were made, upon the several capes and inlets we
passed in our run close along the land to the northward.   Much haze in the afternoon concealed the
tops of the mountains, but the line of coast, with
whose features we had become so familiar whilst
contending against the southern gales we experienced in January, was very plainly in sight.
Tucker Inlet was named after the master of the
Erebus, as was Cape Cotter after that officer of the
Terror; Cape Hallett after the purser of the Erebus, and Moubray Bay after the clerk in charge of
the Terror; Cape M'Cormick, abreast of Possession Island, after the surgeon of the Erebus, and
Robertson Bay, between Cape Adare and Cape
Wood, after Dr. Robertson of the Terror.

I was desirous of making another attempt to
land on the coast near Cape Adare, and with that
object in view we stood towards the cape early
the next morning, passing through many streams   Feb. 21.
of loose ice, until we at length came to a solid pack
extending eight or nine miles from the shore, and

1841.   so cemented together by the late severe frosts as
to defy every attempt to penetrate it.   We therefore steered to the north-west, keeping as close to
the shore as the pack and heavy streams that lay off
it would permit.   Smith Inlet, Cape Oakeley, and
Cape Dayman, were named after the three mates of
the Erebus: Cape Scott and Cape Moore after those
of the Terror: Cape Davis and Yule Bay after the
second masters; and Cape Hooker and Lyall Islets
after the assistant surgeons.   Beyond Cape Davis
the northern extreme of land appeared; it was
called Cape North.   A low point, with three projecting knobs like the tops of mountains, was observed at a great distance beyond Cape North,
whence the land trends considerably to the southward of west; but a dense body of ice interposed
between us, and prevented our following the coast
any further; and as the night was getting very
dark, and we were surrounded by numerous icebergs, at 9 P.M. we hauled off to the eastward on
the starboard tack, to wait for daylight, to renew
our operations: hopeless as they at that time appeared to be, they were not the less necessary.

Feb. 22.   Early next morning we wore round and stood
towards the land, in order to examine more
narrowly whether any way might be made along
the coast to the westward between it and the
pack.   I was also very anxious to find a place
of security for the ships, where observations on
the approaching term-day might be made, and
in which we might pass the winter in safety, for

1841.

although wintering in so low a latitude could be of no advantage to our next season's work, yet the meteorological, magnetical, and other observations in such a situation could not fail to afford much valuable and interesting information. But here, as on the eastern coast of Victoria Land, as far as we had traced it, we found the indentations of the coast completely filled with solid ice of many hundred feet in thickness. Smith Inlet and Yule Bay appeared two more promising places until we got close to them, when we found them equally impracticable as all the other places we had examined. The line of coast here presented perpendicular icy cliffs varying from two to five hundred feet high, and a chain of grounded bergs extended some miles from the cliffs: they were all of the tabular form, and of every size, from one mile to nine or ten in circumference.

Soon after 6 A. M., when within half a mile of this chain of bergs, the weather came so thick, with heavy snow, and the wind failing us, Lieutenant Bird, whom I had left in charge of the conduct of the ship, being myself unable to remain on deck any longer from excessive fatigue, very judiciously recommended that we should stand off again until more favourable weather for our purpose should arrive; fortunately we did so, and had gained an offing of six or seven miles, when it fell perfectly calm, and the ships were left entirely at the mercy of a heavy swell from the S. E.

At noon we were in lat. 70° 27′ S., and long. 167° 32′ E., and about this time the snow cleared off for two hours, so as to give us a view of a fine range of mountains whose summits we had not before seen; the loftiest of the range I called Mount Elliot after Rear Admiral the Honourable George Elliot, C. B., Commander-in-Chief in the Cape of Good Hope station, whose great kindness to us, and warm interest he took in our enterprize I have already had occasion to mention.

A breeze from the north-east at 6 P. M. enabled us to stand out of a deep bight of the pack into which the swell had driven us; and the barometer standing at 28·5 inches, we could not but expect a storm and dirty weather: I was therefore glad to get some distance to the S. E. before it came on. At noon it shifted to the east, and we tacked to the N. N. E. for the night, expecting it would blow hard from the quarter in which the wind seemed now to have settled, which made us the more anxious to get as clear of bergs and as far from the pack as possible; but, contrary to our expectations, after blowing only a strong breeze for a few hours, it again declined to a light air, which after midnight was attended with thick weather and snow showers, rendering our course amongst the bergs and heavy loose ice somewhat difficult and hazardous, and requiring the utmost vigilance of the officers and crew.

Feb. 23.   The uncertain state of the weather, the light

and variable winds, and thick falling snow defeated
my intentions of examination, and compelled us to
keep off to the eastward the whole day, although
we occasionally got glimpses of the land between
the snow showers.

About noon it fell perfectly calm; we were fortunate in being in a space less encumbered by ice
than usual. Commander Crozier took advantage
of the opportunity of increasing his supply of
fresh water by collecting some of the fragments of
bergs about us, not without great hazard to their
boats, during so much swell, but fortunately without any serious accident. We sounded in one
hundred and eighty fathoms, in greenish clay and
coral; we inferred from the shallowness of the
water that all the bergs in sight were aground, as
none of them were less than one hundred and sixty
feet high.

Early in the morning a steady breeze blew from
the westward, which increased so much in strength
as it veered to the north-west at noon, as to reduce
us to treble-reefed topsails, reefed foresail, and
staysails: we had been endeavouring all the day
to close the land, and at 4 P. M., when preparing
to run to leeward of what we considered to be a
monstrous iceberg, it became evident to us that it
formed a part of a body of ice which we could distinctly trace as a continuous mass descending from
near the tops of the mountains several miles into
the sea, and terminated by stupendous cliffs; a
deep bay was formed in these extraordinary cliffs

into which we were standing, and which we could perceive was bounded by cliffs of a similar character; but it came on to blow a gale of wind by the time we had got within a mile of the southeast Cape of the Bay; and as we were quite near enough to see that there could be no place in it that would suit our purpose, we wore round and stood away from this dangerous coast for the night.

We had a very good view of Cape North whilst close in with the icy cliffs, and observed that a high wall of ice, of a similar character to that which extends from Cape Crozier, forming the great barrier of 78° ¼ S., and which prevented our further progress to the southward, stretched away to the westward from the Cape, as far as we could see from the mast-head, and probably formed a coast line of considerable extent; a close, compact, impenetrable body of ice occupied the whole space to the northward and westward.

Our magnetic observations here were of very great interest, showing an extraordinary change in the variation from 114° W. to 40° W., amounting to no less than 74° in a space of about three hundred and sixty miles; the dip had also diminished, as might have been expected, to 86°.

Feb. 25.   Still blowing hard from the westward. We wore before daylight, and stood towards the ice, to continue the examination of it; in a few hours we got close up to the pack edge, which filled the whole space between us and the wall of ice projecting to the westward from Cape North, and without the appearance of any water amongst it, so firmly was it packed together: from this position several small islands appeared to the right of Cape North, which will probably prove to be the tops of mountains connected with it, but from their great distance we could not ascertain their continuity, nor could we get any nearer to them owing to the solid intervening pack.

We had in the afternoon a good view of the coast. The whole of the land being perfectly free from cloud or haze, the lofty range of mountains appeared projected upon the clear sky beyond them beautifully defined; and although of a spotless white, without the smallest patch of exposed rock throughout its whole extent to relieve it, yet the irregularities of the surface, the numerous conical protuberances and inferior eminences, and the deeply marked valleys, occasioned many varieties of light and shade that destroyed the monotonous glare of a perfectly white surface, but to which it is so very difficult to give expression either by the pencil or description. It was a most interesting scene to us, as it was truly the best view we had of the northern shore and mountains of Victoria Land, and of which the western extremity was by no means the least remarkable feature.

The prospect now before us, and the but too evident approach of winter, impressed upon my mind the necessity of abandoning any further attempt to penetrate to the westward, and as there was no measure left untried to find a harbour to winter in without success, I determined to make the best of our way to the northward in search of any lands that might lie between Cape North of Victoria Land and Balleny Islands, as it was most important to ascertain whether these were connected, and how far the space between them might be navigable. And although I could not but feel how great was the hazard of detaining the ships any longer in these dangerous regions, and how great must be the anxiety of those upon whom the care of the ships devolved during the long dark nights that prevailed, and the difficulty we might experience in recrossing the pack of two hundred miles in breadth, which we had passed through near the antarctic circle; yet I considered the object to be accomplished of sufficient importance to justify some further degree of risk, and had some hopes that we might find the pack had driven so far to the northward as to leave us a clear passage between it and the easternmost point of the American discoveries.

In pursuance of this determination we made all sail, beating to the N. W., close along the edge of the main pack, until late in the evening, when the wind shifted to the south, and increased so suddenly, that before midnight it blew a violent storm; to prevent passing any land in the night, as well as on account of the great danger of running during the gale, we rounded the ships to on the starboard tack under close-reefed topsails. The gale was, however, of only a few hours' duration, but at daylight the fog and snow were so thick that we could not see beyond a mile at any time, which, together with the very light and variable winds and occasional calms, effectually prevented our making any progress during the day, which closed in upon us during a perfect calm; the heavy swell, and unceasing heavy snow, rendered the darkness of the night so much more perplexing, and our situation most anxious, as we could not tell one minute what might happen the next. An easterly breeze succeeded, and the snow ceased, so that at daylight the next morning we made sail to the northward, just able to fetch along the edge of the main pack under our lee: at noon we were lat. 67° 27′ S., long. 167° 49′ E., and here we tried for but did not obtain soundings with two hundred and ten fathoms of line: the light easterly winds, which had prevailed for some hours, was followed by a strong breeze from W. N. W., which freshened up to a gale before dark, and continued to blow with great force throughout the night; these sudden changes of wind, and frequent alternations of gales and calms, occasion the navigation of these regions so late in the season to be a cause of continual anxiety of mind: attended, as they almost invariably are, by thick weather, constant snow showers, and a heavy swell, it is difficult to say whether the gales or the calms are the more embarrassing and dangerous. In the calms it is true you are less likely to meet with dangers, on

s 2

1841.   account of passing over less space during their continuance, but in the event of drifting down upon the pack or a chain of bergs, you are left totally at the mercy of the waves, the high sea generally preventing the use of boats to tow you clear of them, and defeating every effort to take advantage of any feeble air of wind that in smooth water might prove effectual; and it is this constant heavy swell that renders the navigation of the antarctic seas so much more hazardous than that of the arctic ocean.

Feb. 28.   At daylight we wore and stood towards the pack; the land was reported at 6 20 A.M., the same abrupt western termination we had before seen, and the pack soon afterwards appeared. We were close in with the edge of it by noon in lat. 69° 57′ S. and long. 167° 5′ E., when it appeared from the northward one unbroken mass of ice with many large bergs amongst it, and so firmly cemented together by the late severe cold, (the thermometer during the night having been down to 14°, and at noon only reached 22°,) that not the smallest hole of water could be perceived amongst it: we therefore wore round and stood to the northward; and as we ran close along the pack edge we passed through several long streams of young ice, which being broken up the heavy swell offered but little obstruction to our progress; whales were seen in great numbers coming out from under the ice to "blow," and then returning under it again to feed or for protection.   At six o'clock in the evening we got the last glimpse of Victoria Land; Mount Elliot could be discerned dimly through the mist at a distance of seventy miles; it was blowing a strong gale at the time, but we continued our course until midnight, having seen far enough a-head before dark to ensure not running into danger.   At 11 30 P.M. we saw forthe first time the Aurora Australis bearing (magnetic) west. It consisted of two segments of a broken arch, at an altitude of 15°, from which bright coruscations shot upwards to the altitude of about 60°; the upper points of these rays were more beautifully attenuated than I ever remember to have seen those of the Aurora Borealis: the vertical beams had much lateral motion, and frequently disappeared and reappeared in a few seconds of time: we could not perceive any exhibitions of colour.

Day.	Position at Noon.		Temperature of the Air in Shade.			Mean Temperature of Sea at Surface.	Temp. at 9 A.M.	
	Lat. S.	Long. E.	Max.	Min.	Mean.		Air in shade	Dew point.
1	77·06	188·27	34	19·5	27·0	30·7	28	21
2	77·45	187·00	32	24·5	28·2	30·2	31	24
3	77·17	185·28	29	23	25·4	30·2	26	22
4	77·00	192·18	23·5	15	20·7	28·7	23	22
5	77·11	192·48	16·7	13	15·1	28·7	16	15
6	77·01	188·26	23	14	18·7	28·8	17	15
7	77·01	186·35	29	19	24·6	29·2	27	18
8	77·39	187·05	32	23	26·4	29·2	29	24
9	77·56	190·15	28	16	21·0	28·9	28	22
10	77·32	186·38	27	19·5	22·6	28·5	25	20
11	76·11	187·53	22	18	19·9	28·7	20	16
12	76·51	184·56	26	20·5	23·6	29·0	24	24
13	76·54	183·16	31	26	29·6	30·5	31	31
14	76·23	178·15	33	29	30·2	30·2	30	30*
15	76·03	170·15	29	26	27·2	28·6	28	28
16	76·32	166·12	32	26	28·0	28·6	29	28
17	76·35	165·21	29·5	25·5	27·5	28·9	29	24
18	76·06	166·11	30	21·5	26·2	28·9	28	23
19	75·03	168·45	27	21	23·9	28·9	26	25
20	73·10	171·26	24	21	22·2	29·1	22	19
21	71·05	169·58	26	23	24·7	29·4	25	18
22	70·27	166·40	26	22·5	24·1	29·0	24	24*
23	70·17	167·32	24·5	22	23·3	28·9	23	23*
24	70·15	167·35	27·5	20·2	24·6	29·0	27	27
25	70·06	167·27	25	19	21·3	28·9	22	19
26	69·52	167·53	31	23	29·0	29·4	30	30*
27	69·24	167·55	29	16	24·8	28·9	28	28
28	69·57	167·05	26	14	20·2	28·9	21	29
			34	13	24·28	29·18		

* Snow falling.

ABSTRACT OF THE METEOROLOGICAL JOURNAL KEPT ON BOARD HER MAJESTY'S SHIP EREBUS.—FEBRUARY, 1841.

Day.	Barometer.			Winds.		Weather.
	Max.	Min.	Mean.	Deflection.	Force.	
1	29·088	29·025	29·069	S.Westerly	2	5 b.c.g.*
2	·260	·095	·201	Northerly	2	A.M. 2 b.c.p.s. / P.M. 3 b.c.
3	·232	28·888	·059	A.M. N.W. / P.M. N.E.	3	0 g.
4	28·900	·832	28·859	E.S.E.	4	A.M. 0 g.p.s. / P.M. 4 b.c.
5	·912	·869	·898	S.E.	3	A.M. 3 b.c.m. / P.M. 1 b.c.g.p.s.
6	29·076	·879	·899	S.E.	4	5 b.c.
7	·245	29·077	29·184	S.S.E.	3	4 b.c.g.
8	·263	·232	·247	A.M. N.Ely. / P.M. N.Wly.	2	A.M. 3 b.c.p.s. / P.M. 5 b.c.
9	·293	·264	·278	A.M. Westerly / P.M. N.E.	2	3 b.c.m.
10	·458	·259	·340	N.N.E.	2	A.M. 5 b.c.g. / P.M. 1 b.c.o.g.
11	·508	·146	·393	N.N.E.	5	A.M. 2 b.c.p.s. / P.M. 0 g.q.p.s.
12	·125	28·577	28·867	N.E.	A.M. 7 / P.M. 5	0 m.q.s.
13	28·534	·284	·372	E.N.E.	A.M. 7 / P.M. 5	0 m.q.s.
14	·847	·403	·636	N.N.E.	3	0 m.p.s.
15	29·171	·852	29·013	East	A.M. 5 / P.M. 3	0 g. / 0 g.p.s.
16	·210	29·151	·178	S.Westerly	1	3 b.c.g.
17	·172	·054	·106	A.M. Westerly / P.M. East	2 / 3	2 b.c.g. / 5 b.c.
18	·048	28·907	·008	S. Easterly	2	4 b.c.g.
19	·014	·841	28·949	A.M.Southerly / P.M. East	4	3 b.c.g.
20	·051	·816	·910	S.S.E.	5	A.M. 1 b.c.g. / P.M. 4 b.c.q.
21	·067	·670	·924	East	4	0 g.
22	28·646	·478	·531	A.M. East / P.M. North	2	0 g.s.
23	·753	·563	·681	Northerly	2	0 g.s.
24	·667	·558	·605	W.S.W.	A.M. 4 / P.M. 6	0 g. / 5 b.c.g.
25	·777	·589	·668	W. by S.	A.M. 6 / P.M. 3	4 b.c.q. / 2 b.c.g.
26	·613	·487	·552	N.W. by N.	2	0 m.s.
27	·819	·568	·704	A.M. E. by N. / P.M. W. by S.	4	A.M. 0 m.p.s. / P.M. 2 b.c.q.g.
28	·962	·680	·820	S.W.	6	5 b.c.q.v.
	29·508	28·284	28·9268		3·39	

* For the explanation of these symbols, see the Appendix.

CHAPTER IX.

THE Aurora Australis continued to appear at intervals in bright colourless coruscations, reaching
from the horizon to 30° of altitude in a W. by S.
(magnetic) direction, until 1 30 A. M., when it
was concealed from our view by light clouds
which rose in that quarter.

With a strong breeze from the westward, and
fine clear weather, we continued the examination
of the pack edge, passing through great quantities
of pancake ice, which formed rapidly under the
protection of the pack, at a temperature of 20°, at
which the thermometer stood with trifling variation
the whole day. A heavy swell throughout the
pack proved to us that it consisted of loose pieces,
although to the eye at a little distance it appeared
as one unbroken mass, and we occasionally ran the
ships in amongst it as far as we could venture without hazard of getting frozen in or beset. I have
no doubt that in the summer season it might be
penetrated to a great distance, and it is very probable that eventually the south magnetic pole will
be attained by persevering to the S. W. through
this vast tract of ocean, which separates Victoria
Land from the Balleny and other islands or lands
discovered near the antarctic circle by Biscoe, Balleny, Wilkes, and D'Urville. We saw a great

1841. many whales whenever we came near the pack edge, chiefly of a very large size; and I have no doubt that before long this place will be the frequent resort of our whaling ships, being at so convenient a distance from Van Diemen's Land, which affords every means and facilities for their equipment; and thus we may also hope to become by degrees, through their exertions and enterprise, better acquainted with this part of the antarctic regions, which the setting in of the winter so much earlier than we expected had prevented our accomplishing so satisfactorily as I wished.

At night the aurora was again seen. It was different from those exhibitions I have seen of it in the arctic regions, in the greater length of the vertical beams, and the frequency and suddenness of its appearances and disappearances, more like flashes of light; it was again also perfectly colourless, had considerable lateral flitting motion, and formed an irregular arch about thirty degrees high, whose centre bore west (magnetic). From this it would seem that, as in the northern regions, the principal seat of the aurora is not in the higher latitudes, and probably in the latitude of 68 S. it will be found principally to obtain.

In passing through the streams of ice that lay off the pack edge during the night, our ships sustained some very heavy blows; and soon after midnight March 2. the shackle of the Terror's bobstay was thus broken: as soon as they made the signal we hove to, that they might replace it. This operation, however, was one of great difficulty, owing to the darkness of the night; the ships' bows and rigging being thickly encrusted with ice, and so much swell as to endanger the lives of the brave fellows that were engaged for nearly two hours, slung over the bows, up to their necks in water at every plunge the ship took, before they could accomplish it; and this with the thermometer at twelve degrees below freezing. We made all sail at daylight along the pack edge to the north, with a light breeze from the westward; and at noon were in lat. 68° 27' S., long. 167° 42' E., the dip 85° 19', and variation 34° 32' E. We had no soundings with four hundred fathoms line, the temperature at that depth 36°; the surface 28° 2', and the air 27°. We met with fewer streams of ice off the pack, and were favoured with very fine weather, the thermometer having risen to a more comfortable temperature.

At 5 P.M. land was seen, bearing N. 62° W., of which before dark we could clearly distinguish the features. It had the appearance of two islands nearly joining, and the whole subtended an angle of seventeen degrees, of great height, and very distant: the centre of the northern island terminated in a high peak. I named it Russell Peak. The southernmost I named Smyth Island, after my friend Captain William Henry Smyth, of the Royal Navy, President of the Royal Astronomical Society. Although I believe these islands to form a part of the group discovered by Balleny in February 1839, yet it is not improbable they may prove to be the tops of the mountains of a more extensive land.

We stood towards the land, passing through

1841.

streams of heavy ice, until 10 50 p. m., when we found the newly-formed ice so thick, and the heavy pack also so close, that we had some difficulty in wearing round to get out again, and this not without sustaining some severe shocks: after an hour's struggling we got into a more open space, and hove

March 3. to for daylight. As soon as it appeared we wore round and again stood in towards the land, which we saw at 6 30 A. M., bearing W. N. W., but was soon after covered by clouds, and completely shut out from our view. At 8 A. M. we were obliged to steer more to the north, the pack being too close for us to proceed any further to the westward, and soon after noon we were much embarrassed by light variable winds, with thick snow and a heavy swell; so that it was difficult to keep the ships so close together as to ensure our not separating and at the same time not to endanger their falling on board of each other, being at times quite unmanageable. And although we took advantage of every light breeze to draw off towards the open water, we were frequently unable to keep the ships' heads in the desired direction; and we were now also surrounded by many bergs and heavy pieces of pack ice that were difficult to avoid.

At 10 30 p. m. a fresh breeze arose from the eastward, and as the night was tolerably clear we continued our course to the N. W. under easy sail.

March 4. Land was again seen at daylight bearing S. 38° W. to S. 68° W., and from this point presenting the appearance of three distinct islands, and distant, by

estimation, between thirty and forty miles. By
the peculiar form of Russell Peak we knew it to
be the same land we had seen on the two previous
days; but owing to thick weather coming on, we
did not get observations, and are therefore unable
to assign its exact position; approximately it
is in lat. 67° 28′ S., and long. 165° 30′ E. The
third island was named Frances Island. We continued our course until 8 A.M., when we found we
had run into a deep bight of the main pack, and a
high sea was getting up; so we hauled off to the
N.E. At this time we observed strong appearances
of land directly to the westward, high and broken
into islands; but it soon after became quite thick
with snow, so that we lost sight of them, and the
breeze freshening to a gale we were obliged to
carry a heavy press of sail to weather the lee point
of the bight we had got into. The deep plunges
the ship gave frequently brought her bowsprit into
violent contact with heavy pieces of ice that it was
impossible to avoid, and our dolphin striker was
carried away. The Terror's bobstay and bowsprit
shrouds were also carried away, but fortunately we
had at that time gained a more open space, where
we hove to for her to repair her damage and to
secure her bowsprit.

At noon we were in lat. 66° 44′ S., long. 165° 45′
E., so that without doubt the land we saw in the
morning was that discovered by Balleny, to which
his name was given by Captain Beaufort, the hydrographer to the Admiralty; and I think it right to
publish here the extract from the Log of the Eliza

1841.

Scott, the ship in which Balleny made his discoveries (belonging to Mr. Charles Enderby and some other gentlemen), with which I was furnished from the Hydrographic Office before leaving England in September, 1839, Balleny having arrived only a few days before our departure.

Feb. 9.
1839.

" At 8 A.M. clear weather. Steering west by compass in latitude 66° 46′ S. got sights for my chronometers, which gave the ship in longitude 164° 29′ E. At 11 A.M. observed a darkish appearance to the S.W. At noon the sun shone brightly; observed the latitude to be 66° 37′ S.; saw the appearance of land to the S.W., extending from west to about south; ran for it; at 4 P.M. made it out distinctly to be land; at 8 P.M. got within five miles of it, when we saw another piece of land of great height. At sunset we distinctly made them out to be three separate islands of good size, but the western one the longest: lay to all night off the middle island, and at 2 A.M. of the

Feb. 10.

10th bore up for it. Ran through a considerable quantity of drift ice, and got within half a mile, but found it completely icebound with high perpendicular cliffs. I wished to run between the middle and western island, but was compelled to come out again to the eastward, as from the western island to the eastern one, on the west or rather south-west side, the ice was in one firm and solid mass without a passage. The weather at sunrise was very threatening; at 6 it came on thick, since when we have been compelled to stand off. I make the high bluff western point

of the middle island to be in lat. 66° 44′ S. and 　1839.
long. 163° 11′ E.　A lunar at two o'clock agrees
with the above longitude by chronometer.　The
weather continued moderate, but very thick to the
end.

" Thick weather.　At 1 A. M. had to hoist out a 　Feb. 11.
boat to tow the vessel clear of an iceberg, which
we were close to, but could not see, and no wind.
At 11 A. M. cleared, and we saw the land bearing
about W. S. W., and of a tremendous height, I
should suppose at least twelve thousand feet, and
covered with snow.　We are inclosed with large
icebergs in every direction.

" At noon we had a very indifferent observation,
which gave the latitude 66° 30′ S., and it immediately came on thick.

" This morning the weather thickens and clears 　Feb. 12.
occasionally.　At 2 A. M. saw the land, bearing
S. S. E. about ten miles.　The west point of the
west island bore W. N. W.　At eight o'clock the
land completely icebound.

" At noon tacked, and worked in-shore to look
for harbours or beach.　At 4 P. M. abreast of the
small island; the eastern island, now on a different
bearing, appeared a large one.　At 6 P. M. went on
shore in the cutter's (Sabrina) boat, at the only
place likely to afford a landing; but when we got
close with the boat it proved only the drawback of
the sea, having a beach of only three or four feet
at most.　Captain Freeman jumped out and got a
few stones, but was up to his middle in water.
There is no landing or beaches on this land; in

fact, but for the bare rocks where the icebergs had
broken from we would scarce have known it for
land at first, but as we stood in for it we plainly
perceived smoke arising from the mountain tops.
It is evidently volcanic, as specimens of stone, or
rather cinders, will prove; the cliffs are perpendicular, and what in all probability would have
been valleys and beaches are occupied by solid
blocks of ice. I could not see a beach or harbour,
or any thing like one. Returned on board at 7 P.M.,
and got the vessels safely through the drift ice
before dark, and ran along the land."

Indications of land are frequently mentioned in
the Log of the Eliza Scott during the following
fortnight as she sailed to the westward along the
parallel of the sixty-fifth degree of latitude, and on
Feb. 26. the 26th, when in lat. 64° 40′ S., and long. 131° 35′
E., and therefore only a few miles to the westward of
the high barrier of ice seen by D'Urville on the
30th of January of the following year, and named
by him Côte Clarie*, the Log states, "that at
8 A. M. it cleared off a little, and we thought we
saw land to the eastward, tacked, and stood for it.
At 11 30 A. M. made it out to be fog hanging over
some icebergs." Thick weather, with snow and
sleet, followed, which prevented a further examination of this part of the coast. From nearly this
position Lieutenant Wilkes says, "On the 7th
(February, 1840) we had much better weather,
and continued all day running along the perpendicular icy barrier, about one hundred and fifty feet

* Voyage au Pole Sud, tome viii. p. 177.

high. Beyond it the outline of high land could
be well distinguished. At 6 P.M. we suddenly
found the barrier trending to the southward, and
the sea studded with icebergs. I now hauled off
until daylight, in order to ascertain the trending of
the land more exactly. I place this point, which I
have named Cape Carr, after the first lieutenant of
the Vincennes, in long. 131° 40′ E., lat. 64° 49′ S."*

There can therefore be no doubt that it really
was land Balleny saw; and which will probably
prove to be a continuation of D'Urville's Terre
Adelie, discovered by him on the 19th of January,
and approached so near on the 21st as to enable
some of his officers to land on a small islet off its
shores. This land was seen by Lieutenant Wilkes
just a week afterwards, but he was then uncon-
scious of its having been previously visited by the
French navigator.

" Appearance of land " is mentioned again in the
Log of the Eliza Scott on the 2d of March, when in
lat. 65° S., and long. 122° 44′ E., and the last point
where Balleny saw land with certainty is thus recorded in the Log.

" March 3.—At 4 A.M. found the ice so close, and
getting more compact, we tacked in hopes of getting
between it and the land; but the weather was so
thick we soon lost sight of it. At 8 it cleared off:
found ourselves surrounded by icebergs of immense
size, and to the S. W. the ice was completely fast, and

* Narrative of United States Exploring Expedition, vol. ii.
p. 321.

every appearance of land at the back of it, but no getting through the ice to it; we were obliged to steer to the N. by E. along the edge of the pack. Another proof of its being land was the fact of the rapid increase of the variation, which on this day was 44° 11′ W. At noon we were in latitude by observation 65° 10′ S., and longitude by account 118° 30′ E."

The vessel had run fifteen miles to the northward since 8 A. M., and was therefore in lat. 65° 25′ S., when they saw the land to the southward. It was named Sabrina Land, after the cutter which accompanied the Eliza Scott throughout this bold and hazardous cruize.

According to Lieutenant Wilkes's chart, the Vincennes must have passed this land, in nearly the same latitude as Balleny did, during the night of the 10th, or the thick snowy weather of the following day, and without seeing it, as no mention is made of it in the narrative. I suppose, therefore, he has placed it on his chart on the authority of Balleny, but under a different name. He has called it " Totten's high land."

I have inserted these several extracts with the view to do justice to the exertions and courage of Captain Balleny and his companions, and to prevent their being deprived of their due share in the honour of a discovery, for the priority of which the Americans and French are contending with each other, and to which, should this land eventually prove to be a continent extending to Kemp and Enderby

Land, as they suppose, it follows that neither of them have the smallest claim whatever ; although equal praise is due to them for their exertions and perseverance as if they had really been the discoverers, for at that time they could not have known that Balleny had been there the year before them.

There do not appear to me sufficient grounds to justify the assertion that the various patches of land recently discovered by the American, French, and English navigators on the verge of the Antarctic Circle unite to form a great southern continent. The continuity of the largest of these " Terre Adelie" of M. D'Urville has not been traced more than three hundred miles, Enderby's Land not exceeding two hundred miles : the others being mostly of inconsiderable extent, of somewhat uncertain determination, and with wide channels between them, would lead rather to the conclusion that they form a chain of islands.   Let each nation therefore be contented with its due share, and lay claim only to the discovery of those portions which they were the first to behold.   But if future navigators should prove those conjectures about a continent to be correct, then the discoveries of Biscoe in the brig Tula in January 1831, and those of Balleny in 1839, to which I have so fully referred, will set at rest all dispute as to which nation the honour justly belongs of the priority of discovery of any such continent between the meridians of 47° and 163° of east

1841.   longitude, and those of our immortal Cook in the meridian of 107° W., in January, 1774; for I confidently believe with M. D'Urville, that the enormous mass of ice which bounded his view when at his extreme south latitude was a range of mountainous land covered with snow.*

March 4.   But to resume our narrative. As soon as our damages were repaired, we made all sail to the N. E., on account of the wind having increased to a gale from E. S. E., placing our ships in a very critical situation; for on the chart which Lieutenant Wilkes was so good as to send me of the discoveries of the expedition under his command, entitled a " Tracing of the Icy Barrier attached to the Antarctic Continent discovered by the United States Exploring Expedition," is laid down a range of mountainous land extending about sixty miles in a S. W. and N. E. direction; its centre being in lat. 65° 40′, and long. 165° E., with the eastern extreme of the barrier in 167½° E., and thus presenting a formidable lee shore in our present position. We were therefore in a state of considerable anxiety and uncertainty for some hours as to whether the ships could weather the land and barrier. We pressed all the canvass on them they could bear, but lost much ground in the frequent necessity that occurred to bear away to leeward of the numerous icebergs we met with during the thick weather which prevailed. In the evening we

* Voyage au Sud Pole, tome ii. p. 7.

recrossed the Antarctic Circle, having been to the southward of it since the 1st of January, a period of sixty-three days.

As night advanced, the cry of the penguin was heard above the storm, which, added to the increasing quantity of heavy loose ice we met with, contributed to increase our apprehensions of dropping down upon the land or barrier under our lee, although we have frequently met with these birds at several hundreds of miles from any known land.

The extreme darkness of the night, and the thick weather preventing our seeing to any distance before us, kept all hands in a state of anxious vigilance throughout the continuance of the gale. Fortunately it began to moderate, and shifted to the southward before midnight, and the weather became so much clearer, that we could see bergs or loose ice in time to avoid them without difficulty; and thus relieved of all our anxieties, we kept under easy sail until daylight. The barometer, which had been so low as 28·4 inches, as usual gave notice of the approach of this favourable change of weather; and when day broke it was a very fine morning. We were now desirous of sighting the land which had been the occasion of so March 5. much fatigue and uneasiness to us during the stormy night we had passed, and our course was shaped accordingly.

By observations at noon we found ourselves in latitude 65° 34′ S., and longitude 167° 40′ E., and

therefore as nearly as possible in the latitude, and
between forty and fifty miles distant from the N. E.
extreme of Lieutenant Wilkes's land : we were also
twenty-two miles to the northward of our reckoning;
but I ascribe this error less to the effects of a current
than to the uncertainty of our reckoning, occasioned
chiefly by running to leeward of the many bergs
we had to avoid during the gale. In our dull sailing
vessels we dared not attempt to weather the bergs
during a fog, for if they were close enough to
be seen, we had no chance of passing them to windward ; and from the great strength of our ships,
we did not apprehend any damage from the streams
of fragments that are almost invariably found
under their lee; but in vessels not so well prepared
to encounter ice, it is always the safest plan to pass
to windward of the bergs when practicable.

We had a moderate breeze from the eastward,
and a beautifully clear day, so that land of any
great elevation might have been seen at a distance
of sixty or seventy miles. As we advanced on
our course in eager expectation of "making the
land," our surprise and disappointment may be
imagined when no indications of it were to be seen
at sunset, although we were not more than twelve
or thirteen miles from its eastern extreme, as laid
down on Lieutenant Wilkes's chart; and we began
to suspect that from having had but little experience of the delusive appearances in these icy
regions, he had mistaken for land some of the
dense well-defined clouds which so continually

hang over extensive packs of ice,—a mistake which
we had ourselves, on many occasions, to guard
against, when appearances were so strong, for
several days in succession, that few in either ship
could be persuaded that it was not really land until
we actually sailed over the spot. It being a fine
moonlight night, we continued our course, with a
light easterly wind, and before midnight gained
the position of the eastern point of the supposed
land, and shaped our course to the S.W. under
moderate sail, along the mountain range.

At day-break, as we had a most extensive view
in every direction, the sky and horizon being perfectly clear, the mast-heads of both ships were
crowded with officers and men anxious to get the
first glimpse of the anticipated shores, but neither
mountains nor barrier were to be seen.

An "appearance of land" was, indeed, reported
to me by Lieutenant Sibbald, the officer of the
forenoon watch, at 10 A.M., but it was so feeble
when I went to the mast-head, that I was quite
unable to distinguish any thing but a dark misty
appearance. It is inserted by him in the log-book
as bearing from S.S.W. to S.W. by W., and being
in the exact direction of Balleny Islands, which
had been seen by us on the morning of the 4th,
it is by no means impossible that he was right,
although they must have been at a distance of
between seventy and eighty miles. There is no
mention of any appearance of land in the log-
book of the Terror.

T 4

At noon our observations placed us in lat. 64° 51′ S., long. 164° 45′ E., dip 83° 30′, variation 29° E. We were therefore very nearly in the centre of the mountainous patch of land laid down in Lieutenant Wilkes's chart as forming a part of the " antarctic continent."

The wind soon after this time falling light, we rounded to and tried for soundings, but could not reach the bottom with six hundred fathoms of line, beyond which we could not determine with any degree of certainty, on account of the ship having considerable drift. The temperature at that depth was 37°·2, that of the surface 29°·2, and that of the air having risen to 31°, felt quite warm to us. It was indeed a perfect Mediterranean day, and the remainder of it was passed in continuing our search after the supposed land, steering a course now more to the westward, and then north-west, until darkness put an end to our search.

At 10 P. M. the wind increased from the northeast, with the appearance of thick weather, dense clouds rising quickly in that direction; our topsails were double-reefed, and sail otherwise reduced so as to admit of the ship being more easily managed by the watch, in case of suddenly meeting with any quantity of loose ice, of which a brightness in sky to the westward gave us reason to suspect the presence in that quarter. We had seen sufficiently far before dark to remove any idea of finding land, but as pack ice can never be seen more than ten or twelve miles from the mast-head, we

were obliged throughout the darkness of night to
proceed at a slow pace, steering to the north-
west.

Early in the morning, whilst running before a
strong easterly breeze, we found ourselves embayed
in a deep bight of the pack, which was seen stretching across our bows, as far as the true north. We
were also at this time much hampered by extensive
fields of pancake ice, which at this period of the
season always form near the margin of a pack; we
immediately hauled to the wind, but had great
difficulty in extricating the ships, although still
favoured by a fresh breeze.

At noon we were in lat. 65° 31′ S., long. 162° 9′ E.,
and again in clear water, but it soon after fell quite
calm, and the heavy easterly swell was driving us
down again upon the pack, in which were counted
from the mast-head eighty-four large bergs, between S. and N. N. W., and some hundreds of
smaller dimensions.

We found we were fast closing this chain of
bergs, so closely packed together that we could
distinguish no opening through which the ships
could pass, the waves breaking violently against
them, dashing huge masses of pack ice against the
precipitous faces of the bergs; now lifting them
nearly to their summit, then forcing them again
far beneath their water-line, and sometimes rend-
ing them into a multitude of brilliant fragments
against their projecting points.

Sublime and magnificent as such a scene must

have appeared under different circumstances, to us it was awful, if not appalling. For eight hours we had been gradually drifting towards what to human eyes appeared inevitable destruction: the high waves and deep rolling of our ships rendered towing with the boats impossible, and our situation the more painful and embarrassing from our inability to make any effort to avoid the dreadful calamity that seemed to await us.

In moments like these comfort and peace of mind could only be obtained by casting our cares upon that Almighty Power which had already so often interposed to save us when human skill was wholly unavailing. Convinced that he is under the protection and guidance of a merciful God, the Christian awaits the issue of events firm and undismayed, and with calm resignation prepares for whatever He may order. His serenity of mind surprises and strengthens, but never forsakes him; and thus, possessing his soul in peace, he can with the greater advantage watch every change of circumstance that may present itself as a means of escape.

We were now within half a mile of the range of bergs. The roar of the surf, which extended each way as far as we could see, and the crashing of the ice, fell upon the ear with fearful distinctness, whilst the frequently averted eye as immediately returned to contemplate the awful destruction that threatened in one short hour to close the world and all its hopes and joys and sorrows upon us for ever. In this our deep distress " we called upon the Lord,

and He heard our voices out of His temple, and
our cry came before Him."

A gentle air of wind filled our sails; hope again
revived, and the greatest activity prevailed to
make the best use of the feeble breeze: as it gradually freshened, our heavy ships began to feel
its influence, slowly at first, but more rapidly
afterwards; and before dark we found ourselves
far removed from every danger. "O Lord our
God, how great are the wondrous works Thou hast
done; like as be also Thy thoughts, which are to
us-ward! If I should declare them and speak of
them, they should be more than I am able to
express."*

After a day of such fatiguing anxiety we passed
a peaceful night, running to the westward under
moderate sail, favoured by a fresh south-east breeze
and the bright light of the full moon, increased at
times by brilliant exhibitions of the Aurora Australis.

Approaching the main pack early in the morning
to resume its examination, we had to make our
way through extensive fields of pancake ice, too
tough to be penetrated except by the assistance of
the strong breeze that aided us. Our course along
the edge of the pack was governed by the direction
it took, and which led us much more to the northward than we wished; but any attempt to penetrate
to the westward would have been quite in vain,

March 8

* Psalm xl. 6, 7.

and sometimes in the course of this examination, when having during thick snowy weather got into some of the deeper indentations of the pack, we were compelled to run back to the eastward. A halo was seen round the sun at 9 15 A. M. with a parhelion on each side, at a distance of 23° 16′, the altitude of the sun's centre being 24° 30′.

At noon in lat. 64° 39′ S., long. 162° 47′ E., we had no soundings with six hundred fathoms of line; the temperature of the sea was taken at that and several intermediate depths below the surface, as was also the specific gravity of the water brought up from those depths.

In the afternoon the wind veered to the northward, and the snow which had been falling at times during the day was by the immediate increase of temperature turned into rain; to us a very agreeable indication of our having reached a milder climate.

As our proximity to the pack prevented our making any progress to the westward with a northerly wind, I took advantage of the opportunity of stretching to the eastward; as by this measure we not only extended our researches for land, but got into a space more free from bergs and loose ice, and therefore during the continuance of such unfavourable weather were in a situation of comparative safety.

March 9.   By noon the next day we were in lat. 64° 20′ S., and long. 164° 20′ E., and therefore about seventy miles north of the land laid down by Lieutenant Wilkes, and not far from the spot from which he must have supposed he saw it; but having now searched for it at a distance varying from fifty to seventy miles from it to the north, south, east, and west, as well as having sailed directly over its assigned position, we were compelled to infer that it has no real existence.

I have entered thus minutely into the details of our search for this land as recorded in my journal at the time, and in accordance with the report I made to the Lords Commissioners of the Admiralty on the subject immediately after my return to Van Diemen's Land.

It becomes my duty now in justice to Lieutenant Wilkes to give his explanation of the circumstances which led to his placing this range of mountains on the chart of his discoveries which he sent to me; as also to repel the assertion he has made, that we had sailed over land said to have been discovered by our own countryman, Balleny; although it cannot but be a matter of surprise that after so much discussion, and by no means a very temperate one, he has not entered upon the question, nor in any way alluded to the discoveries of Balleny in the Narrative of the United States Exploring Expedition, which has been published by the American government under his direction, but has merely removed the land from his chart of the antarctic continent, with no other notice of it than that " Lieutenant-Commandant Ringgold thought he could discern to the south-east something like distant mountains," and which I should have believed had been

the authority upon which Lieutenant Wilkes had
originally placed the land on his chart, had he not
asserted to the contrary; because Lieutenant Ringgold in his report to his Commodore, as quoted by
him in his defence at the court-martial, states, that
" very lofty ridges of ice, and the loom usual over
high land, were visible along the southern horizon
over the barrier;" and he adds in evidence, "I
made no positive report that it was, nor mentioned
in the log, because I was not positive that it was
land, though I have very little doubt about it."*
And this assertion was made after he knew we had
sailed over the spot.   But Lieutenant Wilkes dis-
avows this discovery of Lieutenant Ringgold, and
states in his "Synopsis of the Cruise of the United
States Exploring Expedition," delivered by him
before the National Institute, on his return to
America in 1842, p. 21—"During our cruise, as
we sailed along the icy barrier, I prepared a chart,
laying down the land, not only where we had
actually determined it to exist, but those places in
which every appearance denoted its existence,
forming almost a continuous line from 160° to
97° East longitude, I had a tracing-copy made of this
chart, on which was laid down the land supposed to
have been seen by Bellamy [Balleny], in 165° E.,
which, with my notes, experience, &c. &c., was forwarded to Captain Ross through Sir George Gipps
at Sydney, and I was afterwards informed was

* Defence of Lieut. Charles Wilkes, p. 28.

received by Captain Ross on his arrival in Hobart Town, some months previous to his going south."

The first few lines of this passage would have afforded me another proof that the land on Wilkes's chart was that seen by Lieutenant Ringgold, being precisely in that position, and certainly not near that seen by Balleny. The letter and an exact copy of his tracing will be found in the Appendix. On this chart I have placed Balleny Islands in their proper position, in order to show how impossible it must have appeared to me that Ringgold's Mountains could ever have been intended for them; and the track of our ships along the range of mountains; and these are the only additions or alterations I have made.*

Again, p. 26, he observes, "As I before remarked, on my original chart I had laid down the supposed position of Bellamy Islands or land in 164° and 165° East longitude, and that it was traced off, and sent to Captain Ross. I am not a little surprised that so intelligent a navigator as Captain Ross, on finding that he had run over this position, should not have closely enquired into the statements relative to our discoveries that had been published in the Sydney and Hobart Town papers, which he must have seen, and have induced him to make a careful examination of the tracks of the squadron, laid down on the chart sent him, by which he would have assured himself in a few

---

* The originals are deposited in the Hydrographic department of the Admiralty, and may be readily referred to.

1841.

moments that it had never been laid down or claimed as part of our discovery, before he made so bold* an assertion to an American officer, that he had run over a clear ocean where I had laid down land; and I am not less surprised that that officer should have taken it for granted, without examination, that such was the fact."

These two extracts contain all the explanation that I have seen, except a letter addressed to the editors of the " Spectator," in reply to that of Captain J. H. Aulick, the American officer above alluded to. I had the pleasure of meeting him at New Zealand, and, in justice to him, I consider it proper to insert the following extract from his letter. After quoting the above paragraph from Lieutenant Wilkes's Synopsis, he says, " From the above statement, and in the absence of any explanation, it might well be inferred that both Ross and myself must be, to say the least, very shortsighted and dull of comprehension, not to have been able to see that it was Bellamy's (Balleny's) and not Wilkes's land that he (Ross) had run over.   But in the statement above quoted, Mr. Wilkes has done us injustice, by omitting to mention one very important fact in this connexion, namely, that in laying down the land of Balleny on the chart he sent Captain Ross, *he neglected to affix thereto the name of its discoverer*, or to distinguish it in any way from his own land, there traced out, and almost connected with it.   He also

* He elsewhere calls it an *unfounded* statement: p. 18.

sent Captain Ross a letter with his chart; but
unfortunately the name of Balleny or his land is
neither mentioned nor even hinted at in this letter.*
In short, no intimation in any manner whatever
was given Ross by Lieutenant Wilkes *that he did
not claim the discovery* of *all the land* marked on
his chart; and to this cause alone is to be ascribed
the error into which Captain Ross was, I think,
unavoidably led.

"Mr. Wilkes says Ross ought to have examined
the accounts of his discoveries published in the
Sydney and Hobart Town papers, before he made
so bold an assertion to an American officer. But,
with such evidence as the chart and letter of Mr.
Wilkes in his hands, I apprehend it could hardly
have been seriously expected that he should search
the newspaper accounts (which probably he never
saw) for other or better information on the
subject.

"On my visit to Captain Ross on board the
Erebus, he spread this chart before me in the presence of Captain Crozier and two of my own officers.
It was distinctly drawn out on tracing paper; the
whole appearing to be, so far as I observed, one
connected operation, representing nothing but the
result of his own (Wilkes's) explorations. Ross,
believing it to be such, had transcribed it at length
on his chart, which he also placed before us†,

* See Appendix.
† Upon which Balleny Islands were laid down in the posi-

and pointed out the tracks of his vessels marked on it in red ink, and *passing directly over the spot assigned to the land;* which we all considered as laid down by Lieutenant Wilkes to represent the north-eastern limit of his supposed antarctic continent, and where he (Ross) said they had a clear sea as far as the eye could reach. Such was the evidence on which my belief of his report was founded. To my mind it was conclusive, and I cheerfully leave it to the judgment of others to determine whether or not, under all the circumstances here stated, it be just cause of 'surprise' that Captain Ross should have boldly asserted that he had run over a clear ocean where Lieutenant Wilkes had laid down the land; and that I should have taken it for granted, *without further examination*, that such was the fact.

"In making this statement, I can say, with perfect sincerity, I am actuated by no unkindness of feeling towards Mr. Wilkes; but, fully persuaded as I am that the erroneous statement for which he publicly censures Captain Ross, and shows a little temper towards me, was the result of his own negligence alone, I considered it due to that distinguished navigator, as well as to myself, that the matter should be publicly explained.

(Signed)   "J. H. Aulick."

I cannot sufficiently express my thankfulness to Captain Aulick for his honourable and generous

tion assigned by the discoverer, and the date of their discovery, 1839.

defence of my conduct during my absence; and I
have quoted thus largely from this letter because
his very clear and candid testimony gives so much
weight to the few additional remarks which I must
here make, in order to show that I did not make
any "erroneous statement" whatever. I must first
refer to the only passage that bears on the subject
in Mr. Wilkes's answer to the above letter.*

He says, " On my arrival at Sydney from the
antarctic cruise, I was introduced to Captain Biscoe,
the discoverer of Enderby Land, and believe he
gave me the first information of the English discovery, and its position, which I placed on my
chart, marking it 'English Discovery.' My impression is, that the copy which I ordered to be
made (from my own original) was a perfect one;
and on the original chart the English discovery is
detached and separate from ours, and stands alone.
At the time I sent my letter to Captain Ross, I
did not know the English discoverer's name; but
whether the English discovery was so marked or
not, is of but little consequence, for Captain Ross
knew of Balleny's discovery before he left England,
and therefore must have seen at once the latitude
and longitude to be identically the same with those
of Balleny; and I am satisfied the only erroneous
conclusion Captain Ross could have been led into
by it was, that I had verified Balleny's discovery."

In the tracing copy of his original chart, which

---

* Both letters are printed in full in the Appendix.

Lieutenant Wilkes sent me, the whole of the land, as stated in Captain Aulick's letter, "was drawn out as one connected operation, representing nothing but the result of his (Wilkes's) own exploration."

There was no land laid down where Balleny had discovered it; nor could I ever have supposed he had verified that navigator's discovery, because I could perceive by his track that he was never within one hundred miles of it.

The several passages which I have quoted from the writings of Lieutenant Wilkes might lead some to the impression that, from want of proper consideration, or of common sense, or from feelings of rivalry or jealousy, I had endeavoured to injure the reputation of a distinguished officer, and to underrate his valuable labours. But, conscious of having taken every pains to arrive at a just conclusion, before I asserted that we had sailed over some land which, to all appearance, was laid down on his chart as his discovery, I must detain my readers for a few minutes in order to explain distinctly the grounds of that conclusion; so that all may have an opportunity of judging of the groundlessness of the imputation, and that I may fully exonerate myself not only in the eyes of my brother officers of the American and British navies, but of all who have taken an interest in the question. In addition to the statement of facts made by Captain Aulick, to which I must be permitted especially now to refer, there are only three points with which he could not have been acquainted when he replied to Lieutenant Wilkes, to which I need advert; namely—

1. The true position of Balleny Islands, as given by Balleny himself.
2. Lieutenant Wilkes's knowledge of their true position.
3. That the land in question was not laid down in that position, and therefore could not possibly have been meant for it.

These three points will be discussed under one general head. Lieutenant Wilkes in his last quoted letter states that "Captain Ross knew of Balleny's discovery before he left England, and must have seen at once the latitude and longitude were identically the same with those of Balleny." Had the latitude and longitude of the land on his chart been, as he states, identically, or even nearly the same with those of Balleny Islands, I should feel that the blame of making an "*unfounded*" statement would justly rest upon me for not having detected their identity. But this statement of Lieutenant Wilkes, made so long afterwards, when he must have been fully aware of the real position of Balleny Islands, shows that he confuses two distinct portions of land. He is alluding to that which he says he marked in his original chart as " English discovery," and of course in the position Balleny assigned to it; but this land he did not put upon the tracing he sent to me. The land that we sailed over is laid down upon his chart at least seventy miles from them, and is exactly in

1841.

the position of the mountains said to have been seen by Lieutenant Ringgold; and it is therefore probable that when he became acquainted with Balleny's discovery he had some doubts of the existence of these mountains, and removed them from his original chart, but omitted to do so in the copy of it which he sent to me. This is the only way I can account for the mistake; for at the time he sent me the chart I knew that he had authentic information of the true place of the Balleny Islands; as, on my arrival at Sydney, I was told by Mr. M'Leay, the late colonial secretary, and also by his son, Mr. W. S. M'Leay, that, meeting Lieutenant Wilkes soon after his return from the antarctic cruise, they told him of Balleny's discovery. He seemed to doubt their statement; but the next day they called upon him, and placed in his hands No. 629 of the "Athenæum," published in November, 1839, and pointed out to him the account there given of the discovery: on reading which, in their presence, he exclaimed, "*Then all our labour has been in vain.*"

The following is a copy of the paragráph alluded to: — "In July, 1838, two small vessels belonging to Messrs. Enderby and other merchants sailed from London on a voyage to the South Seas, with special instructions to push as far as possible to the southward in search of land. Touching at Amsterdam Island, Chalky Bay, in New Zealand, and Campbell's Islands, the vessels proceeded to the southward, and reached their extreme south latitude 69° in 172° 11' E. longitude, full two hundred

and twenty miles further to the southward than
the point which Bellinghausen, in 1820, had been
able to reach in this meridian. *Continuing to the
westward, on February 9th* (1839), *in lat.* 66° 44′ *S.,
and long.* 163° 11′ *E., they discovered five islands,
since named Balleny Islands,* from the name of the
master of the Eliza Scott."

Now, knowing that Lieutenant Wilkes was in
possession of this exact information soon after his
arrival at Sydney, and that his chart and letter
were forwarded to me nearly a month after he had
the Athenæum in his possession, from New Zealand,
I cannot understand how he could possibly have
intended a mountainous reef of land, extending
between fifty and sixty miles in a S.W. and N.E.
direction, and placed in lat. 65° 40′ S., and long.
165° E., to represent the five small islands of Balleny, which lie in lat. 66° 44′ S., and long. 163° 11′ E.,
and which we saw on the 4th March in the position
assigned to them by their discoverer.

Nor have I since heard of or seen any statement
that could assist me in coming to a different opinion
from that I have above expressed : on the contrary,
all I have heard since, more especially the statements of Lieutenant Ringgold before the court
that tried Lieutenant Wilkes, in endeavouring to
justify their claim to the priority of discovery over
the French navigators, " that on the 13th January
(1840), when in lat. 65° 8′ S., and long. 168° E.," as
quoted in Lieutenant Wilkes's narrative * ; " from

* Vol. ii. p. 291.

the numerous sea-elephants, and the discoloration
of the water and ice, they were strongly impressed
with the idea of land being in the vicinity; but
on sounding with one hundred fathoms no bottom
could be found: Lieutenant Commandant Ringgold felt convinced, from the above circumstances
and the report that penguins were heard, that land
was near, *and thought he could discern to the south-east
something like distant mountains,*" just in the position
of the mountainous land laid down in Wilkes's chart,
over which we sailed, but not near that of Balleny
Islands, cannot but tend to confirm the conclusions
I had before arrived at; for I can hardly understand
how, professing as he does to have " prepared a
chart, laying down the land, not only where we
had actually determined it to exist, but those places
in which every appearance denoted its existence,"
could have omitted to place on such a chart the
land which Lieutenant Ringgold thought he saw,
and who has since declared himself " to have very
little doubt about it," and therefore I can have no
doubt that the land must have been placed upon
the chart on this authority, or upon none whatever.

I trust, at any rate, so far as I am concerned,
that I have clearly shown that I could not be expected to suppose,—for no one who has read these
statements can even now suppose, — that the land
marked on Lieutenant Wilkes's chart which we
sailed over in the Erebus and Terror could have
been intended to represent Balleny Islands: first,
because of its being placed at least seventy miles

from their real position; second, because it is placed
so near the tracks of the American expedition as to
have been well within sight from their ships, as
near as many other portions of their antarctic continent, and therefore would lead to the belief that
it actually was seen from them; third, from its
being included in the map of the exclusive operations of that expedition, involved in the same barrier (which also has disappeared), without any mark
to distinguish it from their other discoveries, and
that it was sent to me, together with them, to
show the extent of land that Lieutenant Wilkes
claimed as the discoveries of the expedition under
his command.

Having now fulfilled my task of exculpating
myself from any blame on this to me very painful
transaction, I leave others to judge whether the
" *unfounded*" epithet which Lieutenant Wilkes has
applied to my statement may not be applied to his
with more propriety. I have endeavoured also to
do justice to the memory of a brave and enterprising British seaman, by showing how completely
the results of our researches have verified the discovery he announced to the world, and in some
degree removed any false impression that may have
resulted from the statement which has been circu-
lated in America, that we " had sailed over land
discovered by our own countryman, and not over
any part of the antarctic continent of the American
expedition."

I cannot refrain from observing that the practice

1841.   of "laying down the land, not only where we had actually determined it to exist, but in those places also in which every appearance denoted its existence," is not only entirely new amongst navigators, but seems to me likely to occasion much confusion, and even to raise doubts in many minds whether the existence of some portions of land that undoubtedly were seen might not also be of an equally questionable character with those laid down from appearances only, unless some distinctive mark were given by which they could be known from each other.

I had never entertained the smallest doubt that *every* portion of land laid down on Lieutenant Wilkes's chart (with the exception above alluded to) had been clearly and distinctly made out to be land without the possibility of a question on the subject until I read that paragraph, and I must confess that after a very careful perusal of his narrative, and with his chart before me, I feel myself quite unable to determine in a satisfactory manner how much of the land was really seen by him with the degree of certainty that gives indisputable authority to discovery; and lest I should make any mistake on a point of so much importance, I have only placed the discoveries made by D'Urville, Balleny and ourselves in those parts on the general South Polar Chart, and must refer the reader for those made by Lieutenant Wilkes to the chart sent to me, which will be found in the Appendix, and his own narrative; and I may here further remark,

once for all, that the whole line of coast laid down
as our discovery, was really and truly seen, and its
continuity determined in such a manner as to leave
not the smallest doubt on the mind of any officer
or man of either of the ships, and that no part has
been laid down upon mere appearances or denota-
tions except in those places where it is distinctly
marked " appearance of land."

CHAPTER X.

In the instructions drawn up for my guidance by
the Committee of Physics of the Royal Society,
it is stated, that " M. Gauss, from theoretical considerations, has recently assigned a probable position in lat. 66° S. and long. 146° E. to the Southern
Magnetic Pole, denying the existence of two poles
of the same name, in either hemisphere, which, as he
justly remarks, would entail the necessity of admitting also a third point, having the chief character-
istics of such a pole intermediate between them;"
and again, " it is not improbable that the point indicated by M. Gauss will prove accessible; at all events
it cannot but be approachable sufficiently near to
test by the convergence of meridians the truth of the
indication ; and as his theory gives within very moderate limits of error the true place of the northern
pole, and otherwise represents the magnetic elements in every explored region with considerable
approximation, it is but reasonable to recommend
this as a distinct point to be decided;" and although our researches had proved that the result of
M. Gauss's theoretical considerations was not so
correct with respect to the situation of the South
as it was to that of the North Magnetic Pole, probably owing to the want of a sufficient number of
trustworthy observations from which to draw his

1841.
March 9.

deductions; and although we knew the true position of the South Magnetic Pole to be nearly in 76° instead of 66° S., yet as observations at the point indicated by M. Gauss might prove to be of more than ordinary magnetic interest, I determined to devote a few days to endeavour to approach it as nearly as possible, although, from the very late period of the season, I could not entertain the smallest hope of attaining to the spot itself; nor was it of so much importance to do so now, as both the American and French expeditions had at a more favourable period of the season made magnetic observations in its neighbourhood, concurring to show that the Magnetic Pole is situated much further south than he had supposed.

The wind was blowing so strong from the northward, with a high sea running, that we could hardly maintain our ground; we had constant snow and thick weather, but were fortunately in a space more clear of bergs and loose ice than usual, so that we felt ourselves to be in a position of comparative comfort and security, at noon we were in lat. 64° 20′ S., long. 164° 24′ E.

In the afternoon a shoal of porpoises, several white and many blue petrels and Cape pigeons were seen, as were also two whales. The snow ceased, the weather became clear, and as we approached the pack a strong blink indicated its position before March 10. dark; but we stood on through the night until 3·30 A.M., when, meeting with broad streams of ice, consisting of very heavy pieces, and many bergs, we wore and stood off again, our object now being merely to contend, as well as our dull sailing ships could do against the adverse wind which continued to blow with considerable violence the whole day, during which we passed many bergs, much worn away by the long continued action of the waves, and in consequence presenting more variety of figure than any we had before met with in the southern ocean: with the thermometer very little below the freezing point, we greatly enjoyed the high temperature of a milder climate, notwithstanding the occasional showers of snow that fell during the day. At 3 P.M. we again wore, and stood to the S.W., expecting the wind from that quarter, the barometer, at the same time, indicating the approach of fine weather. But still the westerly swell prevented our making any considerable progress, and the whole of the next four days was spent struggling with but small effect against the strong westerly and south-westerly wind that prevailed, taking advantage of every slight change of wind to attain our object, and occasionally getting sight of the main pack when we stretched to the southward of the 64th degree of latitude.

At noon the 14th, we were lat. 62° 42′, long. March 14. 156° 51′ E. The mercury in the barometer at that time had attained the unusual height, for these latitudes, of 29·5 inches, at which it stood steadily until midnight, (the wind then shifting to the north, accompanied by a very thick fog,) when it again fell, as rapidly as it had risen, until at noon the following day it had reached 28·8 inches. We had so often before this time experienced such sudden oscillations of the barometer, that we were in consequence prepared to expect the sudden and violent squall which, however, came on so furiously as hardly to afford us sufficient time to close reef our top-sails, and furl all the other sails. It was of only four or five hours' duration, and had the good effect of driving off the fog. We had for several days seen only a very few bergs; a circumstance that surprised us greatly, as great numbers were met with in these parts by the American expedition during the preceding summer. They must have either been destroyed by the violence of the winter storms, or drifted away to the northward without their places having been supplied by others from the southern lands. It was a comfortable circumstance for us, and rendered the service less hazardous and anxious than it otherwise would have been, for had we found them here in any considerable numbers during the long dark nights that now prevailed, with a constant succession of storms and foggy weather, it would have been utterly impracticable to have persevered in the navigation, and have obliged us to relinquish our present object. We made sail as the wind gradually abated; but it had raised a high, short, irregular sea, in which the ships rolled and pitched uneasily: with difficulty we kept their heads in the right direction until 8 P.M., when it fell perfectly calm, and the

swell took complete command of them, carrying 1841.
us away, during the whole night, upon a course
directly opposite to that we wished to go.

At four the next morning we had a light wind March 16.
from the north-eastward, which gradually freshened
to a pleasant breeze, veering to the southward as it
increased in strength; once more we had all studding sails set, running to the westward, but not
within sight of the pack, although a strong blink
to the southward clearly indicated that it was at
no great distance in that direction: we passed
many straggling pieces of ice, and several bergs,
but they were by no means numerous; and at noon
were in lat. 64° 14′ S., long. 154° 40′ E.   Again, as
on the previous evening, we had a calm from eight March 17.
o'clock until four the next morning, the breeze
following the same course as yesterday, beginning
in the north-east, veering to the south-eastward
about noon, and declining to a light south-westerly
wind at midnight.   We sailed through a great
quantity of young ice as we closed the pack, and at
length it became so thick, where there was much
heavy ice amongst it, that we could not get within
two or three miles of the pack edge, and
owing to the heavy swell, and difficulty of steering
amongst the ice in which the ships were involved,
they received some very heavy blows, but fortunately without doing any other injury than removing some of the copper: the pack presented much
the same appearance as that we had sailed along in
our way from Cape North of Victoria Land to

Balleny Islands; for although at a distance it seemed to be a compact solid-looking mass, still on closer inspection we could make out that it also was composed of heavy loose pieces, amongst which the undulations of the ocean could be perceived, as far as we could discern from the mast-head; and the rolling motion of the larger pieces clearly showed that the frost had not yet been sufficiently severe to perfectly bind them together into an unbroken field: we continued to run to the westward, as close along the edge of the pack as the strong pancake ice permitted, until dark, when we hauled off into clearer water for the night. The Aurora Australis was seen for about a quarter of an hour, about 11 P. M. bearing west by compass, shooting up bright coruscations to the altitude of forty-five degrees: in some parts it appeared in a diffused light along the edges of the clouds.

March 18. Being calm at noon, when in lat. 63° 51′ S., long. 151° 47′ E., we tried for soundings, but could not reach the ground with six hundred fathoms. The temperature at that depth, 39·2; at 450 fathoms 38·5; at 300 fathoms 37·5; at 150 fathoms, 35·5; at the surface 30·4; and the specific gravity of the water throughout 1·0272 at the temperature of the freezing point. With a moderate breeze from the north-east, we made good way to the westward during the afternoon and evening; and although it became thick with snow towards midnight, we continued our course through the night under moderate sail, and by keeping a vigilant look-out

avoided the bergs and heavy ice we were sailing
amongst.

As we were now approaching the meridian of
the pole indicated by M. Gauss's theory, although
in a somewhat lower latitude, such magnetic
observations as depended not on the weather were
made in uninterrupted succession, and the variation of the compass was observed whenever
the sun was to be seen between the clouds
which covered the sky nearly the whole day. At
noon we were in lat. 64° 20′ S., long. 148° 45′ E.,
dip 84° 27′ S., var. 15° 45′ E.: standing to the
S. W. under all sail, direct for the point we were
seeking, we made the heavy pack edge at 8 P.M.,
and bore away along it to the westward, through
streams of young ice and loose pieces from the
pack; the sky was overcast, but there was sufficient light from the moon to enable us to run
without hazard during the night.

At seven the next morning, when in lat. 65°   March 20.
15′ S., and long. 144° 53′ E., and therefore only
forty-five miles north of the spot, our observations gave a dip of 85° 5′, but the variation
could not be observed, owing to the clouded
state of the sky, between the evening of the 19th,
when in lat. 64° 24′, and long. 148° 27′ E.,
it amounted to 16° 41′ E., and the evening
of the 20th, in lat. 65° 4′, and long. 142° 49′,
when it was 12° 37′ E.; the main pack prevented
our nearer approach to the interesting point, but
our observations perfectly corroborate those we

made in the highest southern latitudes, as to the real position of the magnetic pole, although we were here about six hundred miles from it, and will therefore not have been made in vain: they differ, however, more than I expected from those obtained by Lieutenant Wilkes the preceding summer, making due allowance for the difference of our geographical positions; thus, in lat. 67° 4′, long. 147° 30′ E., his observed dip amounted to 87° 30′; whilst ours, in nearly the same meridian, 147° 15′ E., and in latitude 64° 56′, was only 85° 3′, being at least a degree of difference greater than our distance apart would justify. In his letter to me it had been first written 86° 30′, and then altered to 87° 30′, so that I may be mistaken which he meant it to be, especially as 86° 30′ would be a very near accordance with our observations. I have not been able to ascertain the dip observed by the French Expedition at this spot.

One only object now remained for us to accomplish before seeking a milder and more congenial climate: on our voyage between Kerguelen Island and Van Diemen's Land, we had crossed the line of no variation in latitude 46° S., and longitude 134° 30′ E.*; it appeared to me desirable to ascertain its situation in as high a latitude as circumstances admitted, and to recross it in our way to Hobart Town in an intermediate latitude, and by thus determining its place at three distinct and nearly

* See page 104. of this Volume.

equidistant points, the nature of the curve by which
it reaches the magnetic pole might be computed.
As we found the easterly variation to be diminishing rapidly, we might expect, if favoured by circumstances of wind and weather, to accomplish our
purpose without any very considerable expense of
time : and as our crews continued to enjoy the same
good health they had preserved during the whole of
the severe season of antarctic navigation, I felt the
less hesitation in prolonging their labours in these
latitudes a few days longer for so important a purpose.

A fresh south-easterly breeze favoured our
wishes, and we had a good run to the westward
before the darkness of night compelled us to reduce
our speed as we sailed along the margin of the
main pack.

At daylight we again made all sail, but the
wind had shifted to the S.W., so that we could not
maintain so high a latitude as we desired; at
noon we were in lat. 64° 7′, and long. 140° 22′ E.,
in which position we could not get soundings
with six hundred fathoms of line; the temperature at 600 fathoms was 38·7 ; at 450 fathoms 38; at 300 fathoms 36·5 ; at 150 fathoms
34; at the surface 30·8; that of the air 27°.
Many large icebergs were passed during the
day; penguins, cape pigeons, and the blue petrel
were about us in great numbers, and a large shoal
of porpoises was seen going to the westward.

March 21.

1841.

Observations of the Dip and Variation, made on board H.M.S. Erebus, between the 18th of March and 6th of April, 1841.

Date.	Position.		Dip S.	Variation.	· Remarks.
	Lat. S.	Long. E.			
Mar. 18	63·52	151·50	84·06	— 20·15	The sign · — de-
19	64·16	149·15	84·20	— 16·40	notes easterly,
20	64·56	147·14	85·03	—	and + de-
	65·15	144·53	85·05	—	notes westerly
	65·04	142·46	—	— 12·37	variation.
21	64·26	140·46	84·55	— 6·57	
22	63·20	139·43	84·05	— 5·58	
	62·42	138·20	84·00	— 4·05	
23	62·20	136·26	83·45	— 1·12	
	62·06	136·07	83·30	— 0·27	
					Cross line of no
25	60·23	131·38	83·10	+ 8·09	variation.
26	59·10	130·00	82·36	+ 8·32	
28	57·20	127·49	81·45	+ 8·47	
29	56·16	130·46	81·00	+ 5·46	
30	55·10	131·30	80·20	+ 1·34	
	55·07	132·40	80·00	+ 1·05	
					Re-cross line of
31	54·05	134·30	79·30	— 1·44	no variation.
Apr. 1	52·56	135·24	78·50	— 1·03	Anomalous ob-
2	51·12	136·55	77·40	— 4·39	servation.
5	44·52	143·38	73·20	— 6·00	
6	44·06	145·42	71·40	— 10·06	

The above table of Magnetic Observations is inserted here to show how rapidly the easterly variation diminished, until we crossed the line of no variation during the night of the 23d, in latitude 62° 0′ S., and longitude 135° 50′ E. ; thence how quickly the westerly variation increased until the 28th, when in lat. 57° 20′ and long. 127° 49′ E., it amounted to 8° 47′ W. ; and again, how regularly it dimi-

nished until we recrossed the line of no variation
in lat. 54° 30′ S., and long. 133° 0′ E.

The Aurora Australis was seen at 2 A.M., a broad
band of yellowish light in the north-east. It was
again visible at night from nine till near midnight,
bearing from N.W. to E. (magnetic), at an altitude
of ten degrees, shooting long narrow streamers of
colourless light towards the zenith. In the course
of the day we passed several bergs of large size;
and in the evening we were fortunate in getting
good azimuth by means of Sirius and Procyon, by
which we found the variation had decreased to
4° 5′ E.

Pursuing our course to the N.W. with a favouring
breeze, our latitude at noon was 62° 12′, longitude
136° 18′; and late in the evening we crossed the
line of no variation in latitude 62° 0′ S., and longitude 135° 50′ E. At 7° 20′ P.M. observed a bright
arch of the Aurora Australis, W.N.W. and E.S.E.,
extending across the zenith, of a yellow colour, its
edges tinged with a purple hue: in a quarter of
an hour the centre of the arch gradually declined
to the N.N.E., and disappeared ten degrees above
the horizon: a succession of similar arches formed
at an altitude of about ten degrees in the S.S.W.,
their extreme points being also W.N.W. and E.S.E.;
the centre of each arch gradually rose towards the
zenith, which several of them passed before they
disappeared; but generally they became more
faint at the altitude of 45°, no longer preserved a
regular form, but broke up into small streamers,

1841.　and disappeared on reaching an altitude of 70°, the lustre of the larger stars was much dimmed as it passed over them, but they could be distinctly seen through it; some of the smaller stars were totally obscured by the brighter and denser portions of the Aurora; this splendid display was, as usual, followed by a fall of snow, and bright diffused auroral light illumined the edges of the clouds from which the snow fell.

March 24.　Still running to the north-west to increase the westerly variation, we were unfortunate in not obtaining observations; throughout the day it blew a strong gale of wind from the eastward, with thick falling snow, so that we could seldom see a distance of half a mile before us, and most providentially we did not meet with any bergs. The barometer fell rapidly, and at 10 P.M. stood at 28·33 inches; the gale at that time had considerably abated, and the wind shifted to the north; the snow had given place to a thin mist, slightly lighted up by the Aurora, which only occasionally peeped through in obscure patches, but afforded us as much light as would the moon at quadrature, and which was to us of great advantage.

March 25.　At 4 A.M. two icebergs were seen directly ahead of us, but fortunately we had time to avoid them; three others were seen soon afterwards, when the weather was clearer: being becalmed at noon, in lat. 60° 22′ S., long. 131° 28′ E., we tried for soundings with six hundred fathoms: the temperature as indicated by the thermometer at that depth, 40·5°, nearly one degree higher than the mean temperature of the ocean, may have been occasioned by a sudden jerk in hauling it up; the thermometer was, as usual, compared with the standard before and after the experiment, and found to have a small unvarying correction.   At 450 fathoms, the temperature was 39·5°: at 300 fathoms, 38°: at 150 fathoms, 37°: at the surface, 35°: several icebergs were in sight at the time, but none within five or six miles.

The Aurora again afforded us considerable light at night, in the absence of the moon, but did not break through the clouds which obscured the sky, and from which very fine snow was constantly falling until nearly 8 P. M., when it appeared from E. N. E. to N. W. of a yellow colour, forming an arch twenty degrees high, and at times exhibiting vivid flashes of a bright pink colour: it dispersed in a quarter of an hour.   We continued to make good progress to the north-west during the two following days.   In the evening of the 27th we witnessed a most brilliant exhibition of Aurora Australis, which I shall here insert in detail from the copious notes made at the time by myself and the officers, only first remarking that the constant but light snow of the morning was turned into small rain by the temperature rising at 11 A. M. to 36°: the rain ceased at 7 P. M., after a calm of two hours, and a breeze from the S. W. that followed partially cleared the sky.   " At 7 50 P. M. bright coruscations of the Aurora appeared in the west;

the streamers rose from a base at 20° above the
horizon to an altitude of 70°. At 8 15 it formed
a double arch from W. S. W. to E. N. E. at the
horizon, the altitude of their centres in the S. S. E.
being 38° and 53°; they continued visible forty-
five minutes, descending slowly to the S. S. W.
At 9 15 P. M. it again appeared W. N. W. and
E. S. E. in concentric arches of diffused light, with
apparently a rapid internal motion, like a current
passing through and lighting up thin mist. The
centres of these concentric arches first became
visible in the S. S. W. at an altitude of 30°, rising
in succession slowly to the zenith, and thence declining in the N. N. E. to an altitude of 50° at 9 50,
when the S. S. W. semi-hemisphere was perfectly
clear, and the Aurora was very dimly seen to the
N. N. E. At 9 53 a bright diffused light suddenly
appeared from behind a dark cloud, and two or
three minutes afterwards pink and green colours of
considerable intensity were seen amongst it, principally at the edges, and before 10 o'clock bright
streamers darted upward from the cloud to the zenith, forming coronæ, and exhibiting bright flashes
of all the prismatic colours, green and red being the
more frequent and conspicuous: this Aurora had
much motion, darting and quivering about the sky
in rapid flights, and in every direction. It sank in
a few minutes beneath the horizon to the S. S. W., in
the contrary direction to the series of successive
concentric arches of diffused light before mentioned.
Some very thin clouds now covered the E. S. E.
portion of the sky, and a deposit of very fine snow

followed.   Heavier clouds soon after rose in the
west (to windward), and although we observed
no more vivid exhibitions of the Aurora, it continued faintly visible until midnight.   Between 10
and 11 P. M., when the sky was very clear in the
S. W. quarter of the hemisphere, only one falling
star was detected, although carefully watched for.

It blew a strong breeze from the northward all
day, so as to prevent our making much way to the
N. W.; and finding from good observations during
the forenoon that we had increased the westerly
variation to 8° 47', I did not consider it necessary
to stretch any further to the westward.   We therefore wore round at 11 15 A. M. for the purpose of
recrossing the line of no variation, and of visiting
the spot assigned, in my instructions, to one of the
foci of greater magnetic intensity, which I had been
prevented doing on our way to Van Diemen's Land
from Kerguelen Island.   At noon we were in
lat. 57° 21' S., long. 127° 35' E.: during the day
we observed several large flocks of a small dark-
coloured petrel, which we took to be the young of
the Cape-pigeon proceeding to the northward: by the
length of time they took to fly past us, we estimated
some of those flocks to be from six to ten miles
in length, two or three miles broad, and very densely
crowded together, literally darkening the sky during
the two or three hours they were passing over and
about us.   A few stormy petrel were also seen.

At 10 30 P. M. a single flash of forked lightning
was seen in the N. N. E., and at the same time an
arch of Aurora extended across the zenith from the

horizon W. N. W. and E. S. E.; it was then blowing a strong north-westerly gale. Between midnight and 1 A. M. eleven falling stars were observed
in the S. W. quarter, and the Aurora was seen and
described in the Log-book by the officer of the watch,
Lieutenant Sibbald, as follows: " 0 30 to 2 10 A. M.
observed bright coruscations of the Aurora, forming
a succession of arches bearing from west to south
at the horizon, passing gradually over to the N. E.,
each being visible from four to six minutes. At
3 A. M. observed bright coruscations directly over
head in the form of a crescent, and of all the
colours of the rainbow, visible four minutes."

The gale lasted throughout the day, with violent
squalls; but we made good way under close-reefed
topsails and reefed courses. Several large flocks
of the dark-coloured petrel were again seen to-day,
and some large shoals of porpoises, all going to the
northward.

At 1 30 A. M. we passed two narrow lines of heavy
ice, the fragments of the numerous bergs about us,
and dangerous to merchant vessels keeping so high
as the 56th parallel of latitude at this period of the
year, on their way to Van Diemen's Land.

The Aurora Australis was visible throughout
the night, but without exhibiting any very striking
features, generally appearing in a white, diffused,
sometimes arched light.

Soon after noon, when in latitude 55° 9' S., and
longitude 132° 28' E., we hove to, and tried the
temperature of the ocean at various depths, as
we knew from our observation of the 25th, that

we were getting very near to the line of equal temperature throughout its whole depth, which encircles the globe between the fiftieth and six-tieth degree of south latitude. The temperature at 600 fathoms was 39·8: at 450 fathoms, 39·8: at 300 fathoms, 39·5: at 150 fathoms, 39·: and at the surface 38·5: so that no doubt a few weeks earlier we should have here found the mean temperature to prevail, although at this season of the year it was still a short distance to the north-ward; but we had no opportunity of determining its place more accurately.

During the 30th and 31st we pursued our course to the north-eastward, favoured by a moderate north-westerly breeze and fine weather. Between the periods of our observations on the evening of the 30th and evening of the 31st we again crossed the line of no variation, and having been fortunate in getting numerous azimuths, the point where we passed over it may be deduced with great exact-ness.* The Aurora appeared in great brilliancy during the night of the 30th; its various phases are minutely noted in the Log-book, and will be found of great value whenever the reduction of the magnetometrical observations at Van Diemen's Land shall be proceeded with. A few icebergs were seen, but not in sufficient numbers to give us any un-easiness.

Just before midnight of the 31st the wind shifted to the S.W., and we made all sail before it.

* See Table of Observations, page 310 of this Volume.

1841. ABSTRACT OF THE METEOROLOGICAL JOURNAL KEPT ON BOARD HER MAJESTY'S SHIP EREBUS. MARCH, 1841.

Day.	Position at Noon.		Temperature of the Air in Shade.			Mean Temperature of Sea at Surface.	Temp. at 9 A.M.	
	Lat. S.	Long. E.	Max.	Min.	Mean.		Air in shade.	Dew point.
	° ′	° ′	°	°	°	°	°	°
1	69·04	167·45	22	19	20·2	28·8	22	15
2	68·27	167·42	27	16·5	21·9	28·5	24	24*
3	67·45	167·01	15·5	11·7	13·7	28·2	14	12
4	66·44	165·45	27	16	23·6	28·8	23	23*
5	65·34	167·47	27	23	25·1	28·8	27	18
6	65·51	164·45	31	24·5	26·6	28·8	30	25
7	65·29	162·10	32	24	26·7	28·8	29	29
8	64·38	162·53	32·5	22·5	28·8	29·3	28	24
9	64·20	164·15	33·5	30·5	32·1	30·9	32	32*
10	64·06	163·20	31·5	28·5	29·7	30·0	31	31*
11	64·03	163·09	32·5	28	30·1	30·0	31	29
12	64·12	161·20	33	25	28·8	29·4	33	28
13	63·28	159·35	32	25	28·7	30·2	31	31
14	62·42	156·31	30	26·5	27·9	29·4	28	25
15	64·01	155·57	32	21	26·7	29·2	32	32*
16	64·10	154·40	23	20·5	21·6	28·6	24	22
17	64·22	152·58	25	21·5	23·0	28·6	24	24*
18	63·51	151·47	31·5	24	28·3	30·1	29	26
19	64·21	148·45	31·8	21	27·5	30·0	31	31*
20	65·15	143·45	23	17·5	20·6	28·7	20	17
21	64·07	140·22	27·5	21·5	23·3	29·0	24	20
22	62·58	139·18	33·5	27	31·2	31·1	32	27
23	62·12	136·18	35·5	32	33·5	32·3	34	34*
24	61·11	133·52	33·5	32	33·1	33·5	33	33*
25	60·22	131·28	39	33	34·4	34·2	36	35
26	59·24	130·03	37·5	32	34·4	34·7	36	33
27	58·03	128·40	36	32	34·4	35·5	33	33*
28	57·21	127·46	39	35·5	37·2	36·3	39	39
29	56·28	129·57	39	35	37·2	36·6	39	35
30	55·09	132·28	44	36·5	39·7	38·0	40	38
31	54·04	134·31	41	38	39·6	38·5	41	41
			44	11·7	28·69	31·12		

* Snow or rain falling.

ABSTRACT OF THE METEOROLOGICAL JOURNAL KEPT ON BOARD   1841.
HER MAJESTY'S SHIP EREBUS.— MARCH, 1841.

Day.	Barometer (corrected).			Winds.		Weather.
	Max.	Min.	Mean.	Direction.	Force.	
	Inches.	Inches.	Inches.			
1	28·897	28·711	28 789	S.W. by W.	5	5 b.c.v.*
2	·794	·560	·632	S.W.	3	A.M. 0 g.p.s. / P.M. 4 b.c.g.
3	·740	·585	·666	Southerly	{A.M. 4 / P.M. 2}	2 b.c.q. / 0 g.p.s.
4	·678	·365	·476	East	{A.M. 4 / P.M. 6}	0 g.p.s.
5	·967	·696	·873	S.E.	4	A.M. 4 b.c.g.p.s. / P.M. 3 b.c.g.
6	29·001	·871	·957	East	1	5 b.c.v.
7	·028	·754	·858	N. Easterly	{A.M. 4 / P.M. 1}	0 g.s. / 3 b.c.g.
8	·167	·912	29·055	N. Westerly	{A.M. 3 / P.M. 4}	3 b.c.m. / 0 d.s.
9	28·880	·615	28·726	N.W.	{A.M. 5 / P.M. 3}	0 m.s. / 1 b.c.g.
10	·698	·536	·623	West	5	0 g.q.p.s.
11	·807	·588	·707	Westerly	3	2 b.c.g.p.s.
12	·574	·492	·528	Westerly	3	2 b.c.g.p.s.
13	29·211	·457	·796	South	{A.M. 7 / P.M. 5}	0 g.q.p.s.
14	·538	29·231	·441	S.W.	4	3 b.c.g.
15	·263	28·848	·989	S. Westerly	4	A.M. 0 m.s. / P.M. 0 c.
16	28·963	·722	·844	S. Easterly	2	0 g.
17	29·002	·739	·872	Easterly	3	A.M. 0 g.p.s. / P.M. 0 g.
18	·144	·976	29·067	{A.M. S.W. / P.M. East}	1	1 b.c.g.
19	·061	·716	28·835	Easterly	{A.M. 3 / P.M. 5}	0 m.s. / 0 g.p.s.
20	·014	·817	·905	S.E. by E.	5	0 g.q.
21	·264	29·030	29·164	S.W.	3	0 g.p.s.
22	·242	28·854	·068	Easterly	3	A.M. 2 b.c.g. / P.M. 1 b.c.g.p.s.
23	·122	·953	·024	East	2	0 m.p.s.
24	·085	·332	28·692	E.N.E.	5	0 p.s.
25	28·726	·430	·614	E.N.E.	2	3 b.c.g.
26	29·166	·748	29·023	S.W.	3	2 b.c.g.p.s.
27	·223	·819	·011	E.N.E.	3	A.M. 0 m.p.s. / P.M. 2 b.c.q.d.
28	·242	·736	28·897	N.N.W.	6	3 b.c.q.d.
29	·309	·755	29·088	N.W.	7	4 b.c.g.q.
30	·683	29·313	·445	N.W.	3	5 b.c.
31	·741	·458	·640	N.N.E.	3	A.M. 3 b.c.g. / P.M. 0 g.m.r.
	29·741	28·365	28·8808		3·64	

* For the explanation of these symbols see the Appendix.

Favoured by a moderate breeze from the south-west, we shaped our course for the focus of maximum total intensity, as indicated by the general course of the isodynamic lines in Colonel Sabine's chart of the southern hemisphere, lying in about lat. 47° S. and long. 140° E., a position which we had not been able to attain during our run from Kerguelen Island to Van Diemen's Land, but which we now had in our power of approaching with greater advantage, by a course directly across the isodynamic oval surrounding it. The last iceberg was seen from the mast-head this morning when in lat. 53° 30' S.: it was of small size.

The wind increased to a strong breeze, and we had a good run during the night.

Being nearly calm in the forenoon of the next day the boats were lowered down, and soundings were obtained in one thousand four hundred and forty fathoms : our latitude at the time being 52° 10' S. and long. 136° 56' E. The weight employed on this occasion was 336 lbs., and the instant of each hundred fathoms passing off the reel was taken as usual, and is given on the following page, by which the increased friction of the line throughout the descent of the weight may be observed. The observations of the temperature which follow serve to show we had crossed the line of mean temperature since our experiments on the 30th March, and that the influence of the sun's heat was here felt to the depth of 450 fathoms.

TIME BY CHRONOMETER.

Let go at	..	-	3ʰ 22ᵐ 19ˢ.				
100 fathoms passed out at	22		57	occupied 38ˢ running out			
200	-	-	23	45	-	48	
300	-	-	24	54	-	69	
400	-	-	26	10	-	76	
500	-	-	27	31	-	81	
600	-	-	28	55	-	84	
700	-	-	30	27	-	92	
800	-	-	32	7	-	100	
900	-	-	33	48	-	101	
1000	-	-	35	36	-	108	
1100	-	-	37	31	-	115	
1200	-	-	39	29	-	118	
1300	-	-	41	31	-	122	
1400	-	-	43	34	-	123	
1500	-	-	45	40	-	126	
Struck ground in 1540 at			46	48	-	68	

1540 fathoms passed out in 24   29

The boat was kept moored to the bottom some time to ascertain if there was any current, but it was not perceptible. The line was then cut, not being sufficiently strong to draw the weight up again.

In the afternoon the temperature and specific gravity of the sea at various depths was tried. The temperature of the surface at the time being 43°; at 150 fathoms, 42°; at 300 fathoms, 41°; at 450 fathoms, 40°, and at 600 fathoms, 39·8°: the specific gravity being the same throughout the whole depth as at the surface, 1·0274, at 43°. A piece of sea-weed, the first we had seen since leaving the antarctic seas, was passed during the afternoon.

VOL. I.   Y

In the evening the breeze freshened to a gale from E.S.E., with thick weather and rain, which obliged us to reduce our sail to close-reefed topsails and reefed foresail.

April 3.   The gale continued throughout the whole of the next day, with frequent squalls and a high sea running, so that our magnetic observations were not made under favourable circumstances, which was the more to be regretted, as we were now fast approaching the focus of greatest intensity.

In the evening, at 10 P.M., we were in lat. 47° 41' S. by an observation of the moon's meridian altitude, and must have passed over the point we were in search of about eight o'clock the next morning.

April 4.   The gale was still blowing with great force, and the sea was running so high as to wash away one of our quarter boats. Very satisfactory observations of the magnetic force were, however, obtained by means of Mr. Fox's invention, and are published in the Second Part of the "Philosophical Transactions of the Royal Society for 1843." They tend to show a smaller relative amount of magnetic force than had been anticipated, and to prove that the focus of greatest intensity lies very much further to the southward than the spot indicated in my instructions, and probably not far from "Terre Adelie" of M. D'Urville. At noon we were in lat. 46° 34' S. long. 140° 36' E., and having now completed all that remained to be done, we steered direct for Van Diemen's Land, which we came in April 6.   sight of at 10 30 A.M. of the 6th, and late in the

evening entered Storm Bay. The light at the entrance of the Derwent was seen soon after midnight, and at nine the next morning the pilot came
on board. The wind was blowing fresh down the
river, so that it took us until late in the afternoon to beat up. Soon after noon the Governor's
barge was seen standing towards us; and our kind
friend, who was the last to leave us on our departure for the south, was the first to greet us with
his warm and affectionate congratulations on our
return. He was received with three hearty cheers
from both ships. The vessels were moored in their
former berths off the government gardens, convenient to the Rossbank Observatory, after an absence of five months.

In concluding the narrative of our first season's
navigation of the Antarctic Seas, I will only
further observe, that, amongst the many events
which had occurred to call forth our gratitude to
God for his guidance and preservation during the
arduous and hazardous operations in which we had
been engaged, it was a source of no ordinary gratification to me to reflect that the execution of the
service had been unattended by casualty, calamity,
or sickness of any kind, and that every individual
of both ships had been permitted to return in perfect health and safety to this our southern home.

APPENDIX.

APPENDIX. No. I.

MEMORANDUM OF THE FITTINGS OF H. M. SHIP EXCELS,
BY MR. ERCK, OF CHATHAM DOCKYARD.

THE ship is fortified externally by solid chock channels,
the spaces between the channels being similarly fitted,
tapering at the extremities, so as to form an easy curva-
ture in a fore and aft direction; the side is doubled with
six-inch oak plank under the channel, increasing to eight-
inch at the wale, which is three feet broad; from thence,
through a space of five feet, the doubling diminishes to
three inches in thickness, of English elm, and the remainder of the bottom to the keel is doubled with three-
inch Canada elm. The quarter galleries are removed, and
the quarter pieces and stern strongly united by planking;
all rails and projections being carefully avoided.

The knee of the head being removed, the bow is terminated by fittings or thick bolsters, leaving no projections at the stern. Braziers, or thick copper, is substituted
for that ordinarily used, extending along the body at the
line of flotation, and entirely covering the bow down to
the keel.

Within-board, the spaces between the bands at the floor
heads, &c., are fitted in with six-inch oak plank; the entire
surface in the hold being caulked, two thicknesses of 1½
inch African board are then worked diagonally over the
bands, &c. at right angles to each other, each layer being
also caulked. The thwartship bulkheads of the fore, main,
and after holds are wrought diagonally of two thicknesses
of 1½ inch African board at right angles to each other, the

Z 4

upper ends rabbetting into the lower deck beams, and the lower ends into four-inch plank, wrought upon the doubling. The bulkheads are caulked on both sides, and rendered water-tight. The wing bulkheads are similarly wrought. The limber boards are likewise caulked down and doubled by a fore and aft plank. Penstocks are introduced in the limbers at the bulkhead, allowing a communication, when required, from one compartment to another, leading to the well. The fore hold is provided with two common pumps, to work on the weather deck; and the well is furnished with four of Massey's excellent pumps.

The bow, internally, is fortified with a solid mass of timber eight inches moulded, canting from abreast the fore-mast to the stemson, square to the body. Between the upper and lower decks, and also between the lower and orlop decks, thick shelf pieces are wrought, terminating under the transom abaft, and meeting at the middle line at the deck hooks forward.

The central planks of the weather deck are six inches thick, laid fore and aft; the remainder of the deck is wrought double; the lower planks, three inches thick, are laid fore and aft; the upper planks, three inches thick, diagonally, having fearnaught dipped in hot tallow, laid between the two surfaces. The beams of this deck are connected by pointers, or diagonally-lopped carlings, from the catheads forward.

Additional crutches and sleepers have been introduced abaft, and diagonal trusses worked between the chocks under the lower deck beams. The ship is otherwise very strongly built, having diagonal iron riders, iron hooks and crutches in the bow, and iron sleepers abaft.

Filling timbers have been introduced in the stern, with an inner transom, kneed to the stern post and ship's side, double-planked inside and out, thus rendering the counter as strong as the bow, to meet the shocks which the extremities are most likely to encounter in the ice.

Chatham,
19th September, 1839.

APPENDIX, No. II.

ELEVATION OF PICO RUIVO IN THE ISLAND OF MADEIRA.

FOUR barometers were employed in this measurement, viz. the two standard marine barometers of the Erebus and Terror, and two portable barometers; the latter were of Newman's construction, with iron cisterns, numbered respectively 94 and 103. The standards were numbered 19 and 20. The corrections for capillarity, the ratio of the capacities of the tube and cistern, and the neutral points, or heights of the mercury, at which no correction was required for capacity, were respectively as follows:—

19. Capillary + ·012; Capacity $\frac{1}{7}$; Neutral Pt. 29·922; Temp. 65°.
20. ———— + ·012; ———— $\frac{1}{7}$; ———— 29·922; ——— 65°.
94. ———— + ·052; ———— $\frac{1}{6}$; ———— 30·130; ——— 55°.
103. ———— + ·052; ———— $\frac{1}{7}$; ———— 30·084; ——— 60°.

COMPARISON OF THE BAROMETERS.

The mean of eight readings, taken simultaneously at intervals of ten minutes, gave as follows:—

	(No. 19.)	(No. 20.)	(No. 94.)	(No. 103.)
Mean Height.	30·172;	30·164;	30·091;	30·142
Capillary.	+ ·012	+ ·012	+ ·052	+ ·052
Capacity.	+ ·012	+ ·012	—·001	+ ·001
Reduction to 32°.	(72·3) — ·118	(71·6) — ·116	(69°) — ·099	(72°) — ·118
	30·078	30·072	30·043	30·077
			+ ·032 Index.	— ·00 ·
Mean of Standards, 30·075			30·075	30·075

Observations were made at the summit of Pico Ruivo, at intervals of ten minutes, during 1½ hours, viz. from ¼ past 7 to 9 A. M., simultaneously with those of the standards on the shore, six feet above mean tide.

	On the Shore.			Summit of the Peak.	
Mean Height. (No. 19.)	30·247 ;	(No. 20) 30·237 ;	(No. 94)	24·265 ; (No. 103.)	24·28
Capillary.	+·012		+·012		+·052	+·05
Capacity.	+·016		+·016		−·117	−·10
Reduction to 32° (70°)	−·112	(70°)	−·112	(46°)	−·038 (46°)	−·03
Index.	−·003		+·003		+·032	−·00
	30·160		30·153		24·194	24·19
Mean corrected heights -	- 30·1565	-	-	-	- 24·1960	
Detached Thermometer	- -	70°	-	-	44°	
Dew Point - -	- -	62°	-	-	42° 7 (3 observations)	
Humidity - -	- -	·63	-	-	·90 (Saturation = 1)	

Whence by Bessel's Tables (*Sci. Mem.* vol. ii. art. xvi.) we find the height equal 6089·08 English feet, if ·00375 (Gay Lussac's determination of the volume of air at 0° C.) be taken as the measure of its expansion for each degree of the centigrade thermometer, and 6094·90 feet, if ·003648 (Rudberg's determination) be taken.

The cisterns of the standard barometers were 6 feet above the sea; therefore 6 feet is to be added for the height of the summit of the peak, making the above numbers 6095·08 and 6100·90 feet.

  " My dear Ross,

" Mr. Bowditch was, I believe, the first to notice that the height which I had assigned to the Pico Ruivo, from the barometrical observations which were made by Captain Clavering and myself during our short stay at Madeira in the winter of 1821-1822, was some hundred feet less than the true height of the peak, as measured by himself a few months after we had visited the island. A similar notice has recently been made by Lieutenant Wilkes, the American navigator; and the observations of Wilmot and Lefroy, which you are about to publish, bear full testimony to the same fact. If I recollect right, Mr. Bowditch ascribed the error into which we had fallen to our guides having conducted us to one of the summits less elevated than the peak; an imposition which it is well known they frequently attempt to practise, for the purpose of saving themselves the fatigue of a part of the ascent. The day on which our excursion was performed was certainly one on which such an attempt was likely to be made, and not unlikely to be successful. It was mid-winter, the paths scarcely discernible from the depth of snow, and the summits for many hundred feet enveloped in cloud. We had been cautioned, however, both by Mr. Veitch and Mr. Blackburne, that the guides were not to be relied on; and the appearances of the ground and of surrounding objects on the Peak itself had been carefully described to us, that we might not be wholly at their mercy. Twice they did attempt deception, and twice the description which had been given to us enabled us to detect and defeat it. The third summit to which they conducted us, and which was considerably higher than either of the others, corresponded so well with the description, that, influenced also in some degree possibly by the solemn protestations of the guides, we believed ourselves to be really at the Peak; and we were confirmed in this opinion on our return to Funchal by Mr. Veitch, who, though he had predicted failure on account of the season of the year and the state of the weather, believed, from our description, that we had actually succeeded. We therefore ourselves entertained no doubt on the subject.

"It is very possible, nevertheless, that Mr. Bowditch's surmise may be the true explanation. There is, however, another mode of accounting for the erroneous height which we assigned, which it may at least afford a useful caution to others to mention. The barometer which I employed was one of Newman's, with an iron cistern, enclosed in a circular wooden case having an opening by which a few inches only of the upper part of the column of mercury could be seen, the lower part of the column being altogether concealed from view. Using the same barometer a few months afterwards, in the mountains of Jamaica, I was not a little surprised to find that the barometer on one occasion stood higher than it had done when examined three or four hundred feet lower down. Immediately suspecting the cause, and having a fine turnscrew with me, I detached the case altogether from the tube and cistern, and then perceived that a separation had taken place in the column of mercury, low down in the tube, arising doubtless from a small quantity of air which had made its way in, in spite of the usual precautions. It was of course soon tapped out, and the barometer being replaced in its case, gave its proper indication. After this experience, on my return to England, I had a barometer made in which the case was so arranged as to permit the whole column of mercury to be in.pected, from the cistern upwards, at every observation; and I have always used it since.

"Now it is certainly possible that a similar occurrence may have taken place on Pico Ruivo. It is true that on the return to Funchal the barometer agreed with its indication at the same place before our departure; but this does by no means preclude the possibility that the column may not have been perfect on the Peak. The escape of air in travelling might be more easy than its introduction. It may be a very rare occurrence when the proper precautions are not omitted, and I dare say it is so. I do not remember an instance of the kind taking place in the barometer which I have since used, and in which I always examine the whole column. But it would appear undoubtedly preferable to have portable barometers so constructed as always to admit of this examination.

"Believe me, dear Ross,
"Sincerely yours,
"EDWARD SABINE."

APPENDIX, No. III.

TABLE REFERRED TO PAGE 97., SHOWING THE DAILY AMOUNT OF EASTERLY CURRENT OBSERVED BETWEEN KERGUELEN ISLAND AND VAN DIEMEN'S LAND, JULY 20 TO AUGUST 5. 1840.

Date.	Course.	Distance run.	Lat.	Long.	Current.	Mean Temperature.	
		Miles.	South.	East.		Air.	Sea.
July 20 sailed from Christmas Harbour.							
21	N. 86 E.	149	48·24	72·57	No observation.	35	35
22	N. 88 E.	157	48·29	76·55	S. 40 E. 10 miles	30	35
23	N. 85 E.	136	48·17	80·15	S. 80 E. 11 „	30	37
24	N. 82 E.	199	47·55	83·41	N. 3 E. 8 „	31	37 A.M. / 44 P.M.
25	N. 85 E.	106	47·46	86·18	No observation.	32	45 A.M. / 41 P.M.
26	N. 77 E.	141	47·12	89·45	N. 68 E. 58 „	35	44
27	N. 87 E.	133	47·18	93·0	S. 10 E. 16 „	43	43
28	S. 88 E.	169	47·28	97·7	S. 67 E35	42	42
29	S. 75 E.	131	48·02	100·17	No current. „	37	38
30	N. 77 E.	102	47·39	102·43	N. 83 E. 10 „	30	36
31	N. 89 E.	150	47·36	106·26	S. 86 E. 32 „	37	36
Aug. 1	S. 87 E.	172	47·45	110·39	S. 76 E. 8 „	36	49
2	N. 86 E.	145	47·35	114·16	N. 65 E. 23 „	40	42
3	S. 84 E.	156	47·51	118·08	S. 66 E. 15 „	39	41
4	N. 86 E.	136	47·42	121·31	N. 30 E. 11 „	35	40
5	N. 87 E.	129	47·34	124·43	No current.	35	44

Average rate of current = 15·8 miles daily.

APPENDIX, No. IV.

REMARKS ON SOME CORALS OBTAINED FROM GREAT
DEPTHS IN THE ANTARCTIC OCEAN, IN A LETTER
FROM CHARLES STOKES, ESQ., F. R. S., F. G. S., &c. TO
CAPTAIN SIR JAMES C. ROSS, R.N.

"Verulam Buildings,
"26 Feb. 1846.

"My dear Sir James,

"I have found much interest in the examination of the
specimens you have sent me which were obtained by
soundings, and the use of the dredge at great depths, and
have to apologise both for delaying so long to send you
some observations upon them, and for sending them now
in so imperfect a state.

"The fragments obtained by soundings from 400 fathoms,
11th August, 1841, lat. 33° 31' S., long. 107° 40' E.,
consist of pieces of shells and small corals, none of which
appear to have been brought up in a living state, with
small angular pebbles very little rounded by attrition.
Among them I find two joints of stems of a small fossil
pentacrinite.

"Among the small sand taken up by the soundings in
400 fathoms, August, 1841, Professor Forbes finds portions
of spines of echinus and of spines of cidaris.

"Of shells, a small broken cerithium, mouth of a Resida,
a Pteropod allied to Peracle, and a fragment of Cleodora.

"Of Annelides, Spirorbis on the stones.

"Many foraminifera, among which are Textularia,
Nodosariæ, and several of orbicular and renoidal forms in
abundance.

"The corals brought up by the dredge from 270 fathoms,
19th Jan. 1841, lat. 72° 31' S., long. 173° 39'E., consist of
three species of Lepralia: Retepora cellulosa—a small piece
in a perfectly fresh and living state: a Retepora or Hornera,

much resembling the Hornera frondiculata of Lamouroux
in similar fresh condition. The polype cells are salient
only at the extremities of the branches. The cells appear
also on all sides of the branches, which must distinguish
it from the species mentioned. The absence of the openings of polype cells from the exterior side of the branches
is made a generic character of Hornera by Lamouroux, but
probably is only of value to distinguish species.

I name this Hornera lateralis.—The genus Hornera was
established by Lamouroux for a division of Retepora, of
which R. frondiculata is the type, but it was not well
defined by him. The generic character, as given by Milne
Edwards, is, ' Polyparium branched, composed of tubular
cells united together throughout nearly their whole length,
with terminal circular openings. The cells all opening on
one surface.'

The cells of the present species are not so decidedly
elongated as those of H. frondiculata, and it may be said
to occupy an intermediate place between Hornera and
Retepora, but this is one of the ordinary difficulties in
arranging species in genera. An instance of such difficulty is seen in the species R. versipalma, which Lamouroux says (*Expos. Method*, p. 41.), ' est tres voisin des
Hornères,' which De Blainville places in the genus
Hornera, and of which Milne Edwards says, (*Anim. sans
Vertèbres*, Second Edition, vol. ii. p. 279.) ' Nous sommes
porté a croire que ce Polype ne doit pas être rangé dans
le genre Hornère, ainsi que le veut M. de Blainville ; il
nous parait se rapprocher davantage des vrais Retepores."

" The present species differs from all that are described
in the opening of the cell which, as is shown in fig. 3*, is
placed laterally immediately below the pointed summit of
the cell. It is only at the unbroken ends of the branches
that this can be seen, as the ends of the cells seem soon to

* Plates of the beautiful drawings will be found in the " Zoology of the
Voyage," now being published under the superintendence of Dr. Richardson and J. E. Gray, Esq.

wear away, and on the general surface of the branches
only circular openings are left, which are hardly at all
prominent.

"In examining into the relations of this species, we have
another proof of the necessity of good figures to determine species. The description given of R. versipalma is
as follows: — "R. nana, ramosissima; ramis ramulosa-
palmatis; palmis brevibus variè versis; interna superficie
poris prominalis scabra; externa sublævigata."

"This description might do for the present species if
taken from a specimen of which the summits of the
branches were not quite perfect, but as the lateral position
of the openings of the terminal cells is not mentioned,
there is good reason to believe that the present is a different
species. It is to call attention to this point that the name
'lateralis' is given to this species, though it is at the
risk of finding this character common to others, when
specimens are found in a perfect state. It is to be observed also that the cells of H. frondiculata have not,
strictly speaking, circular openings, although the tube of
the cell is cylindrical. The end of the tube of the cell
is in the perfect specimens much higher on one side than
the rest, so that the opening becomes elliptic by being
oblique to the line of the elongated tubular cell.

"A new species of Primnoa, which I name P. Rossii.

"A Melitœa, nov. sp. — M. australis.

"A Madrepora? nov. sp. —M. fissurata.

"This is hardly to be considered a true Madrepora, but
I am unwilling to make a genus for it.

"I send herewith drawings of the three corals last mentioned, which are perhaps the most interesting of the whole.
These drawings are carefully and correctly made, and I
will say little of the description of them, as the figures will
be more useful than words. Although we have long known
that a Primnoa from Norway, (of which I will speak pre-
sently,) is found at a great depth, and some other corals
have been taken at from 70 to 100 fathoms; yet it is rare,

as far as our present knowledge instructs us, to find any corals, except perhaps some of the celleporæ at great depths, and I am not aware of any previous instance of a Melitœa or a Madrepora at all resembling those here represented having been found except at a small depth, and in a warm climate; from which I had concluded that they required more of the solar light and warmth than they could obtain at the depth from which you took those specimens. Your Primnoa is, however, to me the most interesting among them. The genus Primnoa was first established by Lamouroux for the single species previously called Gorgonia lepadifera, which is that found in Norway above alluded to. Ehrenberg (in his "Corallenthiere des rothen Meeres") was the first to include in it other species, and he properly added to it the G. verticillaris: he describes also a third species under the name of P. flabellum, but I am not quite satisfied that this species is established. The locality given for P. verticillaris by Ellis and Solander, and by Marsigli, is the Mediterranean. I have good specimens of this species from the West Indies, where they were collected by the late Rev. Lansdown Guilding. I have met with no statement of the depth at which it grows, but have reason to believe that Mr. Guilding did not use means to obtain his specimens (of which I have many) at great depths, and Ellis and Solander would certainly have told us if they had known of their occurrence at a great depth.

"Primnoa lepadifera is found, I believe, only on the coast of Norway. I have specimens nearly two feet in height, which were presented to me by Sir Arthur de Capell Brooke, Bart. who collected them there in 1820. He received accounts of their growing to a much larger size. They are found at great depths, varying from 150 to 300 fathoms. At these depths they grow in company with a large branching Alcyonium of a red colour (A. arboreum), and it is in fishing with lines for the red fish that the specimens are obtained. This fish frequents the places where these corals grow, and the lines getting entangled with the branches of the corals frequently bring up specimens of them, and sometimes the size and strength of the corals is such as to break the lines.

"The drawings represent your species—Primnoa Rossii. Fig. 1. of natural size: fig. 2. portion magnified: 3, 4. polype cells more magnified: 5, 6, 7. polype cell of P. lepadifera.

"The polype cells of Primnoa are membranaceous and covered with calcareous scales, the forms of which are accurately represented in the drawings, and are useful in forming specific characters, as they differ in form and number in each species. These scales do not cover the whole surface of the cells; on the inner side, next to the stem, there is a part devoid of scales, as if being less exposed their protection was not needed. This is shown in the figures of both species. The substance of the cells being membranaceous they are movable in all directions, as is shown by the different positions in which the cells of P. lepadifera have dried, and hence a mistake was made by Ellis, who described the cells as "reflexed," that is, with the mouth downwards, which must have arisen from the position in which his specimen had been hung up to dry, as the weight of the cells would make them fall.

"I will not go into further remarks respecting the different species, but have said thus much because the Primnoas are a rare form of coral, and there is an additional interest in the Norway species occurring at a great depth, as is the case with your new species of the genus.*

"Very truly yours,
"C. Stokes."

---

* I learn from Professor Forbes that he has got from Capt. Sulivan another new species of Primnoa from near Staten Land, in 278 fathoms. — 1st August, 1846.

APPENDIX, No. V.

EHRENBERG'S PRELIMINARY NOTICE OF THE MINUTE
FORMS OF ORGANIC LIFE IN THE OCEAN, THE ANT-
ARCTIC SEAS, AND AT GREAT DEPTHS; WITH A DE-
SCRIPTION OF SEVEN NEW GENERA AND SEVENTY-ONE
NEW SPECIES.

At the Berlin Academy of Science, May, 1844: —

23rd May. M. Ehrenberg communicates to the
Academy some of the results of his examination of
Materials received by him from Captain Ross's Antarctic
Voyage.

Page 4. Section I. South Polar Voyage, 1841—1843.

Captain Ross's Antarctic Voyage in 1841—1843 has
materially advanced our knowledge of those minute forms
of organic life which are invisible to the naked eye, and
the author of this communication feels it incumbent upon
him to lay some of the general results at once before the
Academy, although the complete scientific examination of
the materials cannot be concluded for a long time.

The Royal Society of London having in 1840 appointed
a Committee to prepare a list of physical and meteorological queries and desiderata of special scientific interest,
for the intended Antarctic Voyage and Magnetic Observatories, M. de Humboldt, in a communication to the
Committee printed by them in their report (p. 96.), called
attention to the important bearing of those minute forms
of organic life on the great questions of modern geology,
and described the easy methods of collection and preservation recommended by myself.

z 2

By the scientific zeal of Dr. Hooker (son of the well-known botanist), who was one of the voyagers on board the Erebus, a large collection has been formed and preserved, and forty small packets and three glasses of water from different parts of the ocean from Cape Horn to Victoria Land have been transmitted to me.

I received almost at the same time a similar quantity of materials of the same nature from other parts of the globe from Mr. Darwin.

It seemed right to examine without delay the contents of the water brought from the Polar Sea in 75° to 78° S. lat. 162° W. long.: as another such opportunity can hardly be looked for. Of the dried materials, only a few have yet been examined, chiefly from the most interesting localities, such as samples of deposits from melted Polar ice, and others taken from the bottom of the sea in latitudes from 63° to 78° South, and at depths from 190 to 270 fathoms. The results show, as I had anticipated, that in high Southern as well as in high Northern latitudes, and great oceanic depths, the minute forms of organic life are intensely and extensively developed.

The following details of the preliminary investigation (which are well assured in essential respects) may not be unwelcome to the Academy, and will at the same time convey the thanks of science to the enterprising voyagers who have brought home the materials.

It may be remarked in general, that those materials are very rich in wholly new typical forms, particularly so in new genera, with sometimes numerous species, forming generally the whole of the mass, though sometimes mixed with a little mud and fragments of small crustacea. The new genera and species are distinguished in the subjoined account. The Asteromphali are quite peculiar and very beautiful stellated forms.

Analysis of the different Materials sent by Dr. Hooker from the Antarctic Voyage.

1. Deposit from melted Pancake Ice from the Barrier in 78° 10′ S. latitude, 162° W. longitude.

A. SILICEOUS-SHELLED POLYGASTRICA.

1. *Actinoptychus biternarius.*
2. ASTEROMPHALUS *Hookerii.*
3.   *Rossii.*
4.   *Buchii.*
5.   *Beaumontii.*
6.   *Humboldtii.*
7.   *Cuvierii.*
8. *Coscinodiscus actinochilus.*
9.   *apollinis.*
10.   *cingulatus.*
11.   eccentricus.
12.   *gemmifer.*
13.   limbatus.
14.   lineatus.
15.   *lunæ.*
16.   oculus Iridis.
17.   *radiolatus.*
18.   subtilis.
19.   velatus.
20. *Dicladia antennata.*
21.   *bulbosa.*
22. *Dictyocha* aculeata.
23.   binoculus.
24.   *biternaria.*
25.   Epiodon.
26.   *octonaria.*

27. *Dictyocha* ornamentum.
28.   septenaria.
29.   speculum.
30. *Flustrella* concentrica.
31. *Fragilaria* acuta.
32.   Amphiceros.
33. *Gallionella pileata.*
34.   sulcata?
35. HALIONYX *senarius.*
36.   *duodenarius.*
37. HEMIAULUS *antarcticus.*
38. HEMIZOSTER *tubulosus.*
39. *Lithobotrys denticulata.*
40. *Lithocampe australis.*
41. *Pyxidicula dentata.*
42.   hellenica.
43. *Rhizosolenia Calyptra.*
44.   *ornithoglossa.*
45. *Symbolophora Microtrias.*
46.   *Tetras.*
47.   *Pentas.*
48.   *Hexas.*
49. *Synedra* Ulna?
50. *Triceratium Pileolus.*
51. *Zygoceros australis.*

B. SILICEOUS-EARTHY PHYTOLITHARIA.

52. *Amphidiscus* agaricus.
53.   clavatus.
54.   *Helvella.*
55. *Lithosteriscus bulbosus.*
56. *Spongolithis* acicularis.
57.   aspera.
58.   *brachiata.*
59.   caput serpentis.
60.   cenocephala.
61.   clavus.
62.   collaris.
63.   fustis.

64. *Spongolithis heterocornis.*
65.   inflexa.
66.   *leptostauron.*
67.   mesogongyla.
68.   Neptunia.
69.   *radiata.*
70.   trachelotyla.
71.   *Trachystauron.*
72.   *Trianchora.*
73.   *vaginata.*
74.   verticillata.
75.   uncinata.

C. CALCAREOUS-SHELLED POLYTHALAMIA.

76. *Grammostomum divergens.*	78. *Rotalia Erebi.*
77. *Rotalia antarctica.*	79. *Spiroloculina* ——

Several forms of the genus coscinodiscus have been recognised with their green ovaries, and must certainly therefore have been collected in a living state.

2. Deposit from melted ice while the ships were sailing through broad strips of brown pancake ice.

(Materials from 75 S. latitude, 170 W. longitude.)

A. SILICEOUS-SHELLED POLYGASTRICA.

1. ASTEROMPHALUS *Buchii.*		8. *Dictyochia* aculeata.
2.	*Rossii.*	9. *Eunotia* gibberula.
3. *Coscinodiscus* lineatus.		10. *Fragilaria* acuta.
4.	*luna.*	11.	*pinnulata.*
5.	oculus Iridis.	12.	rotundata.
6.	radiolatus.	13. HEMIAULUS *antarcticus.*
7.	subtilis.	14. HEMIZOSTER *tubulosus.*

B. SILICEOUS-EARTHY PHYTOLITHARIA.

15. *Spongolithis fustis?* Fragment.

These and the preceding mass were sent over in water in the same sealed glass vessels in which they were collected in 1842. Hemiaulus antarcticus was the prevailing form found in the first smaller bottle, which has a rich sediment, almost all the separate atoms of which are independent siliceous-shelled creatures. The larger bottle was only about a quarter full, the larger portion having exuded through the sealed cork: almost the whole of the mass of sediment arrived in Berlin in 1844 in a state which I do not hesitate to call a living state, though all were forms having little or no motion. The Fragilarias predominated (Fragilaria pinnulata); these, though rarely hanging together in the form of a chain, still preserved for the most part their green ovaries in the different natural arrangements. Coscinodisci and Hemiaulus also showed in many cases groups of grains still green in their inside. No motion.

The following Nos. were sent dry : —

3. Taken up by the lead from 190 fathoms depth, in 78° 10′ S. latitude, 162° W. longitude.

A. Siliceous-shelled Polygastrica.

1. Astrromphalus *Hookerii.*	14. *Fragilaria* al. sp.
2. *Buckii.*	15. *Gallionella sol.*
3. *Humboldtii.*	16. Hemiaulus *antarcticus.*
4. *Cuvierii.*	17. *Lithobotrys denticulata.*
5. *Coscinodiscus Apollinis.*	18. *Mesocena spongolithis.*
6. gemmifer.	19. *Pyxidicula.*
7. limbatus.	20. *Rhizosolenia ornithoglossa.*
8. lineatus.	21. *Symbolophora Microtrias.*
9. *lunæ.*	22. *Tetras.*
10. radiolatus.	23. *Pentas.*
11. *Dictyocha septenaria.*	24. *Hexas.*
12. speculum.	25. Triaulacias *triquetra.*
13. *Fragilaria* Amphiceros.	26. *Tricratium Pileolus.*

B. Siliceous-earthy Phytolitharia.

27. *Amphidiscus polydiscus.*	34. *Spongolithis fustis.*
28. *Spongolithis* acicularis.	35. Neptunia.
29. aspera.	36. *Pes mantidis.*
30. brachiata.	37. *Trianchora.*
31. caput serpentis.	38. *vaginata.*
32. cenocephala.	39. uncinata.
33. *clavus.*	

4. From snow and ice taken from the sea in 76° S. latitude, 165° W. longitude, near Victoria Land.

Siliceous-shelled Polygastrica.

1. *Coscinodiscus* lineatus.	4. *Fragilaria pinnulata.*
2. *lunæ.*	5. rotundata.
3. subtilis.	6. al. sp.

The mass consists principally of thickly crowded Fragilaria pinnulata with Coscinodisci, which, when softened in water, allow for the most part their green, perhaps originally brown, ovaries to be recognised.

5. Contents of the stomach of a Salpa, 66° S. latitude, 157° W. longitude, 1842.

Siliceous-shelled Polygastrica.

1. *Actiniscus Lancearius.*	3. *Coscinodiscus cingulatus.*
2. *Coscinodiscus Apollinis.*	4. gemmifer.

z 4

5. *Coscinodiscus* lineatus.　10. *Fragilaria* acuta.
6. 　　lunæ.　11. 　granulata.
7. 　　subtilis.　12. 　rotundata.
8. *Dictyocha* aculeata.　13. HALIONYX *duodenarias*.
9. 　　speculum.　14. *Pyxidicula*.

This contains so very much larger a proportion of Dictyochas than are found in other samples, that they must have been selected by the Salpa, with whom therefore they are apparently a favourite kind of food.

6. Floating spots from the surface of the open sea, 64° S. latitude, 160° W. longitude.

Small loose-textured, tender-threaded masses (similar to the Oscillatorias of our waters) interspersed with small grains. They consist principally of the siliceous, very tender and long side tubes of the quite new and very peculiar genus Chætoceros. The nature of the grains is still obscure. The other forms are interspersed in the loose mass; they all still show their dried ovaries, evidencing that they were collected alive.

SILICEOUS-SHELLED POLYGASTRICA.

1. ASTEROMPHALUS *Darwinii*.　10. *Dictyocha* aculeata.
2. 　　Hookerii.　11. 　Binoculus.
3. 　　Rossii.　12. *Dictyocha* ornamentum.
4. 　　Buchii.　13. 　speculum.
5. 　　Humboldtii.　14. *Fragilaria* Amphiceros.
6. CHÆTOCEROS *dichaeta*.　15. 　granulata.
7. 　　tetrachaeta.　16. HEMIAULUS *obtusus*.
8. *Coscinodiscus lineatus*.　17. *Lithobotrys denticulata*.
9. 　　subtilis.

7. Taken up by the lead from 207 fathoms depth, in the Gulf of Erebus and Terror, 63° 40' S. latitude, 55° W. longitude, among apparently inorganic sand, were found with sometimes distinctly recognisable ovaries:—

A. SILICEOUS-SHELLED POLYGASTRICA.

1. ANAULUS *scalaris*.　6. *Coscinodiscus* subtilis.
2. *Biddulphia ursina*.　7. 　velatus.
3. *Coscinodiscus Apollinis*.　8. *Fragilaria* rotundata.
4. 　cingulatus.　9. *Gallionella sol*.
5. 　lunæ.　10. 　tympanum.

11. *Grammatophora* parallela.
12. HEMIAULUS *antarcticus.*
13. *Rhaphoneis fasciolata.*
14. *Zygoceros ? australis.*

B. SILICEOUS-EARTHED PHYTOLITHARIA.

15. *Spongolithis* acicularis.
16. *Spongolithis* fustis.

8. Taken up by the lead from 270 fathoms, 63·40 S. latitude, 55° W. longitude.

A. SILICEOUS-SHELLED POLYGASTRICA.

1. *Achnanthes* turgens.
2. *Amphora* libyca.
3. ANAULUS *scalaris.*
4. *Biddulphia ursina.*
5. *Campylodiscus* clypeus.
6. *Coscinodiscus Apollinis.*
7.   gemmifer.
8.   lineatus.
9.   *lunæ.*
10.   oculus Iridis.
11.   radiolatus.
12.   subtilis.
13. *Denticella lævis.*
14. *Discoplea Rota.*
15.   *Rotula.*
16. *Flustrella* concentrica.
17. *Fragilaria* Amphiceros.
18.   *pinnulata.*
18. *Gallionella oculus.*
20.   *sol.*
21. *Gallionella* sulcata.
22. *Grammatophora* africana.
23.   parallela.
24.   serpentina.
25. HEMIAULUS *antarcticus.*
26. *Lithocampe* nov. sp.
27. *Mesocena spongolithis.*
28. *Navicula elliptica.*
29. *Podosphenia cuneata.*
30. *Pyxidicula* hellenica ?
31. *Rhaphoneis fasciolata.*
32. *Rhizosolenia calyptra.*
33.   ornithoglossa.
34. *Stauroptera* aspera.
35. *Symbolophora Microtrias.*
36.   *Tetras.*
37.   *Pentas.*
38.   *Hexas.*
39. *Synedra* Ulna.

B. SILICEOUS-EARTHED PHYTOLITHARIA.

40. *Amphidiscus* clavatus.
41. *Spongolithis* acicularis.
42.   aspera.
43.   *brachiata.*
44.   caput serpentis.
45.   clavus.
46.   Fustis.
47. *Spongolithis Heteroconus.*
48.   *ingens.*
49.   Neptunis.
50.   obtusa.
51.   *vaginata.*
52.   uncinata.

C. CALCAREOUS POLYTHALAMIA.

53. *Grammostomum divergens.*

9. Samples from Cockburn Island, the extreme southern limit of vegetation.

SILICEOUS-SHELLED POLYGASTRICA.

1. *Eunotia* Amphioxys.
2. *Pinnularia* borealis.
3.   peregrina ?
4. *Rhaphoneis scutellum.*
5. *Stauroptera capitata.*

Two of these forms are new; two have also been observed in the North, and one is distributed extensively over the earth.

The distinguishing characters of the seven new genera collected in the course of the voyage, viz. Anaulus, Asteromphalus, Chætoceros, Halionyx, Hemiaulus, Hemizoster and Triaulacias are given in pages 19, 20, and 21, of Professor Ehrenberg's communication to the Academy of Science at Berlin: and those of the seventy-one new species in eight following pages, to which I must refer the enquiring naturalist for further information.

APPENDIX, No. VI.

LETTER FROM LIEUT. CHARLES WILKES, COMMANDING UNITED STATES EXPLORING EXPEDITION, TO CAPTAIN JAMES C. ROSS, H. B. M. S. EREBUS.

"U. S. Flag Ship Vincennes, New Zealand,
"Bay of Islands, 5th April, 1840.

"My dear Sir,

"I need not tell you how much I feel interested in your cruise. From the interest you took in the outfit of our expedition, I am sure you well know the interest it excites, and how much this feeling is heightened by a knowledge on my part of what you have undertaken, and have to go through. This prompts me to a desire to be useful to you if possible, and to give you my experience of the last season among the ice, whither you are bound.

"Your cruise will be an arduous one, no matter how you may be enlightened in your course; but you have so much knowledge of the ice, and the manner of treating it, that it appears almost presumptuous in me to sit down to give you any hints relative to it. But, believing as I do that the ice of the antarctic is of a totally different character from that of the arctic, I venture to offer you a few hints that may be useful to you in your undertaking: and although my instructions are binding upon me relative to discoveries, I am, nevertheless, aware that I am acting as my Government would order, if they could have anticipated the case, knowing how deeply it feels the liberal assistance and great interest evinced by all the societies and distinguished men of Great Britain, to promote and aid this, our first undertaking in the great cause of science and usefulness; and I must add, the pleasure it gives to me personally to be able to return, though in a small degree, the great obligation I myself feel under to you and many others, the promoters of your undertaking.

" *Winds.*—The winds for the first fortnight of our time, to the eastward of 140° east longitude, were from the northward and westward, light generally, accompanied occasionally with clear weather for hours, and again with dense fogs of short duration, with a long swell from the same quarter.

" After passing 140° east, or to the westward of it, we experienced fine weather, with south-east winds and occasional snow squalls, lasting but ten or fifteen minutes, and a dry healthy atmosphere.

" The barometer, during our stay on the coast, was always indicative of wind by its depression, and was a true guide. Its mean standing was 29·023 inches, and in a snow-storm it once fell as low as 28·390 inches. The temperature surprised me; we seldom, if ever, had it above 30°, even in the sun at mid-day, or below 22°; and I do not think that three times it was found above 35°.

" Gales come on very suddenly, and are always attended with snow, sleet, and thick fogs, rendering it extremely hazardous; for one must be found, when they do come, more or less surrounded with ice islands: they sometimes last for thirty-six hours. After they set in, you may calculate that they will blow strong for at least half that time. The nearer you are to the land the more violent they are, though not of such long duration. Fine weather

usually precedes them, and we found them to happen, and
the weather to be more changeable, near the full and
change, although I am no believer in the lunar influences
upon the weather.

"*Currents.*—During the whole of our stay along the
icy coast, we found no perceptible current by the reckoning and current log: during a gale of wind I was induced
to believe that some existed, from the short sea that was
formed, thinking there was more than was to be expected.
Tides on such an extent of coast there undoubtedly must
be, but of little strength, or we should have perceived
them.

"In many of the icy bays we were stationary for a sufficient time to perceive them if they had been of any magnitude, and where the current was repeatedly tried.

"The winds have their effect upon the loose drift ice, or
that which is detached from the icy barrier. From a
change of wind from south-east to north, with a fresh
breeze, the Peacock became embayed, and the ice forced
in upon her, which brought about her accident. The
northerly winds are always accompanied with a heavy
swell, and her escape was a miracle, combined with good
seamanship and perseverance. If Captain Hudson's ship
had been as strong as adamant itself, he is of opinion she
would have been ground to atoms by a longer exposure;
her stem suffered to within an inch and a half of the wood-
ends. This was one of the places in which the barrier is
within the floe ice several miles.

"The temperature being so low in the summer months,
there is but little chance of the ice melting or disappearing,
as from accounts frequently takes place in the Arctic
Ocean. Your time being unlimited will allow you to wait
some days in a situation to make experiments.

"I conceive that the ice of the permanent barrier
changes very little from year to year: along the line of
our exploration it looks too solid and fast to be moved by
any thing short of a continued temperature.

"I frequently found myself so closely beset that I thought it next to impossible to escape, and if the wind had not been extremely constant in its direction, I should have been shut up or much injured; as it was, I escaped with scarcely a scratch, although we took some heavy thumps.

"The chart will show you the track of my ship and the state of the barrier, and the localities of seeing the land and approaches to it. I have not had time to insert on it the tracks of the other vessels, but they very nearly agree with ours, and their reports of the weather is very similar to what I have described; it was constructed as I went on, and your copy is a tracing from it. The ice islands are all laid down as we found them; I made the officer of the deck during his watch keep a diagram of them, and they were transferred by me to the chart; this I found gave me more confidence in proceeding among them, and facilitated and rendered comparatively safe my return, if rendered necessary, (I must guard you against supposing they were only as numerous as there represented on the chart; it contains about *one sixth;* frequently upwards of a hundred were counted from the deck, of large size); I would by all means recommend a similar course to be pursued. They undoubtedly change their positions, but not to signify in the time you will be among them.

"*Magnetic Pole.* — I consider we have approached very near to the pole. Our dip was 87° 30′ S., and the compasses on the ice very sluggish; this was in 147° 30′ E., and 67° 04′ S. Our variation, as accurately as it could be observed on the ice, we made 12° 30′ E. It was difficult to get a good observation, on account of the sluggishness of our compasses. About one hundred miles to the westward we crossed the magnetic meridian, and as rapidly increased our west variation as we had diminished that of the east.

"The pole, without giving you accurate deductions, I think my observations will place in about 70° S. latitude, and 140 E. longitude.

"On the meridian of 140° E., latitude 66° 45' S., you will find a small bay, partly formed by ice islands and rocks, which I have named Piner's Bay, and I think among the rocks you may find a snug little harbour. I was driven out of the bay by a gale of wind, sounding about one and a half miles from the shore in thirty fathoms. The icebergs being aground formed a good shelter to it from seaward; I would have been much exposed to have anchored off it, and I had not time to examine it in my boats; a gale came on that lasted thirty-six hours, and a most providential escape we had of it. My object was to trace the land to the westward, and I have done so; a sketch of its position you will see on the chart. I regret being unable to furnish you a more perfect one, but you will be able to decipher it, I hope, and will have information of the points where you may penetrate.

"We had delightful and clear weather ten days or a fortnight along the coast, with the wind at from south-east to south-south-west; the two latter points particularly. The drift ice is in large pieces, so large as to give a ship an awkward thump; but when I found it tolerably open I have run through it to get to clear water, and in hopes of making the land, but our progress was soon stopped by the firm barrier, impenetrable, through which there is no passing. On this point you will, I have little doubt, agree with me.

"I am of opinion that there is little movement of the ice during the season. Strong gales may change its position a little, but I think not materially.

"The only prospect of nearing the land is through a sea well studded with large icebergs, nearly thirty or forty miles in width; and I generally found that we got nearer to the shore in those places than elsewhere. One thing I must tell you, as respects filling your water. You will sometimes find a pond of delicious water on the top of an old iceberg, frozen over, but on cutting through it you will get a supply sufficient for a navy. It will save you fuel, and discomfort and cold to you, your vessels and their crews.

"I was very fortunate in the weather the greater part of the time; and indeed altogether I was scarcely a day without some observation, (except during the gales, of which we had three, occupying about eight days), and generally half a dozen.

"My time for six weeks was passed on deck, and having all daylight, I, of course, had constant employment, and with the many assistants, I could make rapid progress: and you will find that no opportunity ought to be lost in this navigation, if one is to do any thing. One's ship is in constant danger, and the Vincennes, a first-class sloop of seven hundred and eighty tons, it requires all the foresight and activity one is possessed of to look out for her.

"I consider that I have had a most providential escape, and if this ship had not been enabled to do every thing but talk, I should not have been where I now am; but she had inspired me with so much confidence among the coral reefs last summer, that I could put faith in her doing her duty.

"I should have mentioned that in 1838 and 1839 I went south in the brig Porpoise, in order to trace Palmer's Land on its eastern side, (but too late for any trial to reach high latitudes), and hoping that the lateness of the season would enable me to run some distance along it. I got within three miles of the coast, and saw it trending to the south-south-east about thirty miles; but it was so blocked up with ice as to render it impossible to get through; and after other unsuccessful attempts to the south-eastward to get in with the land, I concluded to visit some of the South Shetlands: we had but one day in which we got observations to be relied upon out of ten. If I had been earlier in the season, I should have followed Weddell's track, or coasted the ice of Palmer's Land as far as it could be done. I firmly believe it may be done in favourable seasons, notwithstanding what the Frenchmen may say to the contrary. I know the currents are strong, and plenty of wind must change the ice rapidly, as I then witnessed; I could not afford the time to be frozen up, as my other duties were paramount to passing the nine months in such a torpid state. You are differently situated, and I should advise you by all means to try to penetrate between 35° and 50° west longitude; if you get nothing more, we shall have a chart of the ice, which I should think worth the trouble. Two of the vessels went to 105° west, and met the barrier solid in 70°. It was my intention that they should have gone east from that longitude to Biscoe's Range; they explored several degrees, and had wretched weather, gales attended with very thick fogs and snow. I should very much like to have met you, for I am well aware one can give more information in a few minutes, than an hour's writing will communicate. I hope you intend to circumnavigate the antarctic circle : I made 70 degrees of it, and if my time would have permitted, I should have joined on to Enderby's Land; it is extremely probable that land will be discovered to the eastward of 165° east, and I have no doubt it extends all round, with the exception of 30 or 40 degrees east of 50 west: where there is no land there will be no icy barrier, and little drift ice will be met with; although there will always be found plenty of ice islands, there is plenty of space for them and a ship too. Wishing you all success,

"I am, &c. &c.,

(Signed) "CHARLES WILKES.

"To Capt. James C. Ross,
H. B. M. Ship Erebus."

APPENDIX, No. VII.

"To the Editors of the Spectator.

"Gentlemen, —Lieutenant Wilkes, in his 'Synopsis of the Cruise of the Exploring Expedition,' which I have but recently seen, having made some statements calculated to produce erroneous impressions in regard to myself, I deem it proper they should be explained and corrected, and with that view I ask the favour of you, who I know take a lively interest in all that concerns the character of the navy, to give this communication a place in the columns of your highly respectable paper.

"In the first place, at page 18. of his Synopsis, Lieutenant Wilkes says, 'In speaking of this cruise to the Antarctic, it will be necessary for me to go more into detail than I intended, not only to substantiate our country's claim to the discovery, but in consequence of the unfounded *statement that seems to have been made by Captain Ross to a commander in our navy, and given currency by him*, viz. that Captain Ross had actually run over a part of the ocean where I had reported the existence of land.'

"I am doubtless the commander here alluded to; and the words I have underscored seem to be intended to convey the impression that I was the *only*, or at least *first person*, to whom Captain Ross made this statement, and through whose report alone it obtained '*currency*.' Such is not the fact. The truth is, that Ross's statement was published in the Sydney Herald of the 10th of August, eight days before I met that officer at New Zealand. From that paper it was copied into the 'Madisonian,' of this city, of 12th March last. It had also reached Mazatlan, on the coast of Mexico, whence it was taken to the Sandwich Islands by Captain Bissell, of the Cayuga, and published in the 'Polynesian' of the 2d of October, seven days before my arrival there.* The account I received from Captain Ross was not matter of secrecy, and was of course spoken of by me without reserve at Honolulu. Thus, and through no other agency of mine, it found its way into a subsequent number of that paper; not, however, as an original article, but expressly as a mere confirmation of what had been previously published.† This Lieutenant Wilkes might have learned, if he did not, when he last touched at Oahu, a few days after I left there.

"In the next place, at page 20., he says, 'On my original chart I had laid down the supposed position of Bellamy's Island or land in 164 deg., 165 deg. E. longitude, and that it was traced off and sent to Captain Ross. I am not a little surprised that so intelligent a navigator as Captain Ross, on finding that he had run over this position,

* " To the Editor of the Polynesian. — Captain Ross, in the Erebus and Terror, had been as far south as 78 deg. 4 min., in long. 186 deg. 40 min. W. He made the south magnetic pole to be in lat. 76 deg., 154 deg. long. east. He discovered an active volcano, which he called Mount Erebus, in 77 deg. 31 min. S., 167 deg. 10 min. E.

" This information was brought to Mazatlan from Sydney by an English vessel; the writer had it from Dr. Wiley, of the English navy, who was a passenger on board, and who stated to him that he took this memorandum from Capt. Ross, who was at Sydney when he left.

" He further verbally stated that Captain Ross had sailed over the spot where land is supposed to have been seen by the American surveying vessels. They (the English vessels) saw vast numbers of seal and many whales.   G. W. P. BISSELL."

" Sandwich Islands, September 20, 1841."

† Captain Aulick, of the Yorktown, confirms the intelligence in regard to Captain Ross's discoveries, published in No. 17. of our paper. He met that celebrated navigator a few months since at the Bay of Islands, and from him learned the discovery of two volcanoes as far south as 77 deg. One of them, which he named Mount Erebus, was 12,000 feet in height, and at the time he saw it in active operation, affording a most magnificent spectacle to the crews of both vessels: the other, whose altitude was 10,000 feet, was named after his consort, the Terror. Captain Ross had received the chart sent him by Captain Wilkes, and had cruised over a space of 50 miles in extent in either direction, where land had been laid down by the latter navigator, and found nothing but clear sea.—Polynesian, Oct. 15th, 1841.

should not have closely inquired into the statements rela-tive to our discoveries, that had been published in the Sydney and Hobart Town papers, which he must have seen, and have induced him to make a careful examination of the tracks of the squadron laid down on the chart sent him, by which he would have assured himself, in a few moments, that it had never been laid down or claimed as part of our discovery, before he made so bold an assertion to an American officer (meaning myself), ' that he had run over a clear ocean where I had laid down the land; and I am not less surprised that that officer should have taken it for granted, without examination, that such was the fact.'

" From the above statement, and in the absence of any explanation, it might well be inferred that both Ross and myself must be, to say the least, very shortsighted and dull of comprehension, not to have been able to see that it was Bellamy's, and not Wilkes's Land, that he (Ross) had run over. But, in the statement above quoted, Mr. Wilkes has done us injustice, by omitting to mention one very important fact in this connexion: namely, that in laying down the *land of Bellamy* on the chart he sent Captain Ross, *he neglected to affix thereto the name of its discoverer*, or to distinguish it in any way from his own land there traced out, and almost connected with it. He also sent Captain Ross a letter with his chart,* but unfortunately the name of Bellamy, or his land, is neither mentioned nor even hinted at in this letter, (as may be seen from the copy of it published with his Synopsis). In short, no intimation, in any manner whatever, was given Ross by Lieutenant Wilkes that he *did not claim* the discovery of *all the land* marked on his chart, and to this cause alone is to be ascribed the error into which Captain Ross was, I think, unavoidably led.

" Mr. Wilkes says, Ross ought to have examined the accounts of his discoveries, published in the Sydney and Hobart Town papers, before he made so bold an assertion to an American officer. But with such evidence as the chart

A A 2

and letter of Mr. Wilkes in his hands, I apprehend it could
hardly have been seriously expected that he should search
the newspaper accounts (which probably he never saw) for
other or better information on the subject.

"On my visit to Captain Ross on board the Erebus, he
spread this chart before me in the presence of Captain
Crozier and two of my own officers. It was distinctly
drawn out on tracing paper—the whole appearing, so far
as I observed, one connected operation, representing nothing
but the result of his own (Wilkes's) explorations. Ross,
believing it to be such, had transcribed it at length on his
chart, which he also placed before us, and pointed out the
tracks of his vessels marked on it in red ink, *and passing directly over the spot assigned to the land*, which we all
considered as laid down by Lieutenant Wilkes to represent
the north-eastern limit of his supposed antarctic continent,
and where he (Ross) said they had a clear sea as far as the
eye could reach. Such was the evidence on which my
belief in his report was founded. To my mind it was conclusive; and I cheerfully leave it for the judgment of others
to determine whether or not, under all the circumstances
here stated, it be just cause of 'surprise' that Captain
Ross should have boldly asserted that he had run over a
clear ocean where Lieutenant Wilkes had laid down the
land, and that I should have taken it for granted, *without
further examination*, that such was the fact.

"In making this statement, I can say, with perfect sincerity, I am actuated by no unkindness of feeling towards
Mr. Wilkes; but, fully persuaded as I am that the erroneous statement for which he publicly censures Captain
Ross, and shows a little temper towards me, was the result
of his own negligence alone, I considered it due to that
distinguished navigator, as well as to myself, that the
matter should be publicly explained.

"I am, very respectfully, &c.

"J. H. AULICK."

APPENDIX, No. VIII.

LETTER FROM LIEUTENANT WILKES IN REPLY TO
CAPTAIN AULICK.

"To the Editors of the Spectator.

"Gentlemen,—The editorial notice in the columns of
your paper, in which the remarks of Captain Aulick are
inserted, is so full as respects the discovery of the Expedition, that I should not have thought it necessary to say
another word relative to the subject, if Captain Aulick's
remarks might not give the idea, that the chart and letter
sent Captain Ross by me were disingenuous, in so far
that I had attempted to claim a greater extent of discovery
than the Expedition was entitled to, and that I had taken
occasion to show some little temper towards himself, and
pass 'public censures upon Captain Ross, while *my own
negligence* was the cause alone to which is to be ascribed
the error into which he thinks Captain Ross was unavoidably led.'

"It will, I think, be sufficiently shown, that I had the
warmest feelings towards Captain Ross and the English
Expedition, by the simple perusal of my letter to him,
giving him the information I did. The whole was prepared in much haste, and when my time was much occupied, and I doubt not all will perceive the candour and
frankness with which it was written; and it ought
certainly to go to prove that I was not afraid of rivalry, for
every one knew that Captain Ross was about to explore
our very track, and thus would test our operations. I am
well aware that many have blamed me for sending him
any information; but I have not changed my opinion,
that it was proper for me to do so. As the Commander
of a great undertaking in the cause of science, I was in
duty bound to forward that of another Expedition of a

A A 3

foreign nation, similarly engaged, every way in my power, even at a sacrifice to myself.

"On my arrival at Sydney from the antarctic cruise, I was introduced to Captain Briscoe (Biscoe), the discoverer of Enderby's Land; and I believe he gave me the first information of the English discovery * and its position, which I placed on my chart, marking it 'English discovery.'

"My impression is that the copy which I ordered to be made (from my own original) on tracing paper, and sent to Captain Ross, was a perfect one, and on the original chart the English discovery is detached and separate from ours, and stands alone. At the time I sent my letter to Captain Ross, I did not know the English discoverer's name; but whether the English discovery was so marked or not, is of but little consequence, for Captain Ross knew of Bellamy's discovery before he left England, and therefore must have seen at once the longitude and latitude of that on the tracing were almost identically the same with those of Bellamy's; and I am satisfied that the only erroneous conclusion Captain Ross could have been led into by it, was, that I had verified Bellamy's discovery.

"That I felt and expressed surprise relative to Captain Aulick having taken Captain Ross's assertion on a point (without a full examination of all the data) in which not only the credit of the Expedition, but the country and navy were concerned, is very natural, and I believe all who consider the subject will agree with me.

"I cannot suppose that the words in the Synopsis, '*given currency by him*,' can be tortured into that he (Captain Aulick) was the '*only or at least the first person*' to whom Captain Ross made the statement; but I think and suspect it will strike all, that coming, as it did, from an officer of rank in our navy, it would obtain *currency*, and be generally believed, from that fact alone.

* Bellamy's Land. — EDITORS.

"My authorities are the inhabitants of Oahu, who, on our arrival there, a few days after Captain Aulick left, told us of the report; one and all gave Captain Aulick as the author of it, '*that it must be so, for Captain Aulick had said it, and that there was no continent left for us.*'

"On my return to the United States, Captain Aulick's name was again attached to the report, and being an officer of high standing, gave it weight and currency throughout the Union that otherwise it would not have had. I was desired by a number of gentlemen of high standing, friends of the Expedition, to state the facts for the credit of the Expedition and country, which I have done in my Synopsis.

"I never, myself, thought enough of this attack on the Expedition to have any feeling on the subject as regards Captain Aulick; nor did I intend any thing personal towards him in the remarks in my Synopsis, as I told a mutual friend, some days since, who spoke to me on the subject.

"My language is erroneously quoted when I am made to say, that Captain Ross '*ought*' to have examined, whereas I only express surprise *that he should not closely have inquired into the statements*, as I think any one would have done similarly situated.

"As for Captain Aulick's charge of *negligence* against me, as an apology for Captain Ross's error, I am well assured, from the personal acquaintance I have had with the latter, he never would have made it himself. I can truly say that I rejoice in his success. *With Captain Ross, as an individual, I am not at issue;* but when an unjust attack is made on the Expedition and the results of our hard labours, which belong to the country, I feel it my duty to defend them.

"I am, very respectfully,
"Your obedient servant,
"CHARLES WILKES.

"Nov. 19th, 1842."

A A 4

APPENDIX, No. IX.

TABLES ILLUSTRATING THE ABSTRACTS FROM THE METEOROLO-
GICAL JOURNAL KEPT ON BOARD HER MAJESTY'S SHIP EREBUS,
PRINTED WITH THE NARRATIVE.

FIGURES — *To denote the Force of the Wind.*

0 denotes Calm.

1	„	Light Air	just sufficient to give	Steerage way.
2	„	Light Breeze	with which a well-conditioned man-of-war, under all sail, and clean full, would go in smooth water, from	1 to 2 knots.
3	„	Gentle Breeze		3 to 4 knots.
4	„	Moderate Breeze		5 to 6 knots.
5	„	Fresh Breeze		Royals, &c.
6	„	Strong Breeze		Single-reefs and top-gallant sails.
7	„	Moderate Gale	In which the same ship could just carry close hauled	Double-reefs, jib, &c.
8	„	Fresh Gale		Triple-reefs, courses, &c.
9	„	Strong Gale		Close-reefs and courses.
10	„	Whole Gale	with which she could only bear	Close-reefed main topsail and reefed foresail.
11	„	Storm	with which she would be reduced to	Storm stay-sails.
12	„	Hurricane	to which she could show	No canvas.

LETTERS — *To denote the State of the Weather.*

* b denotes Blue sky. — Whether with clear or hazy atmosphere.

c „ Cloudy. — *i. e.* Detached opening clouds.

d „ Drizzling rain.

f „ Fog — f thick fog.

g „ Gloomy dark weather.

h „ Hail.

l „ Lightning.

m „ Misty or hazy. — So as to interrupt the view.

o „ Overcast. — *i. e.* The whole sky covered with one impervious cloud.

p „ Passing showers.

q „ Squally.

r „ Rain. — *i. e.* Continuous rain.

s „ Snow.

t „ Thunder.

u „ Ugly threatening appearance in the weather.

v „ Visibility of distant objects. — Whether the day be cloudy or not.

w „ Wet dew.

· under any letter denotes an — Extraordinary degree.

By the combination of these letters, all the ordinary phenomena of the weather may be recorded with certainty and brevity.

EXAMPLES.

bcm denotes Blue sky, with detached opening clouds, but hazy round the horizon.

gv „ Gloomy dark weather, but distant objects remarkably visible.

qpdh „ Very hard squalls, and showers of drizzle, accompanied by lightning with very heavy thunder.

F. R.

* The figures prefixed to this letter denote the quantity of blue sky visible in eighth parts of the hemisphere. — 1 4, 8

APPENDIX X.

GEOGRAPHICAL TABLE.

Name and Description of Place.	Latitude South.	Longitude East.
Adam, Mount - - - -	71 23	168 56
Adare, Cape - - - -	71 18	170 45
Anne, Cape - - - -	73 45	170 10
Albert Mountains (centre) - -	76 00	160 00
Balleny Islands - - -	66 44	163 11
Barrow, Cape - - - -	71 12	168 58
Bay, M'Murdo (centre) - - -	77 20	165 00
Mowbray - - - -	72 11	170 30
Robertson - - - -	71 22	170 25
Wood - - - -	74 25	165 30
Yule - - - -	70 39	166 30
Beaufort Island - - - -	76 55	166 58
Bird, Cape - - - -	77 09	166 40
Brewster, Mount - - -	72 53	169 30
Cape Adare - - - -	71 18	170 45
Anne - - - -	73 45	170 10
Barrow - - - -	71 12	163 58
Bird - - - -	77 09	166 40
Christie - - - -	72 17	170 42
Cotter - - - -	72 39	170 50
Crozier - - - -	77 25	169 10
Daniell - - - -	72 53	170 00
Davis - - - -	70 32	166 06
Dayman - - - -	70 40	170 58
Downshire - - - -	71 35	170 58
Gauss - - - -	76 09	162 52
Hallett - - - -	72 25	170 45
Hooker - - - -	70 36	166 28
Johnson - - - -	74 16	166 20
Jones - - - -	73 08	169 15
M'Cormick - - -	71 55	170 58
Moore - - - -	70 49	167 27
North - - - -	70 31	165 28
Oakley - - - -	70 56	167 45
Phillips - - - -	73 00	169 55

Name and Description of Place.	Latitude South.	Longitude East.
Cape Roget - - - -	73 06	170 50
Scott - - - -	70 59	168 02
Sibbald - - - -	74 06	166 47
Wadworth - - -	73 27	169 55
Washington - - -	74 37	165 10
Wheatstone - - -	72 42	170 48
Wood - - - -	71 19	169 32
Christie, Cape - - -	72 17	170 42
Cotter, Cape - - -	72 39	170 50
Coulman Island - - -	73 36	170 02
Crozier Cape - - -	77 25	169 10
Conical Hill - - -	71 14	168 58
Dalmeny, Mount - -	71 05	167 08
Daniell, Cape - - -	72 53	170 00
Davis, Cape - - -	70 32	166 06
Dayman, Cape - - -	70 40	166 50
Doubtful Island (1) - -	75 44	166 10
Doubtful Island (2) - -	71 43	171 08
Downshire, Cape - -	71 35	170 58
Dunraven Rocks - -	71 15	170 40
Elliot, Mount - - -	70 50	166 35
Erebus, Mount - - -	77 33	166 58
Frances Island - - -	67 20	164 20
Gauss, Cape - - -	76 09	162 52
Hallett, Cape - - -	72 25	170 45
Harcourt, Mount - -	72 32	170 04
Herschell, Mount - -	72 04	170 08
Hill, Conical - - -	71 14	168 58
Hooker, Cape - - -	70 36	166 28
Inlet, Smith - - -	70.55	167 33
Tucker - - -	72 46	169 45
Island, Balleny - - -	66 44	163 11
Beaufort - -	76 55	166 58
Coulman - -	73 36	170 02
Doubtful (1) -	75 44	166 10
Doubtful (2) -	71 43	171 08
Frances - -	67 20	164 20
Franklin - -	76 07	168 20

Name and Description of Place.	Latitude South.	Longitude East.
Island, Possession - - - -	71 56	171 10
Smyth - - - -	67 36	165 00
Islets, Kay - - - -	74 00	169 40
Lyall - - - -	70 45	167 20
Possession - - - -	72 00	171 about
Johnson, Cape - - - -	74 16	166 20
Jones, Cape - - - -	73 08	169 15
Kay Islets - - - -	74 00	169 40
Lyall Islets - - - -	70 45	167 20
Lloyd, Mount - - - -	72 19	170 07
Lubbock, Mount - - - -	73 04	169 00
Magnetic Pole - - - -	75 05	154 08
M'Cormick, Cape - - - -	71 55	170 58
M'Murdo, Bay - - - -	77 20	165 00
Melbourne, Mount - - - -	74 25	164 10
Minto, Mount - - - -	71 33	169 16
Monteagle, Mount - - - -	74 00	166 12
Moore, Cape - - - -	70 49	167 27
Mount Adam - - - -	71 23	168 56
Albert (centre) - - -	76 00	160 00
Brewster - - -	72 53	169 30
Dalmeny - - -	71 05	167 08
Elliot - - -	70 50	166 35
Erebus - - -	77 33	166 58
Harcourt - - -	72 32	170 04
Herschell - - -	72 04	170 08
Lloyd - - -	72 19	170 07
Lubbock - - -	73 04	169 00
Melbourne - - -	74 25	164 10
Minto - - -	71 33	169 16
Monteagle - - -	74 00	166 12
Murchison - - -	73 25	166 56
Northampton - - -	72 40	169 15
Parker - - -	71 18	167 24
Parry - - to	79 00	169 00
Peacock - - -	72 11	170 06
Pechell - - -	71 06	167 30
Phillips - - -	73 06	168 15
Robinson - - -	71 44	170 25
Sabine - - -	71 42	169 55

Name and Description of Places.	Latitude South.	Longitude East.
Mount Terror - - - -	77 30	168 34
Troubridge - - -	71 12	168 05
Whewell - - -	71 55	170 18
Mowbray Bay - - - -	72 11	170 30
Murchison, Mount - - -	73 25	166 56
North, Cape - - - -	70 31	165 28
Northampton, Mount - - -	72 40	169 15
Oakley, Cape - - - -	70 56	167 45
Parry Mountains - - to	79 00	169 00
Parker, Mount - - - -	71 18	167 24
Peacock, Mount - - -	72 11	170 06
Peak, Russell - - - -	67 26	164 30
Pechell, Mount - - -	71 06	167 30
Phillips, Cape - - - -	73 00	169 55
Phillips, Mount - - -	73 06	168 15
Pole, Magnetic - - - -	75 05	154 08
Robertson Bay - - - -	71 22	170 25
Robinson, Mount - - -	71 44	170 25
Rocks, Dunraven - - -	71 15	170 40
Roget, Cape - - - -	72 06	170 50
Russell Peak - - - -	67 26	164 30
Sabine, Mount - - - -	71 42	169 55
Sabrina Land - - - -	66 00	120 00
Scott, Cape - - - -	70 59	168 02
Sibbald, Cape - - - -	74 06	166 47
Smith Inlet - - - -	70 55	167 33
Smyth Island - - - -	67 36	165 00
Terror, Mount - - - -	77 30	168 34
Troubridge, Mount - - -	71 12	168 05
Tucker Inlet - - - -	72 46	169 45
Wadworth, Cape - - -	73 27	169 55
Washington, Cape - - -	74 37	165 10
Wheatstone, Cape - - -	72 42	170 48
Whewell, Mount - - -	71 55	170 18
Wood, Cape - - - -	71 19	169 32
Wood Bay - - - -	74 25	165 30
Yule Bay - - - -	70 39	166 30

APPENDIX, No. XI.

(Referred to in p. 17. of Narrative.)

A LIST OF ROCK SPECIMENS, FROM ST. PAUL'S
ROCKS.

No. 1. Hornstone — from summit of white rock, south-
west side.
    2. " Kaolin," veined with serpentine, from side of
do.
    3. The latter rock, from the base, where exposed to
the spray of the sea; in progress of decomposition.
    4. Altered Hornstone — from the rock on the north-
east side.
    5. Veins — intersecting the base of the rock, like small
dykes, black and much hardened.
    6. The same, filled with calcareous deposit, &c.
    7. Masses of conglomerate, confusedly intermingled
with the last four kinds.

END OF THE FIRST VOLUME.

7

LONDON :
SPOTTISWOODE and SHAW,
New-street-Square.

Printed in the United States
125150LV00001B/206/A